TWENTY THOUSAND ROADS

TWENTY THOUSAND ROADS

WOMEN, MOVEMENT, AND THE WEST

VIRGINIA SCHARFF

University of California Press
Berkeley
Los Angeles
London

University of California Press
Berkeley and Los Angeles, California

University of California Press, Ltd.
London, England

Portions of chapter 6 have been reused from the
author's "Mobility, Women, and the West," in *Over
the Edge: Remapping the American West,* edited by
Valerie J. Matsumoto and Blake Allmendinger (University of California Press, 1999).

Library of Congress Cataloging-in-Publication Data

Scharff, Virginia.
    Twenty thousand roads : women, movement, and
the West / Virginia Scharff.
        p.   cm.
    Includes bibliographical references and index.
    ISBN 0-520-21212-6 (alk. paper)—
ISBN 0-520-23777-3 (pbk. : alk. paper)
        1. Women pioneers—West (U.S.)—Biography.
    2. Women—West (U.S.)—Biography.   3. Frontier
    and pioneer life—West (U.S.)   4. West (U.S.)—
    Biography.   5. West (U.S.)—History.   I. Title.
    F596 .S26   2003
    978'.02'082—dc21   2002011191

Manufactured in the United States of America
12   11   10   09   08   07   06   05   04   03
10   9   8   7   6   5   4   3   2   1

The paper used in this publication meets the minimum
requirements of ANSI/NISO Z39.48-1992 (R 1997)
(*Permanence of Paper*).♾

*To Jack and Fran
and Kate and Casey*

CONTENTS

CONTENTS

ACKNOWLEDGMENTS

I HAD NO IDEA WHEN I BEGAN writing about women in the West, twenty years ago, how many roads the subject would take me down, or how many colleagues, friends, and family members would help me along on the journey.

Thanks, first, to the librarians and archivists who showed me the way to the documents: staff at the Zimmerman Library and the Center for Southwest Research at the University of New Mexico; the Massachusetts Historical Society; the Missouri Historical Society; the Wyoming State Archives, Museums and Historical Division; the American Heritage Center at the University of Wyoming; the Coe Library at the University of Wyoming; and the Beinecke Library at Yale University. For help with the maps, I am especially grateful to Nicholas Graham of the Massachusetts Historical Society; Beth Silbergleit at the Center for Southwest Research, University of New Mexico; and Leslie Shores and Rick Ewig of the American Heritage Center.

Next, my heartfelt gratitude to research assistants who have put up with my crotchets, demands, and deadlines with good humor, creativity, and generosity: Michael Anne Sullivan, Pablo Mitchell, John Herron, Andrew Kirk, Catherine Kleiner, Judy Morley, and Janette Catron.

I now have the great luck to serve as director of the Center for the Southwest, in the History Department at the University of New Mexico, and to work with incredible people. To Cindy Tyson, Rebecca Perez, and Scott Meredith, thanks for making work a joy.

My own migration circuits are anchored in the History Department at the University of New Mexico; they take me annually to meet with dear friends and colleagues in the Western History Association, the Southwest Women's History Group, the Teaching Workshop in Women's History at UCLA, the Larom Summer Institute at the Buffalo Bill Historical Center—to all kinds of places where scholars gather. I am endlessly grateful for this peripatetic professional community. The UNM History Department and the College of Arts and Sciences have supported my research in many ways, including a Research Semester Award that gave me work time when I very much needed it. I am especially grateful to Rob Robbins, Jane Slaughter, Michael Fischer, and Bill Gordon for their help, and to Yolanda Martinez, Helen Ferguson, Dana Ellison, and the rest of the excellent History Department staff. I also want to thank Paul Hutton for making the Western History Association the greatest show on earth.

The stories I tell here have seen the light in various forms and venues over the years. Blake Allmendinger, Karen Anderson, Sue Armitage, Beth Bailey, Durwood Ball, Bill Barton, Ned Blackhawk, Melissa Bokovoy, Katie Curtiss, Phil Deloria, Sarah Deutsch, William Deverell, Dick Etulain, John Faragher, David Farber, John Findlay, Janet Fireman, Douglas Flamming, Neil Foley, Chris Friday, Melanie Gustafson, David Gutiérrez, Janice Harris, Deborah Hardy, Robert Hine, Betsy Jameson, Joan Jensen, Katherine Jensen, Cynthia Leung, Mike Massie, Valerie Matsumoto, Pablo Mitchell, Peggy Pascoe, Liz Perry, Lew Perry, James Ronda, Mary Rothschild, Roger Rouse, Vicki Ruiz, George Sánchez, Jane Slaughter, Hank Stamm, Charlie Steen, Sam Truett, Kathleen Underwood, Frank Van Nuys, Kathleen Weiler, and Chris Wilson have all offered helpful comments on chapters and on papers presented at conferences and study groups. Nancy Scott Jackson has gone above and beyond the call of duty in encouraging me on this project. Way back in 1988, Patty Limerick and Paula Petrik came to slightly different conclusions regarding my argument that women's history had much to teach historians of the American West. Mary Murphy was making a similar argument then, as I recall, and she's done me the extraordinary service of reading this manuscript and making careful comments. Thanks, Patty, Paula, and Mary for pushing me off a short plank into deep water.

Three brave souls have read much or all of what appears here, in one form or another, and, moreover, have been the kind of friends who have been willing to listen to my obsessions and harangues for years. I can hardly convey what their generosity, hardheaded kindness, and expert judgment means to me. To María Montoya, Elliott West, and Richard White, all homage is due.

Each chapter of this book opens with a detail of a cognitive or cartographic map of women's movements. Five of the maps are archival; three are original works. Profound thanks to the distinguished architect George Pearl, who created the map for Chapter 6, and to Florian Brożek, the extraordinary young artist who drew the illustration for Chapter 8. The design for Chapter 7 is my own. I included it at the urging of the gifted architectural historian Chris Wilson, who cheerfully assured me that "the visual stuff is easy." With his expert and patient guidance, it was.

No editor could be smarter, sharper, more encouraging, more fun, or (useful in my case) more patient than Monica McCormick. It is a great privilege to join the list of authors she has brought to the University of California Press list in western history. Thanks, too, to the Press team: Sue Heinemann, Anne Canright, and Nola Burger, for a beautiful (and better) book.

Thanks never seem enough for those dearest to one's heart, and most burdened with one's ups, downs, fears, and hopes. To Jon Myers, bass player extraordinaire; soaring songbirds Catherine Kleiner and Bev Seckinger; and my Everly Brothers, Chris Wilson and Richard Sanchez: thanks for keeping the music alive. To my beloved friends Beth Bailey, Melissa Bokovoy, Katie Curtiss, Kathy Jensen, and Jane Slaughter, thank you for putting up, bearing up, and occasionally shutting me up. To the Levkoff, Scharff, and Swift families, there aren't words enough to express my love and gratitude. Bob and Martha Scharff take care of me, a tall order, heaven knows. Jack and Kate Swift have been colleagues as well as wonderful father-in-law and aunt, and I thank them for all the great conversations and citations regarding New England history, Algonquian language, and the power of people and places. I very much miss Janet Scharff, who inspired me to care about women in the first place; Fran Swift, who gave me my first "western women's history" book in 1978 (Isabella Bird's *A Lady's Life in the Rocky Mountains*); and Casey Miller, who knew why women's history matters.

One of the happiest moments of my life was a night when I sat staring at the computer screen, blank and exhausted, and Sam Swift came into my office and told me he was proud of me. The feeling is mutual. Likewise for Annie Swift. You two hold my heart in your hands.

And to Peter Swift, laughing partner, thinking partner, my love forever.

INTRODUCTION

I N 1639 A WOMAN BY THE NAME of Shaumpishuh, "Sachem Squaw of Menuncatuck," sought to sell rights to lands between the Kuttawoo and Oiockcommock Rivers (later, the East River and Stony Creek) to a party of six Puritan men from the New Haven colony. It was not her first transaction. Shaumpishuh's Narragansett band had suffered terrible losses from disease and from Mohawk and Pequot raiders, and they had come to see living near the English as a way of protecting themselves. She and her brother, Momaugin, had earlier sold their New Haven lands to English settlers. In 1639, however, she acted as "sole owner, possessor and inheritor" of all the land sold, acting also "with the consent of the Indians there inhabiting." She drew a map indicating the bounds of the grant and signed the deed of transfer with her mark, a bow-and-arrow symbol. The map, now lost, survived in the copy made by Henry Whitfield, leader of the Puritans, who also drew up the written agreement. For their land, Shaumpishuh and her people received items ranging from coats and stockings to kettles and hatchets, along with "12 fathom of Wompom." She promised further that she and her people would remove themselves from the land thus sold. The Menuncatucks did move, but not far—to what would become East Haven, where they gathered clams and lived in peace with their Puritan neighbors to the east and west. Whitfield and his brethren, meanwhile, enlarged their holdings, an expanse that would come to encompass the towns of Guilford and Madison, Connecticut. In 1641 they dealt, once again, with a Native woman in a position of authority, purchasing land between the East River of Menuncatuck and the Wattammonossock (later Hammonasset) River, sealing the bargain in a deed signed with the marks of Uncas of the Mohegins and "Uncas Squaw."[1]

We cannot know what Shaumpishuh thought of the bargain, or discern from the fragments of evidence we have the daily, weekly, seasonal, and lifetime paths she might have followed to live a life that made sense to her, even in the face of vast change, accustomed as she likely was to moving between garden and gathering place, fishing stream and clam flat, open ground and shelter.[2] But wouldn't it be illuminating to know her story? Such stories help to explain the persistence of people hardly visible to history, people who are supposed to remain silent or to disappear—people like the Mashpee Wampanoag Tribal Council of Cape Cod, who, three and a half centuries after Shaumpishuh sold her land, would find themselves trying to prove to a federal court that, despite a highly transient and fractured history, they still existed.[3]

The story of America is the stately tale of westward movement and continental conquest. But what happens when, mindful of the chaos and contingency of the past, we retell it against the grain—say, from the point of view of a woman who preceded the West, who behaved as a sovereign, who moved at variance from the story as we're accustomed to telling it? What happens when we discover that stories of women in motion are not few, but many, not past, but persistent beyond what we have imagined? The land, I contend, lies a little different.

We understand movement—in the grossest sense, as the desire and capacity to get the body from one place to the next, with some end in mind—in fundamentally gendered terms. Movement belongs to men. Women, supposedly, move seldom and reluctantly, and when they do, it's a departure from their real stories, not a central plot line. The freedom to move is a marker of social power and of legitimacy, and for women, that freedom seems always in doubt. When women move, they surprise us.

In this book I look at a historical phenomenon so ubiquitous it has been all but invisible, yet to do so is not much different from trying to describe the color or the taste of air. I see women moving into and away from, through and around, the shifting ground of the American West. As our glimpses of Shaumpishuh's story suggest, women do move, sometimes willingly, always knowledgeably, and their movements have consequences for history and geography. If we try to see the great events of our history through the eyes of women in motion and action, those events, and the places they happened, look different.[4]

Finding women means looking away from men. Men's movements have assuredly shaped the places women go, their reasons for going or staying, the things they can do in transit, in place. To see women, we have to take an oblique approach to the epic stories of westering men, the tales of undaunted courage. Women have moved in diverse directions, for purposes only sometimes in concert with the national enterprise, sometimes, indeed, in tension with it. And women's movements have often been bound more by the myriad claims of womanhood than by the exigencies of westering.

At the same time, women's lives tangled with the westward expansion of the United States. I shall examine the making, elaborating, and splintering of the American West, between the beginning of the nineteenth century and the end of the twentieth, by mapping the history of women on the move. Women's movements preceded, configured, and survive the West. These movements have, however, been difficult to see clearly, because historical maps—both graphic and linguistic representations of the ways in which people have marked place—have generally been drawn by, for, and about men.

In the pages that follow I endeavor to focus so attentively on women's presence that some readers may lament the relegation of men to the margins, the background, or even to the limbo of silence and erasure. I confess freely: this is a picaresque tale, a sketchy picture. Like the cartographer who leaves out much geographical information in order to present a clearer picture of what she intends the viewer to discover, this narrative is selective, highly colored, and, I hope, vivid and enlightening.

My argument is fairly simple, though the stories I tell are hindered by the ways in which our history has always been rendered. To understand the historical geography of the American West, we have to acknowledge, imagine, and examine the presence, the power, the utterances of women who came before, who both built and resisted American expansion, whose movements to this day, and for the foreseeable future, shape the landscape. We have to take seriously people we too often dismiss as "draftees in the male enterprise" of nation-building, to see the ways in which the West, as a distinctive place and particular process, and ultimately as myth, has waxed and waned and survived as a force in history.[5]

In Part One, "Before the West," I look at two women whose journeys traversed terrain not yet part of the American West, between the beginning of the nineteenth century and the conquest of northern Mexico in 1846. The West came to Sacagawea as a series of face-to-face encounters with the agents of American empire, all male, nearly all of European extraction. Her thoughts and actions, origins and ends, remain mysterious. But the limits of what we can know about her reveal the boundaries of geographies and genealogies shaped by gender, not yet and indeed never to be assimilated into stories of the West.

In 1846 Susan Magoffin rode and walked into a country still owned by Mexico. She was an agent of the American empire, charged with the job of domesticating a series of strange places. Magoffin wrote a remarkable diary of her travels, which would be edited and published eighty years later as a chronicle of destiny, of a nation spreading westward with a force as elemental as the fruitful multiplication of American families. But Susan's own story was something very different, a tale of a woman wrenched from home, brave and resourceful, curious and myopic, often sick and terrified, seeking a hearth in an area of darkness.

In Part Two, "In the West," we see how new systems of transportation, communication, education, and commerce transformed the vast, fractious, fluid landscapes between the Mississippi and the Pacific into an American region in the years between the Civil War and World War II. In 1869 the West arrived in Wyoming on a Union Pacific train. The building of the transcontinental railroad and the reconstruction of the American nation brought new people and ideas into a volatile country, a violent cultural and political "middle ground" upon which white women played a highly unpredictable role, generating at least one stunning consequence: the granting of suffrage to the women of Wyoming Territory. In Reconstruction Wyoming, conquest and emancipation rode together in the effort to bring civilizing women west.[6]

Once such women were established as residents of a regional West, they mapped western places in different ways. In the late nineteenth and early twentieth centuries, educated women like Wyoming's Grace Raymond Hebard and New Mexico's Fabiola Cabeza de Baca found independence and furthered the aims of the western states that sponsored their work and their travels. Hebard, a historian, politician, and genealogist, took part in the mission of linking the West to the nation, mapping herself and other women onto the western landscape. Cabeza de Baca also used the power of her lineage, the school, and the state, but to notably different ends. Seeking, through an Anglo-dominated present, to connect a Spanish and Indian past to a multicultural future, she delineated a New Mexico that followed a south-to-north geography, traced distinctive genealogies, and passed on recipes different from the rest of the West. By preserving what had preceded American conquest, Cabeza de Baca looked past the West.

In Part Three, "Beyond the West," I look at women whose lives, in the second half of the twentieth century, have been shaped more by gender, race, and nation, by modernity and postmodernity, than by the decreasing claims of region. I argue that the civil rights activist Jo Ann Gibson Robinson, a southerner who later became a westerner, brought an American notion of citizenship and a westerner's belief in entitlement to mobility to bear against the solidity of the South. Montgomery, Alabama, the site of the pathbreaking bus boycott of 1955–1956, was the scene of her most famous struggle and achievement, but Montgomery was, for Robinson, only one stop on a lifelong journey. As an African American growing up in the South, in the frigid heart of the Cold War, Robinson had come to know American regionalism as repression and containment. Jo Ann Robinson's life was about personal endeavor, not geographical exceptionalism or genealogical entitlement; movement, not place.

The Cold War container, as we know, could not hold. The lid blew off in the 1960s and 1970s, and Pamela Des Barres was a pioneer of the sexual revolution that kept the steam rising. Striking out boldly from Reseda, California, on a mission of sexual emancipation and personal freedom, she traveled a road that transformed her from groupie to writer, finding her way through the privileges and problems of being a sex object for rock musicians to become celebrated in her own right as an author. In the end, as she hurtled through a volatile landscape, the constraints of gender, not region, bound her. Des Barres's story illustrates both the possibilities and the limits of women's movements at the end of the twentieth century. Her travels led her to follow the pathways of the suburban working mother, driving to the grocery store and to school to the raucous beat of a rock 'n' roll soundtrack. Such journeys create and maintain and transform our world in ways we need to understand.

We should not mistake female mobility for emancipation. But neither should we assume that women's movements, if constrained, are insignificant. At the end of the twentieth century and the beginning of the twenty-first, the hourly, daily, and weekly journeys of women, as much as anything else, delineate the postwestern landscapes of places like Highlands Ranch, Colorado, a burgeoning suburb in the fastest growing county of the United States. What had once been rolling prairie has become not simply a land of cul-de-sacs and For Sale signs but more, a metastasizing landscape of single-family dwellings, strip streetscapes, massive malls, and families inventing new forms of fissure and connection, stretched across the bounds of geography and genealogy. Highlands Ranch prides itself on its connection to the wide-open West of bygone days, but it could be anywhere—Denver, Dallas, Djakarta. In order for such places to come into being, and to persist, women must move.

The West has always been a product of connections between local and global places and processes—and people. Women moved and marked their worlds as shadowy presences, only fleetingly visible to a West that had just begun, spottily and brazenly, to claim and name the places they inhabited and traversed. By the end of the story that follows, the pathways women engraved with their lives had become permanent fixtures in a landscape of mobility that defied and escaped the West, even as they marked the success of the project of settlement that had powered the urge to conquer. Between the dawn of the nineteenth century and the close of the twentieth, the West penetrated the vast reaches of central North America, thrust out, spread, and shattered. Women moved, and the West moved too. Its movements were always coupled, star-crossed, with those of sometimes unwitting, sometimes unwilling, sometimes eager, sometimes even ecstatic women—women who were there when the West came, and are there still, partners in history's dance, as its potency fades.

PART ONE: BEFORE THE WEST

CHAPTER 1

SEEKING SACAGAWEA

Personally, I would like to ask, what is all of this fuss about? She cannot be buried in other places. She is here on the hill in the cemetery. She can only be buried in one place. . . . Fraud is not with the Indians in matters of this kind. They do not put up a story just to have it startling and out-of-place. **James McAdam, to Grace Raymond Hebard through interpreter James E. Compton, Fort Washakie, July 21, 1929**

Some of our people say she was the same woman, others say she was not. **Statement of Mrs. Weidemann, Elbowwoods, N.D., February 3, 1925, to Charles Eastman, in Sioux**

So many women were there that she might have been there and not noticed, but there were women, many of them. **Hebe-chee-chee, to Grace Raymond Hebard through interpreter James E. Compton, Fort Washakie, July 22, 1929**

Se car ja we au Dead. **William Clark, Cashbook for 1825–1828**

BEFORE THERE WAS A WEST THERE, Native American women lived in and traversed and transformed the terrain that would, in time, become the West. But the arrival of the West meant that most of those women would be dislodged and erased, relegated to the status of missing persons. When you go looking for missing persons, you may not find them, but you are bound to find out a lot of other things. That was what happened when I went looking for the Shoshone woman we know today as Sacagawea.

It seems odd to imagine this most famous Indian woman among the "missing." Pocahontas aside, no one has been *more* in evidence as a representative of indigenous women's history than Sacagawea, the Native American woman who went west with Lewis and Clark.[1] Sacagawea has, of course, been an emblem of Indian womanhood for audiences as diverse as turn-of-the-century white women's rights activists and fans of western movies. An image of her appears on the newest U.S. dollar coin. There is no question that she has been represented often and in varied media, from books to sculpture to musical theater.[2]

For someone about whom so much has been said, written, painted, and even sung in years long since her death, some fairly basic pieces of Sacagawea's story are missing. We don't know where or when she was born, and we're not sure where or when she died. We can't say for certain how many children she had; we don't even really know how to say or spell or translate her name. Even this highly celebrated indigenous woman has left a surprisingly faint trail.

But trails appear faint either because they are neglected, even erased, or because those who try to follow them don't know how to read the signs, or because the signs point in different directions. Women's traces have often faded through neglect, and sometimes been deliberately obscured, obliterated, or falsified. Women have added to the difficulty of the search by insisting, all too often and sometimes for good reasons, on covering their tracks. Tracing indigenous women in the nineteenth century means, moreover, coping with white writers' racial and gender stereotyping, cultural blindnesses, and desires to imagine the country they desired not as peopled but as empty. Thus pursuing the search means thinking hard about how to read the signs.[3]

My purpose in seeking Sacagawea was not to write a definitive biography of her, or even to try to analyze everything that has been said or written about her.[4] I wanted first to think about what we might learn by taking seriously the idea that women move through space as well as time. I also wanted to examine the ways in which race—more a potent construct of the human imagination than a biological reality in this world of interethnic interaction—affected women's movements and their legacies. I knew that even if I didn't find the historical woman Sacagawea and prove able to explain precisely where and when and how she had been, I might still learn something about some indigenous women. I would surely learn something about the difficulty and the promise of tracing the lives of women who move around.

Searching for Sacagawea has shown me ways in which Native women's movements and their knowledgeable actions in the early nineteenth century eluded, delimited, created, and transformed the West, at a time when "West" meant little more than the wish, the intent, and the action of extending American domination into a place not everyone agreed should be understood as a part of the United States.[5] This West was made real, in no small degree, through the act of writing things down. Where the power of the written word faded, so too did the West itself.

The more I looked for Sacagawea, this most written-about Indian woman, the more I tried to find the historical person divested of her burden of embodying stereotype and legend, the more I saw shadows of other women who led lives distant from the literary. Her story, the one that leaked into the chronicles of American expansion, seemed to reveal many women, moving around, mastering a host of languages and skills, turning the terrain they traversed into a densely populated, confusing place. Following her often faint, sometimes invisible trail, a trail that often crossed European Americans' tracks but as often led away from them, I found a profusion of women's footprints, leading in many directions. I finally had to ask: Was she one woman, or several, or even many?

Where previous seekers had tried to create a consistent individual woman's biography, I saw overlapping, often irreconcilable stories of a host of women. As Plains Indian women came into focus, the more "the West" receded. Yet the West did not disappear entirely from view. Just as Native women's thoughts and movements revealed both a world before the West and the limits of American authority, so too did such women take part in erecting the West.

I began, as anyone who has gone looking for Sacagawea does, with the testimony of the men of the Corps of Discovery, the transient band of soldiers and civilians sent by President Thomas Jefferson of the United States to explore a large piece of North American territory that the U.S. had recently bought but that it by no means controlled. She was perhaps fourteen, or maybe seventeen, when the men of this expedition first laid eyes on her; as Rocky Mountain frontiersman Charles William Bocker would later remark, testifying to white men's interpretive handicaps, "It is difficult to tell an Indian girl's age or a squaw's age."[6] Several men of the corps kept journals in an effort to fix as precisely as possible their own whereabouts and activities on particular dates. She might well have been among the Indians who greeted Lewis and Clark as they arrived at the Mandan-Hidatsa villages, not far from where the Knife River joins the Missouri in present-day North Dakota, near the place she lived with her French husband, Toussaint Charbonneau, and his other young Shoshone wife, said by some to have been named Otter Woman.[7] But whether or not Sacagawea had seen the men of the expedition before, their written journals suggest that she came to their attention on November 11, 1804.[8] On that day, as on most to follow, the Americans of Lewis and Clark's Corps of Discovery would refer to her not by name but according to the conventions of race and sex, in this case as one of "two squars of the Rock mountains, purchased from the Indians by a frenchmen."[9]

The expedition had established itself in winter quarters in a fort adjacent to the Mandan-Hidatsa villages. Charbonneau, who had lived and worked in Indian country for at least a decade, was looking for employment. He hoped to use his claim to fluency in Hidatsa, his knowledge of a more widely understood sign language, and his experience trapping and trading among indigenous people to hire on as an interpreter with the American expedition commanded by Captains Lewis and Clark. After some negotiation, Charbonneau signed on with the Corps of Discovery and moved with his wives into the Americans' fort.

For nearly the next two years, written records testify to where Sacagawea was and what she was doing. She traveled westward with the expedition to the Pacific Ocean, and back as far as the Mandan villages. But no one, herself included, could have known in November 1804 what her presence would come to mean to Lewis and Clark's Corps of Discovery, or to later generations. So it is perhaps not surprising that no one bothered to write down her name.

Even had they done so, Lewis and Clark and the others who kept journals were such haphazard spellers that on the few occasions when they later tried to render her name into English their representations were more remarkable for variety than for clarity. In the years since, a fierce battle has raged about the proper meaning, pronunciation, and spelling of that name: Tsi-ki-ka-wi-as (Hidatsa, "Bird Woman"); Sakakawea (Anglicized Hidatsa); Sah ca gah we ah (Clark's sometime usage); Sa cah gar we a (Lewis's attempt); Sacajawea (Nicholas Biddle's spelling, based on advice from Corps of Discovery member George Shannon, a rendering from the Shoshone meaning "Canoe Launcher").[10] Clark had such trouble wrapping his tongue around her name that he sometimes called her, simply, "Janey."[11]

Generations of American schoolchildren learned to know her as "Sacajawea, Guide of the Lewis and Clark Expedition." Each time I refer to her here as "Sacagawea," I rub against my own ingrained habit. The woman I learned to call Sacajawea, and now struggle to call Sacagawea, did not read or write, and did not pronounce her own name with English inflections. Indigenous women's names often reflect clan affiliation, but no scholar has suggested that the name Sacagawea was either a Shoshone or Hidatsa clan name. Shoshone naming practices reflect people's experiences and accomplishments more often than their clan associations. Sacagawea never attained familial status among the matrilineal Hidatsas; she was captured young, and never adopted by the Hidatsas before being sold, or lost, to Charbonneau.[12] Later Hidatsas, as we shall see, insisted that she had never been their captive at all.

In the years after she parted from the Corps of Discovery, according to Shoshone, Comanche, and white testimony, she went by a number of different names, also in different languages. She had been known in Comanche as Pohe-nive, or Grass Woman; Nyah-Suqite, meaning "The Flirt"; Wadze-Wipe, or Lost Woman; and Porivo, or Chief. And then in Shoshone, she was known as Yanb-he-be-jo, or the Old Comanche Woman; and in English, as "Bazil's Mother."[13] If the power to specify one's own name is one of the ways we measure individuality and freedom, the capacity of nations and languages to assign people definitive names is a measure of the power of states, villages, and kin groups—although in practice, the names of individuals and of groups of people often change as life goes on and people move around (consider, for example, the fact that American women have conventionally been expected to change their names after marriage). The woman I am calling Sacagawea may well have been called, and have called herself, a number of names. That English-speaking representatives of the United States have never been able to determine, finally, how her name should be pronounced or spelled or translated, let alone whether this assortment of names refers to one person, demonstrates the incompleteness of American domination of this woman, people like her, and the terrain they traversed. Early-twentieth-century Shoshones were careful to explain to interviewers that the woman they knew as Porivo was called Sacajawea by whites.[14] I settle for an imperfect and imposed representation of her name—Sacagawea—to acknowledge that there is much we will never know about her, or many others whose impact on history was no more visible, and no less substantive, than the influence of air upon lungs.

If in 1804 she was called by the Hidatsa name Sakakawea, as many have argued, it was not the first name she had known. She had, after all, been born Shoshone, probably somewhere in what would become the state of Idaho. At the age of nine or ten or eleven or twelve, camped with her band at the Three Forks of the Missouri River in what is now Montana, she endured a calamity that would change her life forever. As Meriwether Lewis understood the story, probably partly through Charbonneau's translation, she and other children and women of her Lemhi Shoshone band were captured by Minnetarees (identified in the 1920s as Gros Ventres, and more generically designated as Hidatsas) and taken, on foot or on horseback, hundreds of miles east to the Missouri River villages. There, she may have spent the next four or five or six years of her life. She learned a new language, new skills and customs, as a captive slave. Barely into her teens, she acquired the designation of "wife of" Charbonneau (who himself went by several names in different languages) when he either bought her or won her in a gambling game.[15]

White men like those of the Lewis and Clark party conventionally referred to married women by their husbands' names, and most mentions of Sacagawea in their journals follow this practice, calling her "the interpreter's wife" or "Charbono's wife." But since she was Indian rather than white, she would also be described in terms of both her race and her gender, as "Charbonneau's squaw" or "the Indian woman" or "the squar." Then as now, such generic and impersonal designations obscured as much as they revealed.

And so, unfortunately, the problem of locating and identifying and then telling the story of Sacagawea is not simply a matter of deciding on her name and going from there. For here was an indigenous woman who was, first by virtue of race and sex, and then because she was in places where writing white men weren't, largely invisible to the information-gathering mechanisms of the United States. Modern nations extend their authority over people and places by turning them into statistics: names, dates of birth, places of residence, dates of death; dots or lines or areas on a map. In her time, the United States was only just beginning to map the territory it claimed, relying heavily on the willingness of such Native people as its agents encountered to share their own stories and maps and their work and their knowledge of the countryside. Nineteenth-century American officials made estimates of indigenous group populations chiefly for military purposes, thus they paid far closer attention to the numbers of adult males than of women or children. And male or female, Indians were explicitly excluded from national census counts, on the grounds that they were not taxed, and not expected to become citizens.

Even when the U.S. government wished most ardently to count Native people, many Indian groups frustrated the government's intention by moving around. The Shoshones, for example, practiced a mixed economy of fishing, hunting, and gathering that required seasonal migrations over substantial distances and a measure of mobility on a day-to-day basis.[16] The Hidatsas, who lived during the winter along with the Mandans in the Missouri River villages, had occupied most of those villages for less than twenty years at the time Lewis and Clark quartered among them. They lived in outlying settlements during the summer, and they ranged and raided over an area covering hundreds of square miles.[17]

Before she went to the Pacific with the American party, the teenaged Sacagawea had covered a lot of ground, unbeknownst to white authorities. Her knowledge of the requirements of travel, her eagerness to journey to Shoshone territory, and her confidence in her own experience and skill in getting around the country the corps was about to "discover" at least matched those of the expedition's men. She readily joined the party even though she was far gone into pregnancy and knew that she would be carrying along and caring for a newborn baby. Neither the captains nor any of the other diarists voiced any reservations about subjecting a new mother and a tiny infant to such an exacting journey, even when she, described as "one of the wives of Charbono," endured a long, painful labor and delivery within the walls of Fort Mandan. They needed her to translate among the Shoshones, thus could make no allowances for feminine weakness. Their view of indigenous women, moreover, led them to believe that she would be able to endure more hardship than most white women, although their white successors on trails westward would rely, similarly, on women's ability to move and to work without making concessions even to the rigors of childbirth.[18]

Sacagawea was by no means the first indigenous woman the Lewis and Clark party encountered. Maybe part of their indifference to her name came from the fact that their travels had already brought them into contact with many Native women who were doing things they regarded as remarkable but whom they never named, instead tending to homogenize and dehumanize them as "squars" or "squas" or "squaws." These women's tracks crossed the expedition's, and Sacagawea's, in many places, and that mingling often provides the first clue to the existence, and the journeys, of so many others.

Sacagawea herself met up with one such woman on August 17, 1805, when the expedition reached the camp of her people, the Lemhi Shoshones, on the eastern flank of the Great Divide. As Lewis reported:

> Capt. Clark arrived with the Interpreter Charbono, and the Indian woman, who proved to be a sister of the chief Cameah-wait. the meeting of these people was really affecting, particularly between Sah cah-gar-we-ah and an Indian woman, who had been taken prisoner at the same time with her, and who had afterwards escaped from the Minnetares and rejoined her nation.[19]

According to their journals, the captains then moved to open discussions with Sacagawea's brother, Cameahwait, while the women renewed "friendships of former days," until Sacagawea was needed to translate for the men. What Lewis failed to acknowledge was that, for a period spanning five arduous months, the Lewis and Clark expedition simply retraced the footsteps of this unnamed Shoshone girl, who years before, as a ten- or eleven- or twelve-year-old, had been taken captive and forced to travel the long road eastward, then seen her chance to escape and, leaving her cherished friend behind, made the journey from the Mandan villages back to her people, on her own. Like Ginger Rogers dancing in high heels with Fred Astaire, this girl did what Lewis and Clark would, but under pressure, and backwards.

We do not know for certain whether Sacagawea's friend was among the Shoshone women who helped Lewis and Clark to inscribe a line of American presence across the continent, by carrying the expedition's baggage across the Great Divide. A number of Shoshone women did that job, with the assistance of Sacagawea and Charbonneau. By the time they reached the Continental Divide, expedition journal-keepers, who had their own ideas about how work ought properly to be divided between women and men, had seen and remarked often on the amount of heavy physical labor Native women did. The journal-keepers expressed views consistent with the Enlightenment belief that women's work provided a marker of a society's evolution from savagery to civilization; the more physical effort women were expected to exert, the lower the society on the evolutionary scale.[20] Clark, who had brought his own bondsman, York, on the journey, compared Teton Sioux women to "slaves." He thought them "Chearfull fine look'g womin" who nevertheless "do all their laborious work & I may Say perfect Slaves to the Men, as all Squars of Nations much at War, or where the Womin are more noumerous than the men."[21] Arikara women, Clark said, were "Small and industerous, raise great quantitites of Corn Beens Simnins &c. also Tobacco for the men to Smoke they collect all the wood and do the drugery as Common amongst Savages."[22] Shoshones, Lewis observed,

> treat their women but with little rispect, and compel them to perform every species of drudgery. they collect the wild fruits and roots, attend to the horses or assist in that duty, cook, dress the skins and make all their apparal, collect wood and make their fires, arrange and form their lodges, and when they travel pack the horses and take charge of all the baggage; in short the man dose little else except attend his horses hunt and fish. the man considers himself degraded if he is compelled to walk any distance; and if he is so unfortunately poor as only to possess two horses he rides the best himself and leavs the woman or women if he has more than one, to transport their baggage and children on the other, and to walk if the horse in unable to carry the additional weight of their persons.[23]

Lewis and Clark may have told themselves that female drudgery marked a society as "savage" and therefore in need of Enlightening conquest, but Lewis admitted that Shoshone women were "held more Sacred among them than in any nation we have seen and appear to have an equal Shere in all Conversation."[24] As they faced the forbidding prospect of crossing the Continental Divide, both captains were glad to avail themselves of Indian women's skill and strength when convenient, as was clearly the case when Shoshone women drove pack horses and carted their excess baggage across the divide.

When one Shoshone woman teamster stopped by a stream and sent her two heavily laden horses forward with "one of her female friends," Lewis asked Cameahwait what was keeping her. The chief explained that she had stopped to "bring forth a child and would soon overtake us," which she did. Lewis struggled to make sense of the new mother's extraordinary strength and mobility. Forgetting his own witness at Fort Mandan to Sacagawea's prolonged and excruciating labor, he relied instead on the well-established scientific practice of treating indigenous women as examples of a species rather than as human individuals. "It appears to me," he wrote, "that the facility and ease with which the women of the aborigines of North America bring forth their children is reather a gift of nature than depending as some have supposed on the habitude of carrying heavy burthens on their backs while in a state of pregnancy."[25] Thus one indigenous woman's achievement was classified as belonging not to the history of conquest, or even to the analysis of human physical conditioning, but instead to the domain of Enlightenment nature study.

While many Indian men's names are recorded in expedition writings, only one woman's name, apart from that of Sacagawea, appeared in any version of those journals. Watkuweis, an elder member of a Nez Perce band, had experienced a life that in many regards resembled the one Sacagawea was living. Her name translated into English as "returned from a far country." She had long before been captured by Blackfeet or Atsinas, taken to Canada, and sold to a white trader, living for several years among whites before finding her way back to the Nez Perces. According to Nez Perce oral tradition, she retained a positive view of whites and convinced the men of her band to assist the Corps of Discovery.[26] Watkuweis's long, multicultural west-to-east-and-back-again voyage, less literally than that of Sacagawea's Shoshone friend, but no less significantly, anticipated that of the expedition. Her words and actions in September 1805, like the work and willingness of Shoshone women, bound North American geography in a new way, linking Indian and white experience in diverse places to the new political order the Americans were trying to establish. But describing her part in stitching the region Americans wanted to name as their West to the eastern core of their country proved too difficult a task for William Clark. Watkuweis would be literally erased: Clark omitted her name from his revised journal entry.[27]

Women like Sacagawea and Watkuweis, and the unnamed Shoshone woman who assisted the corps, played the role of minor and transient characters in the expedition's story. In their own lives, however, and in the lives of the people with whom they worked and loved and fought and moved and resided, these indigenous women were often featured players. Relegated to the timeless and wordless realm of nature in expedition narratives, their history, then, took place mostly out of view of American authority, sometimes in collaboration with American aims, sometimes indifferent to the American presence, and sometimes in resistance to American domination.[28] Wherever they lived beyond the sight and the reach of Euro-American authority should not be regarded now as part of an inevitably Western history. Their bodies, and the bodies of unnamed and unnumbered indigenous people like them, indeed marked not just the extent, but also the limits of the American power required to call a place "our West."

Even Sacagawea herself, who has so often stood as a complicit emblem of that conquest, had a life apart from it: perhaps a very long life. Nothing better reveals the limits of American dominion in her time, a period possibly spanning ninety or more years, than the mystery of what happened to her after she parted from the Corps of Discovery on August 17, 1806. On that moving occasion, Clark acknowledged her role as "interpretes" on the journey to the Pacific and wrote glowingly of Sacagawea's Shoshone-French son Baptiste, "a butifull promising child" whom Clark promised to educate and raise "in such a manner as I thought proper." Clark clearly liked and respected her, and had witnessed her bravery, resourcefulness, and sense of adventure on many occasions. He had watched once, on shore, as one of the pirogues swamped and she managed, with quick wits and reflexes, to save vital instruments, medicines, and papers as they began to float away.[29] One day when the expedition was in quarters at Fort Clatsop in the winter of 1805–1806, Clark determined to lead a small party on a rugged trip to view a beached whale. Sacagawea begged to be taken along, telling the captains that "she had traveled a long way with us to see the great waters, and that now that monstrous fish was also to be seen, she thought it very hard she could not be permitted to see either (she had never yet been to the Ocean)."[30] On Christmas day of 1805, Sacagawea gave Clark the gift of ten white weasel tails, a sure sign of her own esteem for him.[31] She recognized landmarks, carried messages between the captains, and took part, repeatedly, in the laborious process of translating conversations between the Americans and the diverse people they met. On many occasions she had slaked the expedition's hunger with her skill at gathering roots and greens the men would not have even known were there, much less understood were edible. But at their moment of parting, employing the habit of speech that would do so much to obscure her life and the lives of so many women before and after her, Clark referred to her not by name, but as Charbonneau's "Snake Indian wife." Declining to utter Sacagawea's name, he blurred her trail as surely as if he'd thrown a bucketful of sand across her moccasin tracks.[32]

What happened then? Not long after Clark returned to St. Louis, he wrote a letter to Charbonneau at the Mandan villages, imploring him to bring

Sacagawea and Baptiste to St. Louis, where he promised to give Charbonneau land and livestock and pledged to educate Baptiste, whom he called "my little dancing boy." He explained to Charbonneau that "your famn [wife] Janey had best come along with you to take care of the boy until I get him." But he also told Charbonneau, "Your woman who accompanied you that long dangerous and fatigueing rout to the Pacific Ocian and back diserved a greater reward for her attention and services on that rout than we had in our power to give her at the Mandans."[33]

Sacagawea and Baptiste and Charbonneau apparently made the journey to St. Louis in 1810, where Clark sold Charbonneau some land and set about arranging and paying for Baptiste's education. Charbonneau, however, decided to sell the land back to Clark within a few months and to return to trapping on the Missouri. The six-year-old Baptiste remained behind, where he was educated at the expense of William Clark.[34]

Now comes the critical question: Did Sacagawea remain in St. Louis with her son or return to the villages with her husband? Charbonneau had signed on with a trader named Henry Brackenridge, who wrote in his own journal as the expedition departed St. Louis on April 2, 1811:

> We have on board a Frenchman named Charbonet, with his wife, an Indian woman of the Snake nation, both of whom accompanied Lewis and Clark to the Pacific, and were of great service. The woman, a good creature, of a mild and gentle disposition, was greatly attached to the whites, whose manners and airs she tries to imitate; but she had become sickly and longed to revisit her native country; her husband also, who had spent many years amongst the Indians, was become weary of civilized life.[35]

What "native country" did this most mobile and multicultural woman wish to revisit? And should we see Brackenridge's use of the term as an implicit acknowledgment that the trans-Mississippi region was by no means simply part of the United States? As for the unnamed female passenger, surely the "wife" referred to was Sacagawea; after all, she was the only woman who fit Brackenridge's description. In any case, if she was the woman who went up the river with Charbonneau, then it was probably she whose death was described by the trader John C. Luttig, at the Mandan villages, on December 20, 1812: "This evening the wife of Charbonneau, a Snake squaw, died of a putrid fever. She was the best woman in the fort, aged about twenty-five years. She left a fine infant child." The child, unnamed here like her mother, Luttig would later identify as a daughter called Lizette.[36]

Most historians of the Lewis and Clark expedition regard the Brackenridge and Luttig statements as definitive proof that Sacagawea's story ended in 1812. They further cite a notation on the cover of William Clark's cashbook for 1825–1828, "Se car ja we au Dead," as proof of her early demise.[37] But some of those who reckon their histories using different geographies, and featuring different people in starring roles, have told very different, much longer and more complex and contradictory tales. These stories encompass a much wider terrain, a landscape only episodically describable as the American West.

Some investigators wondered whether the Shoshone wife who returned to the villages with Charbonneau in 1811, and died there in 1812, was indeed Sacagawea. She surely had gone with him and with the Corps of Discovery to the Pacific, but at the time of the 1805 departure from the Mandan villages she was, according to expedition journals, not his only Shoshone wife. Those who sought Sacagawea during the early part of the twentieth century lived in and traveled to places that were, by that time, regularly bounded and incorporated into the western part of the United States. At the same time, they questioned the idea that the story of Sacagawea, or of Native women more generally, was nothing much more than a subplot in narratives of the American West such as the tale of the Lewis and Clark party. They asked whether the vagaries of translation and white men's habit of referring to indigenous women by anything but their own names may have affected English-speakers' understanding of what and whom they were seeing, and of what and whom others had seen.

In December 1924 the federal government hired Sioux physician and author Charles Eastman to investigate the life story of Sacagawea. Eastman's job was to settle a dispute among historians in Wyoming, Montana, and the Dakotas over where and when the indigenous woman had died. It was not an idle question. As has so often been the case in the history of the American West, there was government money at stake. The Anglo-American feminist historian Grace Raymond Hebard, of the University of Wyoming, had begun to lobby Congress to appropriate money for a monument to Sacagawea (whom she called Sacajawea) on the Wind River Indian Reservation in Wyoming.[38] Since 1905 Hebard had been collecting evidence among white agents and missionaries at Wind River showing that the woman who had accompanied Lewis and Clark had found her way back to Shoshones at Fort Bridger sometime in the 1850s, and had lived on the reservation at Fort Washakie until her death in 1884. The North Dakota historian Doane Robinson and others insisted that there was no question that Sacagawea had died in 1812, and they took their case to their own representatives in Congress. Opposition to Hebard's position and her efforts was so strenuous that the commissioner of Indian affairs asked Eastman to make an official inquiry.[39]

Eastman examined the documents Hebard had gathered from white informants and then set out on his own tour of Wyoming, Oklahoma, and North Dakota to interview Shoshones, Comanches, and Hidatsas in an effort to learn what Indians knew about the life of Sacagawea. He looked at the Luttig and Brackenridge journals, examined Hebard's evidence from three Christian missionaries he described as "both intelligent and strong men" who "had known Porivo, Bazile's mother or Sacajawea, the Bird Woman," and collected the "testimonies of three different Indian nations, namely, Shoshones, Comanches, and Gros Ventres." Eastman insisted that "we have to accept the tribal traditions and when they corroborate so strikingly well, we must accept it as the truth." But he also relied on his "knowledge of the Indian mothers traits and habits," derived in part from watching Indian women deal with the wrenching experience of seeing their children taken off to government boarding schools.[40]

By March 2, 1925, after a short but intense investigation, Eastman concluded that Sacagawea, known to the Shoshones as Porivo, had, as Hebard argued, lived until 1884, sometimes in a tepee and sometimes in a government-built wooden house, and died at Wind River. The woman who died in 1812, Eastman believed, was Charbonneau's other Shoshone wife, Otter Woman, because

> Baptiste [at age six] was too young to be separated from his mother and in my knowledge of the Indian mothers traits and habits are such that she could not have permitted to be separated from her child at that age, especially those time. It was hard enough up to thirty years ago to get a child of 10 years to leave their Indian parents to go to school. It would have been impossible for Clark to retain Baptiste without his mother.[41]

According to Eastman, sometime after going back to the Mandan villages Charbonneau returned to St. Louis with a new Hidatsa wife named Eagle. He then took his two surviving wives ("Sacajawea," a name Eastman translated as "Bird Woman," and Eagle) and their children, one of whom was Baptiste and the other, Otter Woman's son, to work translating and trapping in the fur trade in western Oklahoma and Kansas. Trouble ensued when Charbonneau brought home yet another young wife, a Ute girl. After a dispute between Sacagawea and the Ute wife, Charbonneau beat the Shoshone woman, and, Eastman explained, "the

Bird Woman disappears." She managed to find her way to a band of Comanches, and lived among them for "26 or 27 years." During this time she married a man named Jerk Meat and bore five more children, the youngest of whom she took with her when she left the Comanches following Jerk Meat's death in battle. After that time, her Comanche son tried and failed to find her, and the Comanches referred to her as "Wadzewipe": Lost Woman. This was the woman, Eastman maintained, who made her way to Fort Bridger, and from there to Fort Washakie on the Wind River Reservation, where she lived until 1884.[42]

It is not difficult to reconcile Eastman's version of Sacagawea's life with Clark's belief, by 1825, that she was dead. For one thing, since she was not literate, she had no way of maintaining personal contact with Clark across long distances, save through intermediaries, Charbonneau in particular. Purportedly, by 1825 she had already run away from Charbonneau, following a severe beating, and was trying to evade pursuit. In such a case, she would have worked frantically to cover her tracks. To have Charbonneau believe her dead would have aided her escape. For his part, it would have been logical for Charbonneau to believe that no lone woman, particularly one who had recently suffered a heavy physical assault, could survive long on the southern plains, in territory she did not know well.

But Eastman's and Hebard's linking of discrete stories does not quite biography make. From 1806 forward, events Eastman and Hebard would try to associate with Sacagawea's life may have happened to or because of her, or for that matter, to or because of a woman or women with whom she had a great deal in common.

While Sacagawea disappeared from Euro-American view in the years after 1806, she, or mobile, skilled Indian women like her, imprinted their presence in several indigenous oral traditions.[43] The stories other Indians told about her, however, varied from tribe to tribe, and within tribal groupings. These stories, like the ones European Americans recorded, were not products of some authentic and unmodified "native" knowledge, but were historical artifacts very much shaped by the past and present politics of gender and nation.

When Charles Eastman visited the Fort Berthold Reservation at Elbowwoods, North Dakota, in the winter of 1925, some of his Hidatsa hosts seized the opportunity to remind him of the history of conflict between themselves and his own Sioux people. Two Hidatsa men, Bull Eye's and Wolf Chief, insisted that if there was any Shoshone girl in their villages with Charbonneau that winter of 1804–1805, she must have been captured not by Hidatsas but by Crows. As Bull Eye's, the grandson of Charbonneau and Charbonneau's third, Hidatsa wife, Eagle, told Eastman, "We never have any Snake captives here. . . . Our friends the Crow Indians are the ones who have battled with them and it is my impression that if there is any Snake captives they must have been taken by the Crow Indians and not by the Gros Ventres. Our tribes were so surrounded by our Sioux enemies it was impossible for our people to go very far from our village, either in hunting or warfare."[44]

"I don't want to dispute the records of Lewis and Clark," Gros Ventre chief Wolf Chief explained to Eastman, presumably in English, on that same interviewing trip to North Dakota, "but they were undoubtedly misinformed." Standing on his authority as "hereditary chief of the Gros Ventre Indians," Wolf Chief said:

> Our people never go to the Rocky Mountains for the purpose of warfare or hunting because we are absolutely surrounded by our enemies. Therefore we could never have taken any captives from the Shoshoni people. It must have been taken by our friends, the Crow tribe, who made war with the Shoshonis and that Charbonneau must have married these Shoshoni women up the river among the Crows and later came down to our tribe with them and remained with us here a little while when the Lewis and Clark expedition came here and found them here.[45]

Although Eastman was present as a representative of the United States, both Wolf Chief and Bull Eye's seemed to regard relations between Indian nations and the United States as marginal matters compared to the history of Hidatsa conflict with the Sioux. Thus Wolf Chief took pains to inform Eastman that Sacagawea played no role in Hidatsa tradition, and Lewis and Clark were little more than minor figures:

> The fact [is] that they were mere visitors here and then taken away by Lewis and Clark as mere employees, that they did not impress our people's minds as important people. And when Lewis and Clark returned here, Charbonneau and his wife did not stay here very long, and then, as you say, went down to St. Louis, Missouri. . . . I think I have told you the reason why my people did not know very much about Sacajawea, the Bird Woman. I repeat, that she was not a member of our tribe and she was not a captive of our tribe and she did not stay here long and our people did not realize that she had taken an important part in the expedition and therefore we did not include her in the milepost of our history. This is all I can tell you.[46]

Not all Hidatsas, however, dismissed the "Bird Woman" as a figure beneath notice.[47] Another Gros Ventre/Hidatsa informant told Eastman a very different story, speaking, as Eastman carefully noted, in Sioux, although she "could have given it to me in Gros Ventres or English, as well." Adopting white naming practices, Eastman identified this multilingual woman only as Mrs. Weidemann (or Waidemann or Weidmann) and interviewed her in the presence of her husband and a Gros Ventre translator. This eighty-year-old woman, however, claimed authority as the daughter of Poor Wolf, the hereditary chief of the Gros Ventres, who "died 26 years ago at the age of 102. He was born about 1797. . . . He is Tribal Historian." Explaining that her father had been present throughout Lewis and Clark's sojourn at the Missouri River villages, and that he had been "of very clear mind up to his death," she told her father's story about "a Frenchman who came down from North with two Shoshoni wives. . . . One was called the 'Bird Woman' or Sacajawea, the other was 'Otter Woman.' . . . who they were we know very little about them." Mrs. Weidemann explained that Sacajawea had gone along with Lewis and Clark but that Charbonneau's other Shoshone wife had remained "at our village, she being not well." When the Corps of Discovery returned to the village, they left the "Frenchman and his wife, Sacajawea," there, but a year or so later Charbonneau and his two wives went down the river with some fur traders. "We never know what become of these Shoshoni Women thereafter."[48]

But as Mrs. Weidemann spoke further, in the language of the people Wolf Chief called "our enemies," she told a story that provided the crucial clue Eastman and Hebard needed to argue that Sacagawea had lived on past 1812. And this clue revealed and relied on the story of yet another indigenous woman who traversed a wide landscape and made her own history, yet remained virtually invisible to American authorities who wished to name her country "West." In about 1820, Mrs. Weidemann said, Charbonneau had married "Eagle, who was very pretty Gros Ventres girl." Eagle then accompanied Charbonneau on "a wonderful trip" down the Missouri River, "and she was gone for quite a number of years, and she returned to her tribe, strange to say, from up the river." Continuing, Mrs. Weidemann told Eastman "the story that Eagle told herself of the trip, which she gave to my father when she came back, and my father has repeated so many times to our tribe and our family that I still remember the substance of it. I will speak it as if Eagle is speaking," she explained:

> When Charbonneau took me down the river among the white people
> we came to a great town called St. Louis. We stayed there a year or so
> when Charbonneau found one of his Shoshoni wives, the "Bird Woman"

Sacajawea, in a little town about St. Louis, called Portage [Portage des Sioux, Missouri]. This woman had two sons with her, one was about 18 and the other 16. The older one was called Bazile, the other Baptiste. They were bright young men and talked French quite well. The Shoshoni woman, herself, talked French too. After a while Charbonneau wanted to take his wife back and I consented, then we lived together for a little while at St. Louis, when Charbonneau was employed by the Fur Company and we were sent southwest on a big river, almost as big as the Missouri River. On this trip we came to a great many trading posts and we stayed at one place for a year, and we stopped another place two years. We came among many Indian tribes that I never heard of, some were called Wichita, some were called Comanches, and Utes, and other tribes who came to trade at these posts where we were. After [a] while Charbonneau, my husband, took another wife, a pretty Ute woman. I did not complain but Bird Woman made serious complaint and made it unpleasant for the Ute Woman. Finally Charbonneau punished her severely and in a day or so afterwards she disappeared. At this time her two boys were away on a trip. . . . When the boys came back they made it very serious for Charbonneau and they were not friends after that.[49]

Mrs. Weidemann explained further that her father had recalled, late in life, that he had heard that "the Bird Woman" succeeded in returning to her tribe, the Shoshone people in Wyoming, and "lived to be a great old age—died at Fort Washakie, Wyoming." Her father had also remembered a time when a party attached to the Missouri Fur Company had stopped at a fort downriver, and that "among the wives of the Frenchmen and employees" was a "Bird Woman" who went up the river with the rest. For Eastman, as for Hebard, this story provided the basis for the claim that the aged Shoshone-Comanche Pohe-nive, who was also Porivo, was Wadze-wipe and even, indeed, Sacagawea of the Lewis and Clark expedition. Mrs. Weidemann was, however, far more circumspect. "Some of our people say she was the same woman, others say she was not. That's all we knew of the Shoshoni guide of Lewis and Clark."[50]

For Mrs. Weidemann, if not for her Sioux interlocutor, the featured player in her story was not Sacagawea but Eagle, whose own adventures were hardly bounded by the Shoshone woman's disappearance. "The following summer," Mrs. Weidemann explained, still speaking as if she were Eagle,

the Fur Companies organized a large body of employees with many packed mules to visit the mountain Indians toward the northwest and Charbon-neau and I and the Ute woman joined the party. We traveled a long while until we reached a great Lake, the whites called it Salt Lake. . . . In the summer we moved Northeast, over the mountains, but before we moved some Utes visited our winter quarter who were related to Charbonneau's Ute wife. When we were moving Charbonneau's Ute wife wouldn't go, but she went home with her relatives. We never saw her again after that. We moved north and east slowly until we reached Wind River, and down the Big Horn until we came into the Yellowstone River; the men made boats and put all the furs in them and we floated down the Missouri River; from there we reached home at the Gros Ventre village.

"This," concluded Mrs. Weidemann, "was the story of Eagle's wonderful trip."[51] It was also, of course, the story of an unnamed Ute woman's wonderful trip and her determination to step out of the frame of the story Mrs. Weidemann would tell to Dr. Eastman in the latter's native tongue. The Ute woman traveled on. We cannot know where, exactly, she went.

Bull Eye's, Eagle's Hidatsa grandson, had nothing to say about Charbonneau's fourth wife, but he was very much interested in the Frenchman's third. Indeed, he insisted that virtually everyone else had got the story of Lewis and Clark's Indian woman interpreter confused, because the woman in question was not a Shoshone named Sacagawea but, instead, his own Hidatsa grandmother! "My grandmother's name," he told Charles Eastman, "is Eagle, but her husband Charbonneau cannot talk Gros Ventres very well so they simply called her Bird Woman."[52]

Mrs. Weidemann, however, explained that "Bull-Eyes mistaken this for the Lewis and Clark trip, therefore, he claims that his mother was the guide on the Lewis and Clark Expedition, which is not true."[53] Though Mrs. Weidemann's story differed from that of Bull Eye's, both she and Eagle's grandson knew Hidatsa traditions of women's journeys through country not yet an American West but still jointly occupied by Indians and whites and their mutual offspring.[54] And both made a point of telling Eastman, with great precision, that Eagle had been killed by a Sioux war party near Glasgow, Montana, in 1869.[55]

Mrs. Weidemann's testimony suggested that Sacagawea might have lived into the 1820s, and have traveled further in regions still not quite under U.S. domination. But Mrs. Weidemann stopped far short of asserting that the woman who died at Fort Washakie, and the woman who had traveled, for a time, with Eagle, were one and the same: "Some of our people say she was the same woman, others say she was not."[56]

Charles Eastman, however, was on a roll. Two weeks after he visited North Dakota, he was in Lawton, Oklahoma, where he interviewed We-sue-poie, a seventy-five-year-old Comanche woman, "concerning the traditions of Porivo, or supposed to be Sacajawea, 'or Bird Woman.'" Eastman found no one among the Comanches who could say just how and when the woman they called Porivo or Wadze-wipe had appeared among them, but We-sue-poie explained that she had "a clear memory of the tradition of her disappearance from this tribe." Porivo, she said, was the

> wife of Jerk-Meat, and she had five children. When her husband was killed she was very much depressed and she had some difficulty with her husband's people. She was not satisfied with her situation, among the band with whom she lived. She had said she was going to leave the tribe but the people didn't think she meant it. One day she disappeared and took with her her youngest child, who was a little girl, on her back, they said. She also took some provision in a par fleche bag. The tribe hunted for her everywhere but found no trace of her. Her son went to the nearby tribes to see if she run to any of these, but no one saw her at all.

However, said We-sue-poie, "we have learned from the school boys who went to Carlisle School that she had reached the Shoshone people and she lived there a number of years and died at a very advanced age."[57] Among those schoolboys was a Shoshone named James McAdam, who in 1929 told Grace Hebard through an interpreter that he had lived with his great-grandmother, Porivo, and his grandfather, Basil, until 1881, when he went off to attend Carlisle. He remembered that she and her sons, Basil and Baptiste, spoke French and that "she herself distinctly told me a number of times that she had relatives in Oklahoma. She said to me, 'You have relatives down with the Comanches in the South.'" When McAdam went to Carlisle

> I saw some Comanche Indians, and I asked them about Sacajawea, or Poheniv, or the Grass Woman, or Porivo—Chief, or Wadze-wipe—Lost Woman. These boys, Comanche Indians from where Oklahoma is, said they knew of Indians in the North, although she, Sacajawea or Porivo, considered herself a Comanche Indian or as belonging to the Comanche branch of the Shoshone Indians. This was the beginning of the direct connection of Sacajawea of the Comanche and of the Shoshones under Washakie and the connection of our Sacajawea with the Sacajawea of the Lewis and Clark Expedition.[58]

By the mid-1920s, when Eastman and Hebard conducted their interviews, Shoshones and Comanches, numbers of them government-educated, had begun to travel back and forth between Oklahoma and Wyoming as relatives tracing their descent from a common great-grandmother. James McAdam visited Oklahoma, where, he recalled, Comanches told him that until they had learned about her fate from Shoshones, they believed "that the whitemen had stolen Wadze-wipe."[59] Baptiste's daughter, Barbara

Meyers ("commonly known as Maggie Meyers among the Indians"), told Hebard, through the interpreter James E. Compton, that she had recently had a three-month-long visit from a Comanche woman who was her cousin and that "the two families visit back and forth from Oklahoma to Wyoming annually."[60]

Thus by the mid-1920s, some Comanches and Shoshones recognized a common ancestor, known to them as Porivo and to local whites as Sacajawea. Their newly forged kin tie provided the rationale for annual intertribal, interstate vacations. But Eastman and Hebard pursued their own drive to assemble a linear biography of a unique person, Sacagawea. They had to fill in silences, push some evidence hard, and ignore information regarding the presence of native women like Otter Woman, Sacagawea's Shoshone captive friend, the Nez Perce woman Watkuweis, the Hidatsa woman Eagle, and a Ute woman whose name we do not know. These women, like Sacagawea, deployed their own movements, speech, and actions in knowledgeable and strategic fashion, and in obscurity.

A number of Shoshone men and women explained to Eastman—and to Hebard, who conducted interviews with several of them in 1926 and 1929—that it was common knowledge at Wind River that Porivo (whom they would later call by the Shoshone name of Pohe-nive, or Grass Woman), who first appeared among them at Fort Bridger in the 1850s and lived with them until 1884, had "come from the Comanches." Two Shoshone women, Te-ah-win-nie (Susan Perry) and Enga Peahrora (daughter of the famed Shoshone chief Washakie), explained that Porivo spoke Comanche dialect, but also spoke French and, according to Te-ah-win-nie, spoke Gros Ventre and Assiniboin as well. She recognized as her sons two men named Basil and Baptiste, both of whom spoke French and claimed to be the products of her marriage to a Frenchman.[61] Basil's son Andrew Basil, better known to the Shoshones as Oha-wa-nud, told Eastman that "I remember very well her story of her life among the Comanches."[62] Thus, it seems reasonable to assume that Porivo, whom all Shoshone interviewees agreed had first appeared among them as a gray-haired, Comanche-speaking adult woman, had made a long and arduous trek from the southern plains to the northern Rockies in years when U.S. government expeditions were still trying to map the country she walked or rode across. She was, no doubt, a resourceful person.

James McAdam would explain, in 1929, that Porivo had told him that she had a French husband she called "Schab-ano."[63] But by then McAdam had had plenty of time to refine his account not only to conform with the stories of his Comanche friends and relations, from as far back as his years in school at Carlisle, but also with an eye to pleasing the interviewers and reservation officials who seemed determined to prove that Porivo was Sacagawea, "Canoe Launcher" or "Bird Woman." Andrew Basil had told Eastman four years earlier that Porivo "never told very much about her French husband, neither did she tell much about her life with the Comanches. She seemed to want that part of her life unknown, except that occasionally, she would tell something of the Comanches."[64]

She seemed to want that part of her life unknown.

Eastman's and Hebard's connection between the Shoshone woman who accompanied Lewis and Clark, the woman who appeared among the Comanches sometime after 1820 and left them after 1850, and the woman who arrived at Fort Bridger in the late 1850s and went on to live at Wind River until 1884 required both Indian mobility and the existence of outposts of the U.S. government. The mobile Native Americans in question were Comanche and Shoshone people who claimed descent from the woman they called Porivo as well as other names. They made use of agencies intended to restrict them—the Wind River Reservation, Carlisle School—to construct a history that could never be verified by state mechanisms.[65] A Sioux government employee and a white feminist professor would come together to promote this story as "official" truth. Their detractors would never buy their account, insisting to the end that Lewis and Clark's "Bird Woman" had met a sad and untimely end, six short years after the peak experience of her life, her trip across the West with the Corps of Discovery. But we may observe that Porivo, and Wadze-wipe, not to mention Watkuweis and Eagle and unnamed Shoshone and Ute women, had some adventures of their own.

One hot July afternoon in 1929, Grace Hebard and James Compton drove out to an alfalfa field near Fort Washakie to interview Hebe-chee-chee, a Shoshone man whose name meant "a very, very old woman." As they sat and talked in Hebard's automobile, Hebard asked Hebe-chee-chee whether Sacagawea had been present at negotiations over the Fort Bridger Treaty of 1868, which had resulted in the creation of the Wind River Reservation. His reply may stand as the honest but frustrating solution to our search for a missing person. "I cannot recall whether Sacajawea was there or not," Hebe-chee-chee told Compton, who translated the old man's words from Shoshone into English for Hebard. "So many women were there that she might have been there and not noticed, but there were women, many of them."[66]

We will never know the truth about Sacagawea; we will never even know her name. But the more we seek her, the more we find indigenous women traversing a territory that was not yet the West. They left an impression on places and people with their thoughts and words and deeds, reacted to the world around them, and too often covered their tracks as they determined, or were forced, to move on. They challenged white men's ideas about what women ought to be, even as white men made barely acknowledged use of their skills, bravery, and strength. They also sometimes challenged Indian men's ideas of how women ought to behave; as Shoshone James McAdam recalled of his great-grandmother Porivo, "There was another reason why the Indians did not exalt over her work— the fact that Indian men did not like to see a woman go ahead of them."[67]

Ironically, the costs of claiming their actions and celebrating their wonderful journeys may have been so high that these nineteenth-century Indian women opted, instead, to say little and move on. Still, they have left traces in the always unreliable, yet undeniable repositories of memory and story. We know little about them, but we do know that they were present, and moving, in a fully inhabited landscape that Americans wanted to call "empty." They explored and discovered, took risks, and made history, most of which we will never know. Their paths intersected with the lines of writing across paper that stored, and lent authority to, the movements and intentions of the agents of the American empire. And sometimes these Native women helped to create that empire, making fires, cooking roots, skinning animals, carrying bundles, bearing children, speaking to friends and strangers. Their American contemporaries lacked the language to describe their lives. And the dearth of our understanding of their experiences tells us in the clearest possible terms that, all too often, where they were, the West wasn't. At least, not yet.

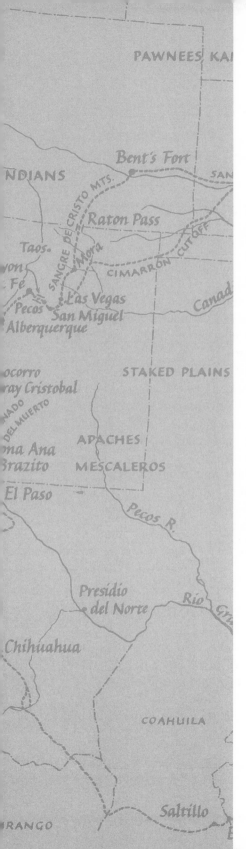

CHAPTER 2

THE HEARTH OF DARKNESS

Susan Magoffin on Suspect Terrain

In her simple and gentle way the young lady deftly raised the curtain from before characters and events of great importance in American history. **Stella M. Drumm, 1926**

Christ himself warns us that we must not fear those who can kill and in any wise injure the body, and can do nothing to the *immortal* soul. But he says "rather fear Ye him who after he hath killed hath power to cast into hell." **Susan Shelby Magoffin, 1846**

I had, for my sins I suppose, to go through the ordeal of looking into myself. **Joseph Conrad, *The Heart of Darkness***

B Y THE 1840S SACAGAWEA'S COUNTRY was under invasion. Americans were swarming to map the terrain between the Mississippi and the Pacific with their movements and their stories. One such American was Kentuckian Susan Shelby Magoffin, eighteen-year-old wife to St. Louis trader Samuel Magoffin and "the first American white woman ever to go over the rude trail of the Santa Fe traders."[1] Susan Magoffin gained a measure of notice as a chronicler of men in the act of conquering. She kept a diary on her honeymoon trip in 1846 and into 1847, across the Santa Fe Trail and southward into Mexico, so keenly observing the country and the events that western historian Sandra Myres called Magoffin's diary "a minor classic."[2] Howard Lamar praised Magoffin as "an intelligent, observant, and tolerant person with a genuinely inquisitive nature," while acknowledging that "commentators have frequently characterized both Mrs. Magoffin and her diary as 'girlish,' 'naive,' and 'charming.'"[3] "She was altogether a darling," wrote Bernard DeVoto, who wove snippets of Magoffin's observations into his compelling 1942 synthesis, *The Year of Decision: 1846.*[4]

The year 1846 was a crucial one for the conquest of what was still half of Mexico but would, within two years, by the authority of the Treaty of Guadalupe Hidalgo, be claimed as the American Southwest. Traders like Susan's husband, Samuel, his brother James, and their relatives by marriage, the Valdez family of Chihuahua, had prepared the path on which the American army rolled into New Mexico and fought its way into Chihuahua before sweeping across to California. The phrase "Manifest Destiny," newly minted in 1845, rumbled across newspaper pages and the chambers of Congress and animated the conversations of boosters and boomers (and dissidents) of all stripes. It was obvious, the phrase suggested, that the United States must occupy land that would soon be identified by the sanguine term "Mexican Cession." Indeed, according to the logic of Manifest Destiny, el Norte de Mexico was already, had always been, American domain that had only to be secured and organized as such.

But in 1846, Susan Magoffin traveled in Indian country and in Mexico. Manifest Destiny was a projection, not a fact. To make it fact, disputed territory had to be domesticated, settled. "White women" (Susan herself once put the term in quotes, marking her own anomaly) played a crucial role in the process of settlement.[5] It was their job to transport, enact, and reproduce the customs of American domesticity, the habits at the heart of American social life. Every recipe and dress pattern, every homily and admonition that westering women advanced carried a little piece of empire along.[6]

"What made Susan Magoffin's trip historically significant as well as colorful and exciting," wrote Howard Lamar, "was not simply that she kept an excellent daily record . . . but that she travelled at a crucial time in the history of the trans-Mississippi West."[7] But in Magoffin's time, the West was not a "trans-Mississippi" entity. It was still a series of encounters ranging from the episodic—bloody or indifferent or curious— to the long-standing—antipathetic or necessary or loving—taking place in widely dispersed, tenuously linked locales. Those engagements and connections were more numerous, more deeply informed, and often more regularized than they had been at the time Sacagawea encountered the Lewis and Clark party. But they still took place among persons who had varying, shifting, and often unreliable geographical loyalties, mental maps, and political allegiances. Susan Magoffin moved through contested country, recording her thoughts and feelings in dozens of places and under wildly vacillating, sometimes baffling, even terrifying, circumstances.[8]

In the language of geology, terrestrial formations adjacent to but geologically unrelated to neighboring structures are called "suspect terrains."[9] Geologists believe that such suspect terrains can reveal tectonic processes along fissures and fault lines, the kinds of activity that can cause earthquakes. At Council Grove in what is now Kansas, Susan Shelby Magoffin entered a first suspect terrain, and for her, the earth began to tremble. At Bent's Fort, in what has become southern Colorado, the world jolted suddenly, waking her to tragedy and loss. The many landscapes of New Mexico took her through a whole series of shifts, and every time she thought she'd found her feet, little tremors shook her composure. As she moved southward into Old Mexico with war raging around her, the strange ground seemed full of little shivers, and at times appeared to shake and yawn and open chasms in everything she'd ever known.

A young, genteel southern, evangelical Christian woman, Susan Magoffin was secure in her race and her class and her creed, but she feared God. She believed in marriage and language and home and hearth, but her mind was uneasy and her body was beleaguered. Death haunted her.

As she traveled, she prepared with increasing fervor to die and to face divine judgment. Manifest Destiny put her where she was. But strip away the tall tale, the heroic march toward the bright telos of continental conquest, and we see how Magoffin journeyed to a different, darker place.

Like Conrad's Marlowe, she was both ingenue and invader. She started out speaking the language of lighthearted escapade: "now for a bit of my wonderful travels so far."[10] Picaresque adventures have a way of wandering into trouble. As she tried to draw domestic circles around her life, to create an American geography of comfort, Magoffin kept running up against the turbulence of strange landscapes, of different people, of military maneuver, of political loyalty, and of her own body. Even as she groped for the familiar, what she could not fathom terrified her.

The ideas and gestures of Manifest Destiny have deeply crosscut Susan Magoffin's trail. And so, before we can follow her journey into darkness, we have to deal with the editor who demoted the author of the diary to the position of "simple and gentle" observer of "events of very great importance." Most readers of Magoffin's diary do not venture to the Beinecke Library at Yale University to see the original or to read the microfilm. Instead, we sensibly opt to let Magoffin's words come to us in published and highly portable form. Anyone can buy, for $12 plus tax, the widely available Bison Books paperback, originally edited and published in 1926 by Missouri Historical Society archivist Stella M. Drumm.

If any volume ever testified to the importance of editorial intervention, this is one. Stella Drumm was an editor on a mission. *St. Louis Post Dispatch* columnist M. W. Childs noted that Drumm's vision of editing "does not mean merely seeing that the commas and periods are where they belong. It means tracing down and identifying each name and place that comes into the record."[11] To Magoffin's original text, some 237 lined pages of writing in a book eight and a half inches wide and ten inches long, Drumm added an avalanche of annotation amounting to a text nearly as long as the diary itself. The typescript of Magoffin's journal covered 153 double-spaced pages of elite type. Drumm added elite-type notes filling an additional 131 pages, which were later converted to footnotes.[12]

The doggedly researched footnotes to *Down the Santa Fe Trail* do indeed deal with names and places, in stunning detail. The footnotes seem to creep from the bottom nearer and nearer to the top of page after page. Drumm's annotations tell stories about any number of people. Curiously, they do not tell us a thing about Susan Shelby Magoffin, who appears in the notes only twice in passing.[13] Drumm directs the reader's attention away from the diarist, nearly pushes the diary itself off the page, and all but renders the author invisible, swamped by the rising tide of editorial commentary. Drumm carefully selected and highlighted certain actors, events, and contexts, ignoring many others, peopling the Santa Fe Trail in her own way. She sought not to tell Magoffin's story, but to commemorate the march of American conquest. Every page of the diary of Susan Magoffin took a manifestly new shape under Drumm's hand.

Trained in library work at the University of Missouri, Stella Drumm worked at the Missouri Historical Society from 1913 to 1944.[14] She was a native St. Louisan from a socially prominent Catholic family, tracing her genealogical roots to Georgia and North Carolina. She was loyal to her family, her class, her town, her state, the South, and the United States. She believed wholeheartedly in Manifest Destiny, lionized those who had carried it forward, and relished the minutiae of its progress.[15] By all accounts, Drumm was an expert in and enthusiast for genealogy, and she carried that interest into all her historical projects.[16]

Genealogy and family are very different things. The study of genealogy makes families appear linear, continuous, and in some sense unchanging, simplifying the messy mixing of human beings into meticulously researched diagrams of names connected by lines. Genealogy erases some intimate connections, and enshrines relationships that may be no more than nominal. People, understood genealogically, appear much more the product of their clear bloodlines than of the chaos of encounter and experience. Thus, genealogy does significant cultural work. The fascination with genealogy in the United States can be usefully understood as an "invented tradition," in Eric Hobsbawm and Terence Ranger's unforgettable phrase.[17]

Drumm's editorial annotations relied heavily on invented traditions, genealogy and military history foremost among them. She meant to commemorate a western history viewed, retrospectively, as the story of a region destined for American incorporation. She devotedly detailed the family connections, personalities, and careers of the American traders and military officers Susan Magoffin encountered in her travels. To a lesser degree, she offered comment on prominent Mexican military men and traders, cast as opponents, advocates, or grudging acquiescents in the American conquest, recording only family relationships among those who came to serve the American nation. By presenting the mobile agents of

American empire nestled in the seemingly lush growth of family trees, and by almost completely ignoring the presence of the Mexican women and children Magoffin met and wrote about, Stella Drumm unsettled the Mexico that Magoffin encountered, replaced villagers with soldiers, and made conquest seem as natural and unstoppable as the presence of parents and the birth of babies.

Susan Magoffin met all kinds of people, male and female, poor and rich, ethnically diverse in the long-established, mixed-heritage world of northern Mexico. Her brother-in-law, the prominent trader James Magoffin, had married into Chihuahua's wealthy and powerful Valdez family, and Susan and Samuel traveled part of the trail with James's brother-in-law, the trader Gabriel Valdez. The Magoffins' relatives included the then-governor of New Mexico, Manuel Armijo. James Magoffin's wife, Doña María Gertrudis Valdez de Beremende, had traversed the Santa Fe Trail from west to east years before Susan Magoffin made her trek, and had died, in Independence, Missouri, only a year before James Magoffin went back to his wife's home country.[18] While Drumm acknowledged such relationships, she obscured the facts of travel from southwest to northeast, and of intermarriage, by pouring out her editorial ink on men, predominantly white American men with family or business connections to Missouri.

Such was not the case with the diarist herself. Wherever Susan Magoffin had the chance to spend time with women, she did so. Indeed, women anchor her narrative in places—Bent's Fort, Santa Fe, San Gabriel, El Paso—in a way that men do not. The editor ignored, and by ignoring erased, the women and the settled social life that Susan encountered.[19] But perhaps it is no great surprise that the meticulous Drumm paid no attention to the women who knew Susan Magoffin. The editor seemed, at bottom, uninterested in Magoffin herself.

Instead, Drumm's textual glosses served as elegiac instruments of national chauvinism, as obituaries. There is finally something monotonous about Stella Drumm's meticulous editing. Her footnotes stand like white marble tombstones in a military cemetery, row upon row, proclaiming the nation with their endless sameness. Military bands and costumed paraders pass by and fade away. Grieving widows and daughters, so heavily veiled that only the fact of some connection to the departed remains, float through the landscape like ghosts. Like battlefields consecrated as war memorials, military cemeteries bury more than the dead interred beneath the surface. When national memory claims territory, it erases all other memories, and crossings, and uses of the land. Homes become battlefields, and boneyards.

The title of Susan Shelby Magoffin's narrative was not *Down the Santa Fe Trail and into Mexico.* It was *Travels in Mexico, Commencing June 1846: El Diario de Doña Susanita Magoffin.* She began, thus, mixing English with Spanish, announcing her journey to a strange country in a language spoken by the men who were taking her there, a party that included both Mexicans and Americans. Foremost among them was her husband, to whom she first refers as Don Manuel, and most often as *mi alma*—my soul. Susan called herself by a diminutive name and put herself in Samuel's hands as she entered a new world, his world, a place on the other side of some kind of fault line: "My journal tells a story tonight rather different from what it has ever done before."[20] Writing in the present, she radiated the innocent excitement that Conrad's Marlowe adumbrated in the past tense as he began his tale of imperial horror: "When I was a little chap I had a passion for maps."[21]

Samuel Magoffin had spared no expense to provide his pregnant wife with as much comfort as life on the trail would allow. In a convoy including fourteen large freight wagons and a baggage wagon, Susan Magoffin set out in her own private carriage, along with a curtained "dearborn" buggy for the separate use of Jane, her maid. Susan's tent, "a grand affair indeed," was equipped with a built-in cedar table, a shelf that she used as a dressing table, portable stools upholstered with carpeting, even a carpet made of sail duck. Her camp bed, she wrote, was "as good as many houses have; sheets, blankets, counterpanes, pillows &c." Their first night on the trail, Susan and Samuel dined on ham and eggs and biscuits, enjoyed with a cup of shrub, an alcoholic fruit beverage that Susan preferred to tea or coffee. "It was sweet indeed," she wrote.[22]

Before long, however, the realities of the road disrupted domestic order. Wagons stuck in mud holes; animals ran off and had to be chased back. Meals were delayed or canceled, and the days were hot and thirsty. The traffic on the trail brought news of the war, of Pawnee resistance. Soon a company of seventy U.S. dragoons arrived, sent, Susan believed, "for the protection of the traders," although, as Stella Drumm explained, the military had doubts about the political and economic loyalties of some of those traders (including the Magoffins?).[23] Still, out on the prairie, Susan took evening strolls while Mexican laborers pitched the tent, putting pebbles in her pocket to take home as "my Prairie curiosities" and picking flowers to press in her journal. Wild roses and raspberries and gooseberries abounded. "It is the life of a wandering princess, mine," Susan sighed.[24]

Soon Susan Magoffin left home behind, to enter Indian country. "We are now at the great rendezvous of all the traders," she wrote. "Council Grove may be considered the dividing ridge between the civilized and barbarous, for now we may look out for hostile Indians." Susan "could not suppress the fear . . . some wily savage or hungry wolf might be lurking in the thick grapevines. . . . I would not tell *mi alma* these foolish fears, for I knew he would ridicule them, and this was torture to me."[25] Imagining herself in a land without real people, and assuredly without true women, she stood silent.

As they moved onto foreign terrain, the Magoffin party grew to forty-five wagons, "a strange compound of Americans, Mexicans and negroes; Horses mules and oxen. This may litterally be considered our start *No. 2*," wrote Susan.[26] The heat gave way to wind and drenching rain. Susan and Samuel managed to keep dry by staying in bed in their tent and pulling up the carpet where the "water ran through the tent like a little spring"; still, the relentlessly cheerful Susan insisted, twice in the space of two pages, that she viewed the downpour as "one of the 'varieties of life.'" And so, "of course it must be enjoyed."[27]

Now Susan's diary detailed not the fulfillment of household routine but the dailiness of departures from domesticity, of rain-soaked sleepless nights, and days without food because no dry wood could be found to start a cooking fire. She continued, faithfully, to describe "scenery" in the convention of travelers' tales, and to insist that she was having a terrific time. She didn't hate the rain; on the contrary, "It is truly fun for me." But it was not comfortable. "*Out on the Prairie with no wood and little water,*" she wrote after a long night of heat lightning and wind.[28]

Perhaps it was the stormy nights, but she began to fear for her own soul. The party traveled when it could, including Sundays, and the days had begun to blur together, taken up with the search for firewood and water, with the arduous job of hauling across swamp and stream and rutted road. On June 28, 1846, she pleaded that "my heavenly father grant me pardon for my wickedness!" That Sunday, Susan had "classed it so much with the days of the week, that I regularly took out my week's work, kniting. Oh, how could I ever have been so thoughtless, so unmindful of my duty and my eternal salvation!"[29] For a young woman who worried that knitting on the sabbath was grounds for damnation, worse, much worse, was yet to come.

They had entered the country of scarce water and insect pestilence. Oxen began to die, miserably, of thirst. The parched, killing heat was better than one alternative. "Now, about dark, we came into the mus-quito regions, and I found to my great *horror* that I have been com-plaining all this time for nothing, yes, absolutely for *nothing;* for some two or hundred or even thousands are nothing compared with what we now encountered." The carriage nearly overturned when the Mexican driver swerved to avoid a dead ox in the road, and when Susan jumped down into the grass, her dress filled with the buzzing, biting mosquitoes, an unforgettable experience denied American men. Susan huddled in the carriage, wrapped up in her smothering shawl to keep the mosquitoes off, recollecting the ordeal in biblical terms. "Millions upon millions were swarming around me, and their knocking against the carriage *reminded me of a hard rain.* It was equal to any of the plagues of Egypt."[30]

Four days later, at Pawnee Fork, Susan lost another piece of home on the range. "What a disasterous *celebration* I have today," Susan wrote on July 4. They'd started the day by climbing Pawnee Rock, a landmark named to commemorate a battle with Indians "most treacherous and troublesome to the traders." Susan wanted to join previous travelers in carving her name in the sandstone face of the rock: "*mi alma* with his gun and pistols kept watch," she noted, and Jane too looked out for Susan as she cut her name amid hundreds, but Susan admitted "it was not done well, for fear of In-dians made me tremble all over and I hurried it over in any way."[31]

Disaster lay ahead. Six miles along they caught up with the rest of the party, and in their haste to cross a creek the carriage flipped and crashed, smashing the top and sides, tossing "guns, pistols, baskets, bags, boxes and the dear knows what else" around, a bottle breaking on Susan's head and knocking her out. The wreck of the carriage seemed to her an omen.[32]

They remained in camp at Pawnee Creek, awaiting permission from the army to travel on, an unaccustomed inconvenience to a veteran in-ternational trader like Samuel Magoffin. There, the United States caught up with them, marching on to war. More soldiers arrived, and more wag-ons, more than doubling the size of the party. The men spent their days hunting the abundant and delicious buffalo. Susan, knowing how de-pendent she was on Samuel, was daily consumed with worry that he would not return from the perilous hunt: "It is a painful situation to be placed in, to know that the being dearest to you on earth is in momen-tary danger of loosing his life."[33]

As she waited anxiously, Susan did what she could to make the campsite "pleasant and homelike." But it was a precarious domesticity in the midst of mobilization. They were waiting for orders from the commander of the Army of the West, General Stephen Watts Kearny, and no one knew which way they would go. Perhaps they would be diverted around Santa Fe, traveling far across the plains behind the army, searching for game and water and fuel in country already scoured bare by the invading force. She admitted finally that she had been feeling "sick" ever since the carriage crash.[34]

Susan must have known that her pregnancy was in trouble. The party hurried to catch up with a doctor on the trail ahead of the Magoffins. "*Mi alma* sent a man ahead to stop the Dr.," who waited for them to travel the twelve hard miles between. Frightened as she was, Susan tried for cheerfulness:

> Now that I am with the Doctor I am satisfied. He is a polite delicate Frenchman (Dr. Masure) from St. Louis. He . . . is called an excellent physician *"especially in female cases,"* and in brevity I have great confidence in his knowledge and capacity of relieveing me. . . .
> The idea of being sick on the Plains is not at all pleasant to me; it is rather terrifying than otherwise, although I have a good nurse in my servant woman Jane, and one of the kindest husbands in the world, all gentleness and affection, and would at any time suffer in my stead.[35]

In the Drumm edition, Dr. Masure and his St. Louis family rated an extensive footnote, but Susan's difficult, ultimately tragic pregnancy did not merit mention.[36] Reticent as the Victorian Susan was about such female bodily matters, the usually voluble editor was even more so.

Susan's condition certainly worried those who traveled with her. When a storm blew their tent down one night, three of the Mexican laborers gave their blankets to Susan and Samuel, earning her deep gratitude. Susan grew to know excruciatingly the hard ground they rumbled over and the rivers they crossed. Her descriptions offered testimony of her physical state. She called a river bank "poorly timbered," and the plains "destitute of everything, even grass . . . painful to the sight."[37]

At last they came upon Bent's Fort, a monument and an oasis in country that had shown Susan a barren face. Seldom had that place seen so many people, so much action, overwhelming the capacity of the Bent brothers to deal with the traffic. The army camped nearby, coming and going among gathering traders and Indian visitors. Nonetheless, William Bent understood instantly how ill Susan was and found room for the Magoffins.[38] Susan pronounced their quarters "quite roomy," with two windows and a dirt floor, "which I keep sprinkling constantly during the day." Poor health and turbulent circumstances made housewifery a burden. By the end of her first day she complained about "keeping house regularly. . . . I beg leave not to be allowed *that* privilege much longer."[39]

Susan goggled at the strange goings-on at Bent's Fort. Here, for the first time, she encountered Mexican women, "*las senoritas,*" one of whom shocked her by combing her hair in the presence of a man, making her ablutions with the aid of "a crock of oil or greese of some kind, and it is not an exaggeration to say it almost *drip[p]ed* from her hair to the floor." One of the women she met was married to one of the Bents, and another was Solidad Abreu, daughter of a former governor of New Mexico and wife of American trader Eugene Leitensdorfer, but Susan did not mention the women by name.[40] If they had womanhood in common, Susan could not see it. To her American eye, the Mexican women were creatures of some exotic species, not sisters, not even fully human on her own terms.

No doubt she was feeling awful, but even physical anguish did not lead her to reach out for help or comfort. The blinders of racism isolated her as surely as the walls of her room, even as the presence of Mexican women seemed to her to mark, indelibly, the strangeness of the place.[41]

Susan had begun to consider her trip a big disappointment. Dr. Josiah Gregg, whose *Commerce of the Prairies* Susan carried along and used as a model for her observations, had gone west for his health in the 1830s, found travel a tonic, and published his observations in 1844. Susan felt she had been misled in imagining that the journey would be good for her. "I should never have consented to take the trip on the plains . . . it is so bad to be sick and under a physician all the time." Kearny wanted everyone to ship out in three days, and Susan wrote that "the idea of getting onto those rough, jolting roads, and they say this is rather *worse,* if anything, than the one we have passed, is truly sickening. I have concluded that the Plains are not very beneficial to my health so far."[42]

On July 30, 1846, Susan Magoffin turned nineteen years old and went into premature labor. "I feel rather strange . . . ," she observed, "this is it, I am sick! strange sensations in my head, my back, and hips." By the next morning her pains had begun in earnest, in agony, attended by Dr. Masure. While she suffered, so very far from home, life seethed around her. The servants quarreled and gambled, the doctor himself complained that he was ill-treated. The fort filled with soldiers getting ready to move out. Traders impatiently awaited word to head west with the army. A party of Arapahos thought to be spies came and went. In this faraway place, the United States massed its resources for war, disrupting international trade in the process of extending empire.

At that great moment for Manifest Destiny, Susan Magoffin fought her own life and death battle. Finally, "*all was over*" and she "sunk off into a kind of lethargy, in *mi alma's* arms." When she wrote again, on August 6, she spoke in the language of horrified epiphany:

> The mysteries of a new world have been shown to me since last Thursday! In a few short months I should have been a happy mother and made the heart of a father glad, but the ruling hand of a mighty Providence has interposed and by an abortion deprived us of the hope, the fond hope of mortals! But with the affliction he does not leave us comfortless!
>
> We have permission to "come unto him when our burden is grievous and heavy to be borne"; we have permission to pray for more submission and reliance on his goodness, and in that petition we have an intercessor with the Father, Jesus Christ, who himself came into the world an infant, after the manner of man.[43]

Susan compared her fate to that of an Indian woman in the room below her, who gave birth to "a fine healthy baby, about the same time, *and in half an hour after she went to the River and bathed herself and it,* and this she has continued each day since." Echoing Meriwether Lewis's observation about the birthing prowess of purportedly primitive women, she commented, "No doubt many ladies in civilized life are ruined by too careful treatments during child-birth, for this custom of the hethen is not known to be disadvantageous, but it is a '*hethenish custom.*'"[44]

Bloodied and heartbroken in a strange place, where soldiers mustered noisily to prepare for war on foreign ground, Susan had come to believe that convention was no sure ticket to heaven. No one could know who was destined for salvation, and who would burn. She even questioned the justice of the American cause. "Though forbidden to rise from my bed," she wrote,

> I was free to meditate, on the follies and wickedness of man! . . . sinking himself to the level of beasts, waging warfare with his fellow man . . . and by his example teaching nothing good, striving for wealth, honour and fame to the ruining of his soul, and loosing a brighter crown in higher realms.— —
>
> All of the Traders followed on after the troops the next three days.[45]

Not all the traders. The Magoffins lagged behind. Susan could not travel yet. Mingling the language of war and childbirth, she complained that she had been "taken prisoner . . . *confined* in a Fort," and she obsessed about souls—hers, Samuel's, her poor, sacrificed baby's. 'What a satisfaction it would be to me now, to know that I shall be as well prepared to leave this mortal, this earthen body as I am to leave this earthen house, and with as much anxiety. That I could know that my daily prayers were not frowned upon by my God, that my Savior's blood pleads not in vain . . . " More than ever, she relied on Samuel, but she worried that they loved each other too much, forgetting their duty to love God above all other things.[46]

At last, however, they started off. The first night out of Bent's Fort, Susan wrote, "I am now entirely out of 'The States,' into a new country." From that vantage point, her homeland looked to her "bright and sunny," and she feared she'd never see "its happy people, my countrymen," again. They inched south and west, up into the mountains.[47]

Susan was feeling better, able to see the countryside rather than only to feel it as pain. She took time to record her observations of her surroundings, to describe in detail the piñon juniper trees that dotted the dry hills, to relish the first rain in three weeks. In Raton Pass she fell into the cadences of the romantic sublime—"most magnificent scenery. On all sides are stupendous mountains." The pines grew taller, the road rockier. It was easier to walk than to ride, bouncing hard over the stony ground. Her sense of humor was coming back. "If exercise will do me any good," she remarked, "I must surely be benefited now." As the road grew "worse and worse," the teamsters unhitched the mules from the carriages and pulled the conveyances themselves. Progress slowed to a few hundred yards a day. While men and animals labored, she and Jane scrambled up a high hill to take in a "magnificent" view of mountains and canyon and the village of Mora, "thriving, with its nice little cottages and court house in the center. Contentment, ease and peace are apparently inmates of this spot." High up and at a distance, Susan felt exhilaration at the sight of neat houses amid so much grand scenery.[48]

The going was slow in any case, but between rocks, mud, and the uncertainties of war, they seemed to stall. Soldiers brought word that James Magoffin was acting as a go-between in negotiations between General Kearny and Manuel Armijo, governor of New Mexico. They were told to expect good things, but were also assured that if traders had to turn around and go home, the Samuel Magoffin party would be the first to hear. To go home, after all they'd been through to come so far, to be at last on the threshold of settled country? We can only imagine Susan's thoughts; she did not comment.[49]

At last, though, they got leave to proceed, and moved out of the cool mountain pass onto the hot plains. Before Bent's Fort, all across Kansas and into Colorado, Susan had imagined two kinds of human company on the land: male itinerants who crossed rather than lived on the plains (traders, soldiers, teamsters), and genderless, but presumably male, "wild Indians" who seemed to come from nowhere and to claim no place in particular. In short, the plains were, to her, unsettled, empty, unwomaned. But now in New Mexico, from that first lofty vista of picturesque Mora, she knew she had entered somebody's homeland. In Santa Fe the Magoffins would set up housekeeping, and Susan's daily rhythms would change from the halting, linear movement of the trail to the repetitive rounds of feminine domesticity. New Mexico was a foreign country, long ago claimed and inhabited by a strange people. Working Spanish words into her everyday speech, Susan endeavored to move onto suspect terrain on local terms.

"We are surely getting close to the settlements," she wrote as they neared Mora itself, when three men rode out to the approaching Magoffin party with "*aguardiente, quesos, y pan*" (brandy, cheese, and bread) to sell. All along the trail, Susan had described in detail what she ate and drank, when she went hungry, where the water was good or bad, where they had shrub or wine with a meal. But this was the first time she faced the choice of eating food prepared by locals, not members of her own traveling ménage. She didn't like it, pronouncing the bread too hard and the cheese "very tough, mean-looking, and to me unpalitable."[50]

Up close, she found Mora disappointingly dirty and poor, the largest house "a little hovel, a fit match for some of the genteel pig stys in the States." She was, however, ashamed of her superior attitude, and she tried to curb her disdain with a moral lesson: "they say my opinion is formed to hastily, for within these places of apparent misery there dwells that 'peace of mind' and contentment which princes and kings have oft desired but never found!"[51]

As they moved on to Las Vegas, the presence of women and children marked the new world into which she had come. There, Susan had her first real taste of New Mexico hospitality, and her first encounter with a community of people who regarded her as a fabulously freakish curiosity. As Susan sat in the carriage, pulling her veil down over her face, a crowd gathered. Samuel, she observed, "could have made money enough to buy out the whole village . . . from the excitement to see his wife a '*monkey show*' in the States never did a better business than he could have done." Through her veil, which protected her from "the constant stare of '*the natives,*'" she gaped back at the throng, "the little ones in a perfect state of nudity," while Samuel and another trader laughed uproariously at the spectacle. They were taken into a big room, where "not only the children, but *mujeres* and *hombres* swarmed around me like bees." The women, "clad in *camisas* and petticoats only," seemed immodestly dressed to Susan, and she was shocked to see some of them nursing babies under their *rebozos*. Once everybody sat down, "out came the little cigarritas, and the general smoking commenced."[52]

Food established cultural continuity, and cultural difference. At Las Vegas Susan encountered a culinary challenge to her own well-conditioned habits and found the going appalling. *Blue corn* (her emphasis) tortillas, wrapped in cloth "black with dirt and greese," a local cheese "entirely speckled over," and "two earthen *jollas* of a mixture of meat, *chilly verde* & onions boiled together completed course No. 1." Without silverware, she was expected to scoop up chile on tortillas, but "I could not eat a dish so strong, and unaccustomed my palate." Samuel, seeing her distress, asked that she be brought some roasted corn, which she "relished . . . a little more than the *sopa*," along with a fried egg. Soon they escaped to their tent, where Susan was happy that "once more I was at liberty to breathe the pure air of the prairie, and to sit alone in my little tent, un-molested by the constant stare of these wild looking strangers!"[53]

Now as they traveled among settlements, Susan blushed at the "truly shocking" garments of the women and children. "The women slap about with their arms and necks bare, perhaps their bosoms exposed (and they are none of the prettiest or whitest)," and when the Mexican women crossed creeks, they pulled up their (already too short) skirts above their knees. The children ran about too often "perfectly naked," a condition she pronounced "repulsive."[54]

Scandalized as she was, Susan tried to imagine a place for herself in this new country. Word came that Armijo had fled Santa Fe and that Kearny was fortifying the city, and Susan reckoned that "we may just fix ourselves there for the winter." At the village of San Miguel she be-gan to hope for friendship, and to adjust to local cuisine. She managed to laugh at herself when someone paid her a compliment in Spanish and she understood. "As usual the villagers collected to see the curiosity," she wrote.

> I did think the Mexicans were as void of refinement, judgement &c. as the dumb animals till I heard one of them say *"bonita muchachita"* [pretty little girl]! And now I have reason and certainly a good one for changing my opinion; they are certainly a very *quick and intelligent people*. Many of the *mujeres* came to the carriage[,] shook hands and talked with me. One

of them brought some tortillas, new goat's milk and stewed kid's meat with onions, and I found it much more palitable than "the dinner at the Vegas." They are decidedly polite, easy in their manners, perfectly free &c.[55]

Finally, on August 31, they arrived in Santa Fe. "I am here in my own house," Susan wrote, "in a place too where I once would have thought it folly to think of visiting." She was home, and she was making history. "I have entered the city in a year that will always be remembered by my countrymen; and under the 'Star-spangled banner' too, the first American lady, who has come under such auspices."[56]

Here, where empire had sunk its anchor, Susan came to a household already prepared for her. Kearny was fully in charge, promising not to "molest . . . the habits, religion, &c. of the people." Susan, for her part, was trying hard to adopt the customs of the country, working on her Spanish and her manners. She and Samuel arrived late at night, and James Magoffin welcomed them with a trader's supper of cold oysters and champagne.[57] James was to head off in the morning for Chihuahua, leading a party in advance of Kearny's army, but Susan and Samuel were to settle in. She found it "truly pleasant to follow after the Mexican style, which is after dinner to close the shutters and take a short siesta. . . . it both refreshens the mind and body."[58]

Instantly, Susan embarked on the familiar routines of domesticity, seeing to housekeeping and receiving a steady stream of callers. Kearny came first, followed by a mysterious "American lady, formerly a resident of '*Illinois.*'" (Susan was clearly not "the first white woman" down the trail, but only the first to leave a record that history has preserved and made available.) She also entertained "a Mexican lady, Dona Juliana . . . a woman poor in the goods of this world, a great friend to the Americans and especially to the Magoffins."[59] Santa Fe boiled with rumors—that former governor Armijo would return; that followers of the departed Mexican governor must flee. Susan, however, felt well protected against invasion or unrest. The army camped on the common across from the Magoffins' house.

Orienting herself within "the little circle of my vision," Susan commenced the "general business of housekeepers," instructing her servants, bargaining for wondrous peaches and grapes and melons with vendors. "How very happy and contented I am," she wrote, " . . . with this new country, its people, my new house, or rather my first house, . . . and last of all, what a good, attentive and affectionate husband I was fortunate enough to choose."[60]

Even as she was celebrating her good housekeeping and her good judgment in choosing Samuel, Santa Fe society made her less dependent on his company. Indeed, her marriage imposed certain social duties upon her as "the only *traderess*," including attendance at a "Spanish ball," where soldiers and Santa Feans mingled. She would describe the dance in detail, fixing on the page an event turned into spectacle, made bizarre and exotic in the recounting. She remarked on the motley antique fashions, the haze of cigarette smoke, and the remarkable presence of "Dona Tula," keeper of the monte house and seducer of "the wayward, inexperienced youth to financial ruin." A guitar and violin played and dancers whirled, and one "dark-eyed Senora" sat with a servant under her feet, "a custom I am told."[61]

Susan revised her opinions about Mexican women when the modest Doña Juliana requested a pattern for Susan's high-necked cape so that she would not have to "go into the *plazo* where there are so many *Americanos,* and her neck exposed." She also made a "protégé" of a young market girl, who brought fresh peas and little cakes. And she entertained a stream of homesick soldiers and traders from St. Louis and Kentucky, who shared the intimacy of being so far from home "in this foreign land where there are so few of our countrymen, and so few manners and customs similar to ours, or in short any thing to correspond with our *national* feelings and *fire-side* friendships."[62] Some visitors brought unsettling news of the war, of political turmoil in Chihuahua. Yet Santa Fe seemed a haven of abundance. She and Samuel were invited by Solidad Abreu to a formal dinner for Kearny, "the first entire Mexican dinner I take." Susan relished the feast of two kinds of soups, "*carne de asado, carne de cocida,* and some other *carnes,*" accompanied with liberal doses of champagne. She particularly liked the desserts, and thought, for the first time, about asking for a recipe. At the end of the meal, Kearny offered a toast to "the U.S. and Mexico—They are now united, may no one ever think of separating." On that comfortable August night, in that most hospitable outpost of empire, women exchanged recipes, and Manifest Destiny extended a grasping hand far to the south.[63]

Kearny's army was getting ready to march to California. The soldiers came to say good-bye, and though most farewells were seemly, one soldier friend had "taken a little more of 'the ingredient' than he can well bear," offending her with his drunkenness. The code of politeness frayed further when another drunken soldier, one she did not even know, staggered into her house: "I do think some of my countrymen are disgracing themselves here," she mused. The departure of the army left Susan lonesome and bored, worrying about wildly shifting rumors from Chihuahua and about her sister Mary, pregnant at home. War was perilous, but so was maternity. She was almost afraid to write to Mary because of her "peculiar situation, having heard not one word whether she might be dead or in fine health &c.," but once she had word that Mary was still alive she wrote her a letter to wish her "well and a happy & safe termination of the long dreaded hour."[64]

Susan had hoped to spend the winter keeping house in Santa Fe, but the hope would not be realized. As the U.S. Army moved west, the Magoffins were to head south, across the cultural fault line that separated the long-established settlements of northern New Mexico, the Rio Arriba, from the volatile terrain to the south, the Rio Abajo. Following Samuel's usual trading route into Chihuahua, they would travel out of Pueblo settlements and into Apache range.[65]

Susan's last Santa Fe visitor was James Magoffin's brother-in-law, the Chihuahua merchant Gabriel Valdez, who immediately fell sick with wracking chills and fever. Susan was a sympathetic nurse but eager to depart. In a sense, Valdez's appearance was a harbinger of what was to come, for now she moved into a strange place, one that reckoned kinship, loyalty, and safety according to geographies and genealogies rooted in Mexico, not Missouri. Here, families lived long-established lives. But here also, Apaches challenged both Mexican and American claims.

On October 7, only five weeks after arriving in Santa Fe, they were under way, accompanied by Valdez and by Samuel's younger brother, William. Once again, people stared at Susan "with as much wonder as if they were not people themselves." Soon came the rumor that brother James's caravan had been raided by Apaches, with everything— "carriage, mules, trunk, clothes &c. &c."—taken, although James survived. Susan thought James's escape must be "a miracle," since as she understood things, Apaches "always want the *scalps,* the principal part of the business."[66]

But this wasn't simply Apache raider territory; this was mestizo country, full of families. Indian villagers came to trade, offering eggs and "sandias" (watermelons), tortillas and grapes, onions and apples in exchange for empty bottles. Her palate had changed over the weeks in New Mexico, and now Susan relished the tortillas, commenting that "with a good dish of Frijoles or any thing of the kind, one does not eat a bad dinner." Yet much as she tried to assimilate, she remained a stranger. Local women peeped under Susan's tent, pulled at her clothes and bedding, asked her why she had no baby. After a time, the constant staring and questioning began to rankle: "*Mirabile dictu*," she wrote. "How these people annoy me."[67]

Still, Susan made some friends who accurately appraised her situation. One "old comadre . . . half Indian, half Mexican" teased her for leaving her family back home, "*just for a husband.*" Susan replied in Spanish, asking "*pues es mejor no?*" (Isn't it better?), making the old woman laugh and agree that "*el marido es todo del mundo a las mujeres*": a husband is the whole world to women.[68]

For Susan, indeed, there were few constants beside Samuel. Word came that Mexican troops were mustering to march northward and that traders on the road to the south were "corraling together and sinking their wagon wheels to the hubs for a breast-work in case of attack," hoping that the American army would send troops to help.[69] When Susan fell sick, Samuel rented a house in the village of San Gabriel. For three weeks she lay ill, but finally pronounced herself "creeping about" and joyously wrote that she had received her first letter from her family in Kentucky. The letter bound the distant home to the faraway place where she somehow survived. It was both lifeline for Susan and one small link in the fragile chain of continental nation-building. "If we live," she wrote, baring her anxiety, "the time is coming around for us to be together again."[70]

Having no idea what the war might bring, Susan resolved to make a temporary home in San Gabriel. This would be no old Kentucky home, but a domicile on local terms. "If we remain here during the winter," she wrote, "I must learn a good many of the New Mexican ways of living, manufacturing *serapes, rabozos,* to make *tortillas, chily peppers . . .*" Her landlady came with her daughter to show Susan the art of tortilla-making, which Susan described at great length, observing, "What a deal of trouble it is too. I had not thought half the work." Susan, in turn, showed the landlady American knitting techniques, which both women found much easier than Mexican knitting styles, and Samuel opened a bale of calico that so thrilled the village women they were "like children in a toy shop . . . nearly run crazy."[71]

There in San Gabriel, the homely practices of domesticity seemed to lend some truth to Kearny's toast, knitting two countries together. But as the inhabitants knew, the national status of the Rio Abajo was anything but settled. The village lay in disputed territory, and local loyalties were tenuous and shifting. On December 1 Susan and Samuel got word that James had been arrested in Chihuahua and was on trial as a spy. Susan prayed, watched the news from the front, and fretted that they could do nothing but remain in San Gabriel, "lying here in a state of silent anxiety, what a day may bring forth we know not, tomorrow may turn us back to Santa Fe." And now they heard that Santa Anna was expected to march on New Mexico. Suddenly, Susan looked around at the neighbors who had shown such kindness and saw a "fickle people" who would "rise on our heads and murder us without regard. This," she observed, "is rather a dark picture to be painting."[72]

And it became darker still. Now she gave in to naked terror for her soul. In a long and anguished Sunday meditation she worried that "I have not prayed with sufficient fervour to have my weak faith strengthened." She had been frivolous and idle. "What must be the wrathful sentence of my Judge above?" she wrote. "Let me flee and hide myself from the thought and 'seek relief in prayer.'"[73]

The movements of the army controlled the fate of the traders. Detained in San Gabriel, the Magoffin party pored over every message, every shred of rumor. William fell ill, and Samuel rode across the river to talk with some troops passing by, on the way to join a larger force to the south. Susan, left to be both housewife and, for the moment, merchant, drove hard bargains with the people who came to trade, all the while frantic with the tasks of nursing and managing her demanding household. Jane coped with the anxiety of the situation by drinking, and Susan, who had formerly rambled the hillsides with Jane, determined that Jane's bad behavior was only "correctable by the rod."[74] It matters little who dealt the beating (William was ill; Samuel, absent, so it was probably Susan); violence had come into the Magoffin home.

When word came that the troops were preparing to march through the Jornada del Muerto toward El Paso, the mass of traders determined to follow. Samuel, however, was equally determined to wait. Susan felt like a sitting duck. "We are alone," Susan lamented, "for they have heedlessly [gone] into the jaws of the enemy. That jornada (a travel of two or three days for those heavy wagons without a drop of water) may be called the enemy's breastwork, the traders are going within it, to be cut to pieces perhaps." Back in San Gabriel, the Magoffins were defenseless against an enemy who would come "when they have devoured that portion of their prey, to destroy [us] as they please."[75]

Who was friend and who was foe? They remained in a region Susan identified as "the American portion of the Republic" of Mexico, but the map could be redrawn at any moment, depending in great measure on the choices local men and women made. "It is a strange people this," Susan wrote. She believed that Mexican men were "in a mass . . . brave," and as individuals, "they will not flinch from danger." But on whose behalf was that bravery to be displayed? A San Gabriel man rode back from El Paso to report that seven hundred Mexican dragoons, "all determined and resolute men," were mustered at the pass, awaiting three thousand more troops from Chihuahua. "'Tis painful to think of it," Susan anguished at the thought of such a mass hurled against the Americans' inferior forces. "They must all be cut to pieces, every thing seized." And then, the enemy forces must "march on to *us* here."[76]

To Susan Magoffin, trusting no one completely except her husband, the prospect of a Mexican attack on San Gabriel meant, above all, losing Samuel, the man who was both her family and her nation. "I shall be torn from the dearest object to me on earth, perhaps both of us murdered, or at best he will be put into one prison, while I am sent to an other without even my bible, or my poor journal to comfort me." What solace could she find? In desperate straits, she looked inward. "I have a *soul*, I have a Savior, the means of prayer are always within my reach." As Samuel paced and worried and waited for messages, Susan prayed and tried to think of something worse than capture and prison. Falling into the hands of the Mexican army was terrible to imagine, but how much more to be feared was the awful power of God? "Christ himself warns us that we must not fear those who can kill and in any wise injure the body, and can do nothing to the *immortal* soul. But he says 'rather fear Yet him who after he hath killed hath power to cast into hell.'"[77]

Anxiety was its own kind of hell. They could not know, from day to day, whether war would reach them or not. "The movements of the army as we hear it is all I can find to write about these days," Susan admitted as the fighting crept closer, disrupting order every place it touched. "The Indians are all around us."[78]

But the tide turned. On Christmas day, American troops skirmished with Mexican dragoons only eighty miles from San Gabriel. Three days later, U.S. forces moved on to take El Paso. Susan described the victors as "elated with their late success." Yet her own world, for the moment safe from armed attack, was invaded by sickness.[79]

As the new year of 1847 dawned, the movements of armies and refugees and traders spread contagion throughout the countryside. People began to come to San Gabriel to ask Samuel for medicine. Disease made no distinction between putative friends and enemies, and neither did Samuel, who sent medicine to the wife of Manuel Pino, one of two rich and prominent brothers who had refused to take an oath of allegiance to the United States when the Americans occupied Santa Fe. When Pino sent fresh pork and mutton to the Magoffins, Susan remarked that "it shows a feeling of pure gratitude which I constantly see manifested among these people for any little kindness done them."[80]

Kindness and conspiracy. While Susan dined on Manuel Pino's pork, Pino's brother Nicolas was put in jail for taking part in a plot to overthrow American rule in Santa Fe. "But for the fortunate disclosure of [the conspiracy]," Susan noted, "we might have been killed before this." Themselves now ailing as well, the Magoffins learned the alarming news that "the Taos people have risen, and murdered every American citizen in Taos including the Gov . . . all the troops from Albaquerque (the regulars) have been ordered to Santa Fe leaving this portion of the territory at the mercy of the mob." The way back to "the States" was now cut off by "a perfect revolution." In the midst of Apache country, the Magoffins' best hope of safety lay in running *south* to Old Mexico, to stop with Samuel's friends and find the American army. Susan was terrified not only by the necessity of "*flying* before" an advancing army of rebels, but also of the endless possibility of betrayal by neighbors she had once imagined might be friends. "My knowledge of these people has been extended very much in one day. There are among them some of the greatest villains, smooth-faced assassins in the world and some good people too. . . . without doubt 'tis the intention of nearly every one of them to murder without distinction every American in the country if the least thing should turn in their favour." The United States was a physical presence, for practical purposes, only where the troops massed. And so now the Magoffins hurried to catch up with the army: "wisdom says 'keep with the fource.'"[81]

Where Susan had once seen warm good feeling, she now saw duplicity and danger. San Gabriel was no longer a place where women made tortillas and tended to their knitting. Now it was a place where men plotted. Manuel Pino whispered with his friends, and Susan thought he "would not hesitate to do a 'deed in the dark.'" The Magoffins cleaned and fired and reloaded their weapons; Susan and Samuel alone had a double-barreled shotgun, a pair of holster and a pair of belt pistols, and a Colt revolver. Susan prayed that they would not have to fight, but she fully expected a battle with someone—the Mexican neighbors, the regular troops, or Indians.[82]

They rolled south, the dreaded Jornada del Muerto up ahead. Susan was in the midst of her own inner darkness, the kind of religious crisis that had seized so many young women of her time, burning across the country to scorch souls in the churches and the camp meetings.[83] "I wonder if I shall ever get home again?" Susan wrote, and then corrected herself for the thought: "'tis all the same if I do or do not. I must learn to look farther ahead than to earthly things. Now that a conviction has been awakened within my dark and sinful soul, how greater is my sin if I suffer it to die away without seeking my Savior's pardon for multiplied transgressions." The time had come to choose between evil and good.[84]

They were moving into the sere, lonesome country of the jornada, a land of wintry "bleak hill sides." In the cold wind and the dust, someone set fire to grass near the baggage wagon; the servants and teamsters beat it out before the flames reached two powder kegs in the wagon. Dry as it was, to save the draft animals they traveled mostly at night. Now the road itself imprisoned her as she jolted on in darkness, "shut up in the carriage in a road I know nothing of, and the driver nodding all the time. . . . I was kept in a *fever* the whole night, though every one complained bitterly of the cold."[85]

Everyone was nervous and touchy. When Susan determined to climb some "beautiful rugged cliffs," Samuel upbraided her for wandering off in Apache country. "*Mi alma* thinks I am wrong to go two hundred yards from the camp," she pouted, but admitted that there was danger. They were now pitching their tent within the circle of the wagons.[86]

Despite their efforts, the Magoffin party could not seem to catch up with the army. As they neared El Paso, Doniphan moved south, taking along "five or six of the most influential citizens as hostages for the good behavior of those remaining." Samuel's "friends in the Pass send him word to come on without fear, that they have always been friendly to him and still are." But now they moved into a land of battlegrounds and graves. Susan knew that the "friends of the prisoners can of course have no very friendly feeling towards us, and if they once get the advantage of us, what must the consequences be?"[87]

Susan passed another Sunday in the grip of her conversion experience. "I am beginning to long for a church to attend," she wrote, wondering if her willingness to undertake the long and difficult journey was itself a sin against keeping the Sabbath. She consoled herself with the thought that her distance from home had brought her to the light. "God in his infinite mercy has come near unto, when I was far off, and called me when I sought not after him." She was a suffering sinner, but penitence would bring divine relief. "Though I am now in darkness," she wrote, "the Lord has said, 'Awake thou that sleepest, and arise from the dead, and Christ shall give thee light.'"[88]

At last they reached El Paso, which opened its doors to the Magoffins and gave them shelter. As in Santa Fe, the presence of women and families signaled sanctuary. First Samuel and Susan stayed in the beautiful *casa* of a generous Spaniard, Don Agapita, and his daughter, twenty-one-year-old Josefita, who quickly befriended Susan. The cooking was excellent and varied, brandy and wine flowed, and Don Agapita told Susan how greatly he sympathized with her "troubles, dangers and difficulties."[89]

Presently they moved to the house of the curate Ramón Ortíz, who had been taken prisoner by U.S. Army commander Colonel Alexander Doniphan, his household left in the hands of his sisters and their children. Despite the political tension, the Ortíz women offered Susan friendship and comfort. Her hosts were "exceedingly kind and exert themselves so much to make me enjoy myself, 'twould be cruel if I did not attend to their solitications." She was learning the delights of Mexican cookery and commented, "I shall have to make me a recipe book, to take home . . . some, indeed all of their dishes are so fine 'twould be a shame not to let my friends have a taste of them too." More of Samuel's friends came to visit, and Susan declared that "we are all getting quite familiar and friendly in our dealings; as our acquaintance extends it is more agreeable, and to me more improving."[90]

So confident was she in her newfound faith, she went to mass, declaring that even a Catholic church was "the house of God . . . I can worship there within myself, as well as in a protestant church, or my own private chamber." During the week, she went visiting. She talked politics with Don Ygnacio Rouquia, a man who admired George Washington and assured Susan that Polk's plan of empire was "entirely against the principals of Washington, which were to remain at home . . . and never to invade the territory of an other nation." Susan was not disturbed by such gentle political criticism. Far more upsetting was another thing Susan heard on her visit to Don Ygnacio's, where she met a Doña Refugio, wife to another of Doniphan's prisoners and someone who had known Samuel before, "a lady much given to talking." Doña Refugio peppered her with questions, asking at one point "if I was never jealous of my husband." When Susan pleaded that she did not understand what the word *zeloso* meant, the woman "was quite particular to explain to me that at that moment he might be off with his other *Senorita*. Oh, how I was shocked, I could have cried my eyes out for any one else to suppose such a thing let alone myself!"[91]

A husband is the whole world to women. And especially to one who had left home and kin so far behind. Susan was devastated by Doña Refugio's nasty suggestion. She insisted that "my own heart tells me he is a husband as true as the world *ever* contained." But the blow shook Susan's faith in Samuel, a man who had lived as much in Mexico as in Missouri, and made her doubt the Mexican women who knew him, perhaps better than she. Now she felt utterly isolated. "I generally tell him every thing that happens in my visiting," she wrote, "but *this,* I couldn't try his feelings so much." The news sent such a tremor through her that she spent the next day "half deranged with headache."[92]

For a whole week, she did not write in her journal, and when she resumed, she reported that "my friends say I am so *triste;* and no wonder." News of the war continued to be alarming. Santa Anna was said to be preparing to invade Texas. A large army from Chihuahua was supposed to be ready to march on Doniphan's small force. Brother James had been transported to Durango, perhaps on to Mexico City, "and who knows what will become of him?" Would Samuel and Susan be captured, deprived of all their worldly goods, and dragged off to prison? Samuel was mad with worry, and Susan could do nothing but pray for him.[93]

There in El Paso, Manifest Destiny looked like deadly folly. Susan no longer thought of herself as a traveler: she was a captive. "We may be seized and murdered in a moment," she wrote, "for we are Americans . . . here entirely against our own will." There was more irony in her domestic situation, amid the uncertainty of the clash of nations, for the curate's family had treated her well even though he was a hostage of the Americans. She, in turn, had come to love them—though James was a prisoner of the Mexicans. Yet even her private thoughts had to be guarded. Later, she added a note that "while at this house . . . I never wrote all I might have done, for fear of my journal being seized had things gone with us differently."[94]

But they were saved. Don Ygnacio Rouquia himself came, with tears in his eyes, to tell Samuel that the Americans had won the long-feared battle and taken Chihuahua. On March 14, 1847, Susan and Samuel departed El Paso, leaving behind the last close Mexican friends she would make on her journey.[95]

Passing into Chihuahua, the Magoffins entered a landscape of war, bereft of the welcoming families and domestic comforts that had replenished them at intervals along their long trek. Chihuahua was occupied by Doniphan's army, "Missouri volunteers who though good to fight are not careful at all how much they soil the property of a friend much less an enemy." Most local families had fled, and the soldiers were bathing in the public fountains, ripping the bark off trees, wreaking havoc on the people's "loved homes . . . their fine houses." When the troops were ordered out, to go home or to move on to Monterrey to join the main body of forces under Zachary Taylor, the Magoffins left quickly, heading for Saltillo, where General John Wool was encamped.[96]

Susan was pregnant again, and exhausted. The toll of travel, the rigors of living in a shifting succession of strange places, the physical wear and tear of surviving one tragic pregnancy and embarking on the fearful uncertainties of another, and the strain of never knowing whom to trust, even among women, began to weigh heavily on her. "I thought I had done some very hard traveling before and in truth I had," Susan wrote, "but this had surpassed all." They rode fast over "the worst roads I ever saw," the dust and jolting nearly unbearable.[97]

Saltillo was an armed camp, not a secure haven. "I've heard of wars and rumours of wars and have been as I thought almost in them, but this is nearer than ever," Susan wrote as she and Samuel mobilized for battle. Artillery pieces were dragged across the city, the citizens organized into companies attached to the military. "I am really tired," Susan confessed; "we have counted and baled up all the money in the house" to send to a safer place. "All the pistols and guns have been cleaned and loaded. I shall say I had a hand in this too." Once the alarm abated, Samuel admitted to Susan that he had planned, in case of attack, to take Susan to the safest possible place and then join the fighting.[98]

The sight of young soldiers passing the town on the way to war made Susan sad and homesick. She wished for a letter from home, but none came. "How lonely it is," she wrote; " . . . I am perfectly isolated." Samuel might be called to fight and die, leaving her "in a stranger land without a protector and heart broken."[99]

And now they heard the worst news of all. James Magoffin was reported killed, murdered in his own house in Chihuahua. Samuel was inconsolable. Nearly a month went by before they learned that James was in fact alive and well. Meanwhile, they wondered and suffered. Not even a letter from home bringing news of the birth of her sister's baby could raise Susan's spirits. Thinking more of herself than her sister, she wrote, "I do think a woman *emberaso* [pregnant] has a hard time of it, some sickness all the time, heart-burn, head-ache, cramp etc. after all this thing of marrying is not what it is cracked up to be."[100]

After fourteen months on the road, Susan had lost her sense of adventure, her capacity to create comfort: she just wanted to go home. Pregnancy made that impossible, "my situation not admitting of a sea voyage for three or four months." When they were ordered to move again, this time to head to Monterrey, Susan took heart in the fact that that city was "so much nearer" the United States, and "letters can be received twice as often." She was glad to hear, too, that at Monterrey she would meet Mrs. Hunter, the American wife of the army quartermaster, "a *lady* . . . with whom I can sit & converse freely."[101]

Once wide open to new people and experiences, eager to make women friends, and eager to make a home in a new country, she now sought comfort in the familiar and shrank from her part in conquest. In Mrs. Hunter (a woman, Susan had been told, who "has seen quite enough of the elephant") she found a "curiosity" like herself, someone "quite as anxious to see a 'white woman' as I am . . . after an entire sepperation of twelve months from female society." They literally fell into each others arms:

> We talked *all* the morning till dinner, and after eating, on account of the great heat, in part, and *to be alone* leaving the gents . . . to take care of themselves, we undressed ourselves and layed down for a couple of hours, loosing not a minute of the time for our tongues were as incessantly in motion as the bell clappers in Mexico, telling of our adventures in travel, anxiety to reach home, the wishes of our friends &c. &c.[102]

This intimate interlude stood alone in Susan's diary, like a flag of surrender in the hands of a shell-shocked veteran. Although General Taylor entertained the Magoffins with cake and champagne, in Monterrey they were not on the ground of warm home, or even polite civil society, but were instead in the country of military occupation. Susan saw houses pitted with cannonball and bullet holes and was shown where American soldiers had been killed. In Santa Fe she had felt protected by the army, but here in battle-scarred terrain the presence of so many heavily armed American men was menacing. Some soldiers subjected to harsh discipline put a bomb in their commanding officer's tent, "intending to kill him. . . . it exploded about 11 O'clock shattering the roof of his tent, his trunk, part of his cott and even piercing the bed cloathing, [but] *he was unhurt*," Susan reported. She added just after, with some evident relief, "Tonight I'm in the packing business again."[103]

"I resented bitterly the absurd danger of our situation," the sailor Marlowe said, when he realized how unreliable were human connections on strange ground.[104]

Now they set out for Matamoras, traveling at night in the smothering heat of September, and Susan was sick of it all. "Till now I've done nothing but travel," she wrote, "every morning up by 1 o'clock and on the road by 3 o'clock jolting over stumps, stones and ditches, half asleep, expecting an attack from Mexicans constantly." In the limbo of country recently conquered but still contested, Susan found the landscape of hell. "We passed the *bones* of murdered countrymen, remains of burned wagons, all destroyed by Mexicans." They had to send to the "burned town of Marine" to get potable water, and there Susan had a truly eerie experience. She met "an old woman witch" who asked to be taken back to the United States. Susan asked her why, pointing out that the Mexicans were at war with the Americans. To that the old woman "neither answered yes or no, but gave me a sharp pinch on the cheek . . . and said '*na guerro este*' [there is no war]."[105]

On into bedlam. In the town of Mier, "the most miserable hole imaginable," they could not find a house and had to share quarters with a "family of men, women and children," along with William and one Captain Thompson. As the Magoffins huddled in the packed room "our trunks piled up serving as a screen," the remarkable Susan found the strength to chuckle, reflecting on such unlikely intimacy with a strange man and invoking the future presence of an absent woman: "if I ever have the pleasure of seeing Mrs. Thompson . . . I shall make her laugh with the scenes of this night."[106]

The final pages of *Travels in Mexico . . . El Diario de Doña Susanita Magoffin* are missing. The last entry we have tells us that the Magoffins "have said good bye to land travel and tomorrow shall take a steamboat for Comargo."[107] But her story, of course went on. As Howard Lamar explains, Susan fell victim to yellow fever in Matamoras, gave birth to a son, and the baby died soon after. "Unhappily," writes Lamar, "the rigors of her Mexican trip appear to have ruined Mrs. Magoffin's health."[108]

Perhaps. Perhaps the hardships of conquest had taken too great a toll on her commitment to keeping house for Manifest Destiny. Or perhaps, instead, she suffered less from travel than from the rigors of womanhood in a time when pregnancy and childbirth killed mothers and children with chilling regularity, with greater frequency than men died in war. She died in Missouri in 1855, after giving birth for the fourth time. She was buried in St. Louis. The child, who lived, was named after her.

The mother left a legacy unusual for a woman of her time. With her blood, her terror, her wit, her bravery, and her often moving words, Susan Magoffin marked a journey through many lands, strange countries, suspect terrains. None of them were—yet—the American West. Indeed, in a sense the frayed edge of Susan's homey comfort, the fading power of the "little circle" of her domestic vision, the unreliability of sisterhood, marked cultural boundaries that counted for as much as the march of Manifest Destiny. Susan had wandered far from sentimental rambles among the raspberries and the roses, into the nightmare world of fleeing families, burned villages, armed men, scattered bones. She longed desperately not to make a home, but to go home.

In Old Mexico, the families would return, and in New Mexico, the women who had preceded Susan Magoffin remained: the hospitable Solidad Abreu, the modest Doña Juliana, the smart little market girl of Santa Fe, the mean-spirited Doña Refugio of El Paso. Binding the land Susan Magoffin had crossed to the American nation would be a task left to later generations, who would live their lives not simply on American terms but by building new worlds on earlier geographies and genealogies and recipes.

PART TWO: IN THE WEST

CHAPTER 3

EMPIRE, LIBERTY, AND LEGEND

Woman Suffrage in Wyoming

Among the Rocky Mountains, seeking to establish an empire, we have inaugurated for the first time in history complete civil and political equality. **Edward M. Lee, Wyoming Tribune, December 18, 1869**

. . . the hardy pioneers of the Rocky Mountains still hold dear the principles and examples inculcated in their minds by their mothers and sisters in their far off eastern and western homes. **Sweetwater Mines, January 9, 1869**

This is the West, sir. When the legend becomes a fact, print the legend. **The Man Who Shot Liberty Valance**

THE ORIGIN MYTH OF THE American West pitted a lone man against empty wilderness. In the end, of course, the man was supposed to win. But the presence of women gave lie to the legend. As we have seen, the West would seek to take place in a collection of occupied realms and terrains in which women lived and moved. Contrary to the myth, the West did not end with the coming of women. Instead, they preceded, and then created it. For the West to come into existence as an American place at all, the presence of women—white women—was required, not simply as isolated transients like Susan Magoffin, but white women by the thousands, come to stay.

The story of the American West is the tale of this mass movement. In this chapter, I turn, for the moment, from biography, pulling back to set the stage, to establish a national context for the making of a region. I then zoom in for a close-up of Wyoming Territory, to portray the convergence of ideas and institutions, people and things, money and machines, that mobilized white women in order to make the West into an American place. At the height of national Reconstruction, women uprooted in the name of empire moved into, and through, one locale of the vast expanse designated for Americanization, a violent place called Wyoming. They entered unsettled territory in more ways than one, with surprising consequences for American women, and for the West they made. In the process, a new legend and a new region would be born.

When Susan Magoffin went south and west from Independence, she traveled in foreign country. But between the time she moved out of and returned to "the States," the political geography of the land she had crossed changed. Britain and the United States settled the question of the boundary between the U.S. and Canada the year she left. Within a year of her return, Mexico ceded sovereignty of half its territory to the United States. The nation's continental destiny appeared fulfilled.

But what would happen in this newly conquered place? What kind of government would it have? Who would rule, and how? What kinds of lives would the inhabitants lead? When Thomas Jefferson unbuttoned his beliefs about the Constitution and consummated the deal for Louisiana, he envisioned the country to the west as an "empire for liberty." As Peter Onuf has explained, Jefferson insisted that "the expansion and perfection of the union—and of American nationhood—depended on fostering republican government on the western frontier, on not recapitulating the tragic errors of the British by establishing a despotic, colonial regime."[1]

Establishing the empire for liberty was a complicated matter. To begin with, it was one thing to claim national sovereignty in a space stretching across many places, and something else entirely to assert uncontested political dominance in all those locales. In the South, secessionists threatened to shut down the organs of the United States government and replace them with other instruments of rule—individual states, perhaps, or possibly a confederation of states. West of Missouri, myriad Indian peoples insisted on their right to operate as sovereign bodies, using every tool available to them, from sex and friendship and diplomacy to unspeakable violence. Meanwhile, those who represented United States power in the western realms fell to shedding one another's blood over whether the American institution of slavery would be hauled into newly claimed territories. How would a government anchored in Washington, D.C., extend its power across such a vast expanse, over diverse people who seemed more than reluctant to accept Washington's authority?

Securing the South ultimately cost a million lives, untold wealth, unthinkable wretchedness, enduring hatred. War was the means, and it was verily hell. The nation brought hell to the place it now claimed as its West too, honed to a bloody edge by the Civil War, in the persons of men and women who dreamed of freedom and prayed for progress, even as they knew too well how to denigrate and hate and fight. Just as Americans had carried the politics of slavery into new places, so too they brought the conflicts of Reconstruction along after the war. Making the nation anew on western terrain was an enterprise scored with struggle among many contenders, people who were sometimes insiders, sometimes outsiders, sometimes on the edge, and sometimes fighting what they had stood for the day before. In such a confusing, often frightening landscape, military conquest and civilian genocide were only the two most horrible tools of national incorporation to be used. Making conquest stick required other, less violent instruments.

The territorial system of government was one crucial device, combining both political and material resources at the nation's disposal.[2] First codified by the Articles of Confederation government in the Northwest Ordinances of 1785 and 1787, the system was a brilliant Enlightenment scheme for the expansion of empire. The earlier ordinance outlined a procedure for surveying land according to a grid system capable of locating, attaching title to, and commodifying regular parcels of land, theoretically anywhere on the globe. The grid, which ignored topography, geology, local culture, folk practice, served as the basis for private property arrangements that would disperse settlers across the American landscape. "By the 1860s," wrote John Stilgoe, "the grid objectified national, not regional order."[3]

The ordinance of 1787 provided for a system of government for land thus claimed, surveyed, and potentially conveyed into private hands. When five thousand male voters had moved into a territory, they could organize a territorial government, elect an assembly, and send a nonvoting delegate to Congress. Most officeholders, including judges and the territorial governor, would be federal appointees. Finally, when the territory reached a population of sixty thousand (excluding Indians), the citizens could write a constitution, elect officials, and apply for statehood on an equal basis with states already existing. Put into the hands of fractious people on contested terrain, the territorial system was unstable at best. At many places in the West, the system broke under the strain.[4]

The United States also deployed the power of capital and technology, embodied in epic fashion in the transcontinental railroad. In 1862 Congress chartered two corporations, the Union Pacific and the Central Pacific, to build a railroad from Chicago to San Francisco. The government dispensed lavish land grants (twenty square miles for each mile of track laid), loaned the companies vast sums to cover the costs of construction, and sent troops to protect the survey crews and construction workers from Indian attacks. For a decade to follow, Congress subsidized railroad projects to create a transportation network in the interior West, linking that great wild space with the more settled regions to the east and on the Pacific coast. Superimposed on top of land gridded into property, and territory bounded and bound for statehood, the long steel rails and short wooden cross ties would stretch the thin, tough warp and weft of a continental nation.

But in the drive to transform the West from a series of discontinuous, if increasingly frequent, encounters in disconnected places into a regularized, apparently natural national domain, the most important resources the nation possessed were human: settlers. No quantity of land offices and armies and railroads and government bureaus could truly unsettle the original inhabitants and domesticate the western lands as American places if Americans (or would-be Americans) declined to go and live in those places. Some of the spaces the government hoped to settle were decidedly inhospitable. The prospects of the Empire for Liberty were ultimately in the hands of unpredictable, unruly, and diverse inhabitants facing novel challenges.

Consider the territory of Wyoming, an enormous place in actuality, but on a schoolroom map little more than a small blank, remote from the nation's capital, its major cities, its neighborhoods. Astonishingly, in 1869 American women first won the right to vote, that fundamental measure of liberty, in this windswept colonial backwater that straddled the Continental Divide. Why? How could such a human rights milestone have come to be planted at such a tense time, and in a place that seemed the very embodiment of the West's origin myth of man against wilderness? The answer to this puzzling question has a great deal to do with the ironies, contradictions, and unintended outcomes of the troubled nation's quest for a continental empire. It is a long and twisted tale. And it has everything to do with women's movements.

By the late 1860s and early 1870s, Americans had begun to weave webs of human action stretching from Washington, D.C., and other locales in the eastern United States to the nodes of white habitation springing up along railroad corridors, to American settlements along the Pacific coast, and in other isolated interior places. Newly strung telegraph wires, mail trains, and wagons bearing the U.S. mail spread messages of all sorts. The movements of people, goods, and ideas coincided to carry many new things to a distant, lofty, forbidding place imperiously called not Cheyenne or Shoshone but Wyoming, after a town in Pennsylvania.[5]

Wyoming Territory was a place contoured by the movements of men and women and children, and by the ideas they transported in their heads, including ideas about gender. The intimate, protean pairings of male and female, like the painfully reiterated lacerations of race, shaped the public world in unexpected and unacknowledged ways. The meanings of manhood and womanhood and of race, in turn, took their myriad forms amid political conflicts, and in relation to often seemingly irrelevant events: the creation of territories, for example.[6]

Manliness and womanliness and racial identity can be particularly unstable and important along boundaries like frontiers, places where human beings find unparalleled opportunities to wonder who they are and what in the world they are doing. Vocal Americans in Reconstruction Wyoming answered those questions by reminding themselves often, and sometimes viciously, that they were white, were male or female, and were nobly carrying the American flag westward. But as much as they seemed to agree on the basic outlines of race, gender, and empire, white Wyoming-ites, anxious and restless, found more than enough to divide them. To see them clearly, we need to employ both the sweeping continental view of the empire builder and the eye for detail of the keeper of local lore.

On July 25, 1868, the federal act organizing the U.S. territory of Wyoming became law. This infant political entity had been carved out of the older and larger Dakota Territory in response to the building of the Union Pacific Railroad, then making its way toward its transcontinental partner, the Central Pacific, across the southern part of what was to be Wyoming. The railroad was the slender but remarkably strong thread that bound this distant and inhospitable place to the nation that claimed it. As the territory's first governor explained in the imperial terms of his inaugural message, "For the first time in the history of our country, the organization of a territorial government was rendered necessary by the building of a railroad. Heretofore the railroad had been the follower instead of the pioneer of civilization."[7]

Most American migrants to Wyoming welcomed the reinforced government presence that territorial status would bring. But they were not always happy about federal officials' plans and policies, especially the government's willingness to honor Indian rights and claims. The U.S. territory of Wyoming was after all, in 1868, very much Indian country, a realm of shifting interests that most American emigrants to the place could barely comprehend, even had they wished to do so. Wyoming was still, and would remain for a few years, a "middle ground" jointly and uneasily occupied by diverse Native Americans, European Americans, European immigrants, African Americans, Mexican Americans, and Chinese immigrants.[8] Wyoming's indigenous population doubtless far exceeded the number of white emigrants in the territory, and whites knew they were outnumbered. As late as 1870, the U.S. marshall computed the non-Indian population of the territory at 9,128 persons, only about one-sixth of whom were female; the *Cheyenne Leader* commented, "The Indians of course are not included. It is sufficient to know we have a great deal too many of them."[9]

Emigrants understood that the distant government was only just then mustering the power to enforce its will upon either resistant Native Americans or the eternally quarreling newcomers to the northern Rockies. Less than a hundred miles from the boomtown capital of Cheyenne, at Fort Laramie, military and civilian agents of the U.S. government were negotiating a peace treaty with representatives of a mobile, fractious, and changing collection of Lakota and Arapaho villages. Much of the northern part of the territory remained under the control of Lakota bands, according to the terms of the Fort Laramie Treaty of 1868, though white prospecting parties protected by American troops repeatedly entered Lakota terrain, particularly the Big Horn country and the Black Hills, in search of gold. In the western part of the territory, miners flocked to camps on the Sweetwater River, most notably South Pass City, Atlantic City, and Miner's Delight. These enclaves bordered, and even intruded into, the Wind River Reservation, established for the Shoshones (and later, Arapahoes and Bannocks) by federal agreement to the Fort Bridger Treaty of July 3, 1868.[10]

In the meantime, violent encounters in places remote from reliable witnesses, law enforcement agencies, or even agreements as to what constituted law in the first place combined with fear, misunderstanding, and hatred. Rumors abounded, transmitted by word of mouth and by telegraph, spreading with amazing speed and exacerbating the already tense atmosphere. Indians and whites attacked one another, each pointing the finger of blame. Whites (and a few blacks) shot and stabbed each other and accused Indians; Indians committed acts of mayhem and insisted that other Indians were guilty. Civil War enmities continued to fester, long after and far away from the war theater, as Confederate die-hards, "Galvanized Yankees," and Union stalwarts moved into the territory in search of a new start. Civilian fortune hunters agitated for the government to send more troops, but they wanted soldiers to protect them, not restrain them when they flouted treaty provisions. Native Americans, for their part, wavered between appealing to U.S. officials to enforce their agreements and trying to drive white invaders from their country. Federal officials, natives, and emigrants alike coped daily with the consequences of living together in misunderstanding and fear.[11]

Territorial laws and treaty agreements were not goals in themselves. They were tools available to people who brought ideas and dreams and ways of life with them to the high lonesome country. Most of the emigrants were "white" men—native-born Americans of various ethnicities and European immigrants—either unmarried or living as if they were single, seeking a temporary livelihood rather than a permanent home.[12] They toiled for the Union Pacific, or wielded pick and shovel on mining claims, or wore the uniform of the United States Army. Railroad laborers and miners went where the work was, and didn't stay long. They saw little reason to cultivate good relations with Indians, or for that matter with each other. They were available to the government in the event of military emergency, depended on federal authority to defend them in turn, and regarded their property and voting rights as natural prerogatives of manhood. But they did not particularly want to be burdened with the weight of empire building. Some, indeed, were actively fleeing the disciplines and punishments of United States law and morality.

These men of the military and mining and railroad frontiers were instruments of American imperial plans, but, unreliable as they were, policymakers generally regarded them as temporary (in)conveniences. They helped to plant American enclaves in Lakota and Arapaho and Shoshone places, but they could not and would not, by themselves, anchor the government's wider regional claims. In fact, they might easily end up robbing the very trains they had laid track for, blowing up vaults in the banks they had built, hiding out in the hills they had prospected for gold.

A smaller contingent of white male emigrants avowed themselves the advance guard of a real, permanent, family-centered "civilization." They explained, in newspaper pieces, sermons, and political speeches, that, unlike their feckless transient brothers, they intended to occupy a savage land in the name of a superior culture, settling the country for all time. They were, they claimed, a "class of men . . . who possessed sufficient energy and stamina to overcome the many obstacles found in their path. Upon men of this kind do we depend for the future development of this country."[13]

Politicians expressed the hope that footloose single males would move on at the earliest possible opportunity, and in the meantime would at least refrain from thievery and terror. At best, they would marry and join the more sedentary ranks of the men, women, and children expected to come to raw new settlements as family members. Families, American leaders hoped, would stay in the faraway places to which they had journeyed and create a more densely populated, continuously American landscape of permanent farms and towns and cities. The dream of a permanent American empire was, at its heart, a dream of harmonious families, fixing themselves in domestic place.

Family harmony, as the middle-class white men who ran the country understood the idea, rested on a particular arrangement of power and affection, within the household and in the larger world. Wyoming's middleclass Victorians said that men and women were destined, by nature, to occupy different, generally separate "spheres" in life. Men, restraining their baser passions in the interest of civil society, were supposed to use their superior intellect and strength to administer the infant territory's public life. Those women who accompanied husbands, fathers, or sons to the mines had long been urged to embody "true womanhood," the feminine ideal that was also an emblem of white, and middle-class, moral superiority and a justification for occupying the West in the name of "civilization." Wyoming's women were to shoulder the burden of upholding national morality as well as creating wholesome, loving, and gentle homes.[14]

Middle-class Americans learned, in their schools, their churches, and from a growing body of novels, advice books, and magazines, that they ought to strive to emulate gender models.[15] Still, they understood that most people fell short of the ideals of the manly man—a person always restrained and responsible, capable of deep concentration, huge fortitude, and warm kindness toward his family—and the true woman—pure, pious, domestic, subservient. Men sometimes failed to curb their tempers, or to control their passions, or worst of all, to provide the means of living for their families. Women sometimes showed unseemly anger, or chafed at the need to obey, or worst again, neglected to take care of their households and children. The vagaries of life often intervened between American men's and women's good intentions and their actions. And ironically, both the most short-sighted selfish impulses and the best-laid plans of women and men had unpredictable results.

In the summer of 1868, thousands of Americans, virtuous in varying degrees, found their way to places in Wyoming, including the small but booming town of South Pass City, the largest of the three isolated Sweetwater mining settlements. Seething with racial and regional tensions, this U.S. outpost would almost inevitably become a staging ground for white Victorian contests over gender. Supposedly vice-prone single white men dominated camp life. They claimed the right to try to make a fast fortune, raise hell, and come and go as they pleased. In their rough and disorderly world, a number of self-consciously upright white women and their respectable male supporters stood for prudence, stability, deferred gratification, and the mission of making a home on the range. South Pass City's wives and mothers were urged to guide their husbands and sons away from activities men were known to embrace in the absence of feminine influence—gambling, drinking, and fighting, for example. And though women were supposed to assert their influence entirely within the confines of the "private sphere" while men took care of public business, that private feminine force was supposed to carry much of the weight of planting the Stars and Stripes in far-flung, wild places.

Like most oversimple yet somehow compelling stories, there is some truth to this one. According to the 1870 census, South Pass City's pop-

ulation was 460, with men outnumbering women four to one.[16] Public
life in the Sweetwater settlements took place in the streets, the gold mines,
and the saloons. In South Pass City alone, seven retail liquor dealers, three
breweries, and one liquor wholesaler did business. According to Chicago
journalist and outraged observer James Chisholm, miners gambled and
drank "to a considerable extent." Indeed, said Chisholm, "a vast amount
of gold dust is ground in the whiskey mill."[17] Judging from the prepon-
derance of saloon advertising in the territory's newspapers, the local bars
dominated social life to a staggering degree. One advertiser maintained
that "there is no better appetizer than one of [this establishment's] cock-
tails taken before breakfast in the morning," and newspaper editors
throughout the territory commonly recommended their favorite bars in
the editorial columns of their papers.[18]

White, middling women who found themselves in places like South
Pass City did what they could to settle in and to "elevate," as they put
it, the tone of local social life. The first Christmas of the Sweetwater boom
found a few stalwarts hanging on through the howling winter, while most
fortune hunters fled. Fourteen settlement women pooled their efforts to
throw a Christmas party the *Sweetwater Mines* described as "the first
social gathering of our people." Bringing in supplies from Salt Lake City
and Cheyenne, the women put on a spread featuring "every description
of pies, cakes, and confectionary . . . turkeys, game, salads and jellies."
They decked the hall (the Sholes Exchange saloon, to be exact) with pine
boughs and provided plenty of champagne in the bargain, although the
Mines was elated to report that though the party went on into the early-
morning hours, no one was drunk! Referring to the women by their ini-
tials (Mrs. S., Miss T.) to preserve feminine modesty, *Mines* editors
crowed: "We have formed a nucleus of female society in our midst that
may give an assurance to some families who expect to visit us next spring
and summer, that the hardy pioneers of the Rocky Mountains still hold
dear the principles and examples inculcated in their minds by their mothers and sisters in their far off eastern and western homes."[19]

In places like South Pass City, however, living up to ideals was often
impossible, and the separation of men's and women's social spheres was
frequently breached.[20] Drunken men were a common sight in the streets
of the Sweetwater camps, and women also sometimes took to the bottle. Only a few weeks before the Sweetwater ladies mounted their sump-
tuous and decorous Christmas gala, one Anna Wright was "arrested by
officer Carson on charge of being drunk and fighting."[21] Like all mining
camps, these towns attracted their share of prostitutes, women obliged

to make money off men's deviations from the path of virtuous Victorian manliness (failings so common that they were, indeed, a secret component of Victorian manhood).[22]

Other women, not prostitutes exactly, still defied feminine convention. One notorious example of such a person, Martha Jane Cannary (more familiarly known as "Calamity Jane"), adventured in the towns along the Union Pacific, working at such unladylike occupations as stagecoach driver and U.S. Army scout. To those most ardently committed to preserving segregated roles for men and women, any female excursion into men's domain must inevitably lead to women's wholesale adoption of male practices (and privileges). Calamity Jane may indeed have inspired a comment in a column in the *Frontier Index*, a "press on wheels" operated by brothers Fred and Legh Freeman, who rode west with the Union Pacific. The *Index* correspondent, railing against the mixing of men's and women's spheres, snarled, "You just as well set a woman upon a stage driver's box, with whip in hand, as to allow her at the ballot box with whisky in her head and oaths upon her lips."[23]

Some women in Wyoming Territory were, of course, disqualified from true womanhood on racial grounds. Wyoming newspapers seldom passed up the chance to proclaim the wickedness of Native American women. The *Sweetwater Mines* ponderously insisted that "the depraved nature of [Indian] women is manifest. We are taught to associate the sex with everything that is lovely, and gentle, and amiable, and kind, but the squaw becomes an instrument in the hands of the buck for the torture of the innocent."[24]

But the *Mines* was mild in its racism compared to its chief journalistic competition, the *Frontier Index*. Most newspapers published in the United States at that time indulged freely in hyperbole, launching lavish libels against the local competition and extravagant malicious falsehoods regarding political opponents. The *Frontier Index*, however, made racist invective its specialty. The paper frequently reprinted stories from newspapers in the South and Northeast vilifying blacks and white Radical Republicans who favored black rights. The *Index* also reported often on anti-Chinese activity in the West and, of course, missed no chance to speak ill of Indians or of government officials who favored any Indian policy short of extermination. The paper characterized Radical Republicans as leaders of a conspiracy against white men's liberty, intent upon using "inferior" nonwhite people to serve their own tyrannical ends. "As the emblem of American Liberty," the editors crowed from the town of Green River, "*THE FRONTIER INDEX* is now perched upon the summit of the Rocky Mountains; flaps its wings over the Great West, and screams forth in thunder and lightning tones, the principles of an unterrified anti-Nigger, anti-Chinese, anti-Indian party—Masonic Democracy!!!!!!!"[25]

The *Index* delighted in printing dispatches, jokes, and anecdotes intended to demonstrate that indigenous women were more carnal and bloodthirsty even than Native men. In a story on a "tragic affair" in a Ute camp near Tierra Amarilla, New Mexico, the *Index* reported that a man named Chino had been shot by another Indian man, but underlined the barbarity of Native women by adding that "the sister of Chino then killed his wife by cutting her head open with a hatchet, to prevent her from marrying anyone else."[26] The *Index* routinely ridiculed and sexualized even dignified behavior in Native women, noting, for example, that "riding along, a companion remarked of a squaw, that 'she walks like a soldier.' I responded, 'Yes, she looks like she's been drilled.'"[27]

Clearly, white Wyomingites' ideas about the proper arrangement of "the races" constructed, and were shaped by, their ideas about ideal relations between men and women. And in truth, even those women best endowed, by virtue of race, class, and education, to assume the mantle and the benefits of true womanhood found the Sweetwater a daunting place to bear the white woman's burden. Reporter James Chisholm boarded, in the camp of Miner's Delight, with a Major Patrick Gallagher and his twenty-four-year-old wife, Frances, who had taken the stage to the Sweetwater in July 1868. Determined to "create domestic comfort under the most trying circumstances," Frances Gallagher would also take it upon herself to teach school.[28] But life was lonely. Only three other women lived in tiny Miner's Delight at the time, none of them close to Gallagher in age, interests, or social position. Chisholm remarked, in the spirit of Victorian sentimentality and chivalry, that "apart from woman in the abstract, for whom I retain an unspeakable veneration, she must be a brave soul who, accustomed to the refinements of life, can voluntarily front the hardships and perils of a mining camp like this, far in the remote wilderness, that she might be the sharer of her husband's fortunes for better or worse." Frances Gallagher could not always keep up the brave front, however. According to Chisholm, who evidently acted as her confidante, "She sometimes pines for home so pinefully that I get quite sympathetic on the subject."[29]

If women like Frances Gallagher found themselves desolate in the face of life on the Continental Divide, the *Frontier Index* admonished: "A modest woman must often neither see nor hear." Neither, according to white commentators, should good women be seen or heard. Even as they

encouraged women to come settle the West, local newspaper editors obscured women's presence, adhering to the Victorian maxim that a
woman's name should never appear in print but twice, once to herald
her marriage and again to announce her death. The *Sweetwater Mines*
reported the birth of a baby girl with regrets that "Nature has so willed
it that the first child born in the Sweetwater shall not become a *miner*. It
may aid, however, in developing the country." In keeping with polite practice, neither mother nor daughter was mentioned by name in the paper,
though the father's name appeared in the birth notice.[30]

Perhaps not surprisingly, not all white women were willing to shut
their eyes and mouths in the name of decorum. As the *Frontier Index*
quipped, "'None but the brave deserve the fair.' And none but the brave
can live with some of them."[31] While Frances Gallagher pined at home,
some Sweetwater women abandoned wifely deference and took their family business into the streets. One South Pass City housewife, a Mrs. Carr,
sent her children to a local saloon to reclaim a husband who had "imbibed somewhat in excess." The man told his child "to deliver the message that he was too drunk to come home and if she wanted him to return home, they would have to come after him with a wheelbarrow. This
they did."[32]

Another South Pass City woman went even further. Janet Sherlock
Smith, whose descendants persisted in the South Pass area long after the
gold mines ceased to yield profit, told historian Grace Raymond Hebard
that she thought South Pass City had been a rather law-abiding town,
given the fact that Methodist-Episcopal services had been held there and
that there had never been a lynching.[33] Nevertheless, Smith's own role
in trying to promote community and civility would become the stuff of
legend. Smith, who was the most successful of the town's handful of
women lodging-house keepers, herself reputedly prevented the only
lynching that might have marred the town's record. A man named Al
Tomkins had shot and killed George McOmie, Smith's own brother, and
a mob gathered in the town's main street to hang Tomkins without benefit
of a trial. James Sherlock, Smith's grandson, explained: "Hearing of the
plot, grandmother in her devout Christian and characteristically kind and
sensible manner, interceded. She said that her loss was already great
enough without having this man's blood on her hands, and she knew
that in living with his own conscience and Divine judgment, the man
would receive his just punishment."[34]

Such women stretched the boundaries of the private sphere, even as
they still provided Wyoming boosters with examples of the kind of moral

white womanhood that empire builders celebrated. When the *Sweetwater Mines* opined that "the wife makes the home, and the home makes the man," the newspaper alluded to a far larger zone of comfort and civilization than any private household could encompass.[35] Still, the prospect that women might go too far, might turn on their male protectors like an angry wife with a wheelbarrow, made the true white woman a somewhat unreliable ally of the imperial white man in Reconstruction Wyoming. Too many of the various inhabitants of Wyoming Territory had come of age in worlds defined by war, and had lived lives in motion. If they dreamed of tranquillity and stability, they were pragmatic about such reveries. "A cynical journalist," offered the *Sweetwater Mines*, "says the reason so many marriages occur immediately after a war, is that bachelors become so accustomed to strife that they learn to like it, and after the return of peace, they enlist in matrimony as the next thing to war."[36]

Power on this periphery of the American empire was obviously up for grabs, even had there been political stability at the core. But the nation, a weak presence in the Rockies and the Southwest and so recently ripped in half, was constructing itself anew. In 1868, the political status of the former states of the American South was as uncertain as that of western territories like Wyoming. War-born political turmoil in Washington, D.C., deferred for some months the arrival in Cheyenne of the men charged with erecting a federally mandated territorial government. The organic act creating the Wyoming Territory was delayed in passage, and stalled further in execution, while Republicans and Democrats battled for control of the federal government.

Thus, although American citizens were moving into the territory, flowing through the railroad boomtowns and flocking to the mining camps, the United States did not really establish a political presence in Wyoming until lame-duck Andrew Johnson, barely hanging on to the presidency after his power struggle with Radical Republicans in Congress, relinquished the office to Ulysses S. Grant. Grant quickly moved to appoint Republicans to fill territorial offices, including Wyoming's first governor, Ohioan John A. Campbell; its secretary (second in command), Connecticut's Edward M. Lee; its senior judges, including John W. Kingman of New Hampshire; and its U.S. marshall, Church Howe of Massachusetts. Both Campbell and Lee had risen to become brigadier generals in the Union army; all four men took their Republicanism seriously, even radically.

These presidential appointees by no means reflected the preferences of those eligible to vote in Wyoming, where party politics divided white men into hostile camps. Before the presidential election, seventeen Democrats in the booming mining hamlet of South Pass City, including one W. H. Bright, equated the condition of the West and the South. The group announced a mass party meeting for "all good and true men, who repudiate the Reconstruction policy of Congress, negro suffrage, and the principles espoused by the Radical Republican Party, and who are in favor of equal and exact justice to all sections of the union."[37] When South Pass City voters went to the polls on September 2, 1869, to vote for a territorial legislature and a nonvoting delegate to the U.S. Congress, fifteen or twenty black male voters, under the protection of U.S. Marshall Howe, defied white Democrats' attempts to prevent them from casting their ballots. Justice Kingman described the scene:

> At South Pass City some drunken fellows with large knives and loaded revolvers swaggered around the polls, and swore that no Negro should vote. . . . When one man remarked quietly that he thought the Negroes had as good a right to vote as any of them had, he was immediately knocked down, jumped on, kicked, and pounded without mercy and would have been killed had not his friends rushed into the brutal crowd and dragged him out, bloody and insensible. There were quite a number of colored men who wanted to vote, but did not dare approach the polls until the United States Marshal, himself at their head and with a revolver in hand, escorted them through the crowd, saying he would shoot the first man that interfered with them. There was much quarreling and tumult, but the Negroes voted.[38]

The Democratic Party, trumpeting its determination to stand for white supremacy and against black rights, swept the territorial elections that year. Wyoming voters chose Democrats to fill every office, including electing William H. Bright to the Territorial Council.[39]

The ensuing discussion over race and rights among white men in Reconstruction Wyoming had all the subtlety and charm of fingernails across a blackboard. The parties staked out their positions in the newspapers. In the overheated rhetoric of the *Frontier Index,* a Republican victory in the presidential campaign of 1868 meant race war—conflict far more complex and confusing, as seen from Wyoming, than a simple battle between black and white. The bill to organize Wyoming Territory, the paper claimed, had been delayed in Congress

> to prevent Wyoming from being settled by conservative white men. . . . A few more such planks in Grant's platform will Africanise and Indianise our

whole mongrel region. . . . four hundred millions of Chinamen . . . [will be] "knocking at our national door" . . . our white laborers and their wives and children will suffer for bread. Americans you will have to subsist (not live) on rats, and rice and drink tea made from the grounds emptied from Chinamen's teapots.

Reminding readers of the war so recently and, in the editors' eyes, so unsatisfactorily concluded, the paper warned that if Grant won,

the war of races will have commenced. Our watchword will be Revolution or Death!
Up with white men, down with the devil![40]

Announcing Grant's election, *Index* editors Fred and Legh Freeman sounded like southern secessionists greeting the news of Lincoln's victory: "The clouds of revolution are lowering. On with it! Freedom to the white race! Off with the crown of the military dictator—Grant!" Such men dreaded the imminent arrival of federal appointees who promised to protect black men's rights and who, in embracing Grant's "Peace Policy" toward indigenous people, appeared soft on the Indian "problem." The Radicals, the *Index* predicted, would give the Indians "full rations as long as they carry on a vigorous and successful war upon the whites, and turn over their outside trade to 'our agents.' Go in, Lo: Thad. Stevens and Ben Butler will back you!"[41]

At least one Republican official, Wyoming governor John A. Campbell, did indeed intend to honor Indian rights. Campbell was responsible for enforcing federal policy toward Indians in the territory, and he all too frequently found himself forced to mediate between white emigrants who had no regard for Indian claims or lives; "friendly" Indians who were hungry, suspicious, and disillusioned; embittered Indians whose rage at the white presence mirrored emigrant hatred; individuals of all races who used the general confusion to pursue their own often disruptive ends; and a remote and corrupt government that generally failed to carry out its treaty obligations. "I believe it to be unwise and wrong to insist on a faithful obeissance of the [Fort Bridger] Treaty stipulations on the part of the Indians without a corresponding faithfulness on our part," Campbell wrote to Commissioner of Indian Affairs Ely S. Parker following a dispiriting visit to the Wind River Reservation shortly after his arrival in the territory.[42]

The convening of the all-Democratic legislature in November 1869 thus boded not only a struggle with the Republican executive over race relations in the territory, but also a tussle for political power between the legislative and executive branches that, ironically, mirrored recent national politics. As the historian T. A. Larson has noted, Campbell vetoed a number of bills sent to him by the legislature, which promptly overrode his vetoes in turn.[43] The conflict over one such bill, a measure prohibiting "intermarriage between white persons and those of Negro or Mongolian blood," demonstrated differences between Wyoming Republican and Democratic positions on racial issues. The Democrats' position seemed clear enough: the "white race" must be protected from "mongrelization," by means ranging from extermination to antimiscegenation laws. Republicans, however, seemed less certain of how race relations ought to be negotiated. In his veto message, Campbell refrained from offering opinions on interracial unions, explaining that he was unsure "how far it may be expedient or well to attempt to govern social life and taste by legislative prohibitions." Nevertheless, he reasoned that "if it be wise policy to prohibit intermarriage between persons of different races . . . I can see no reason for excepting any race from the operations of the law." The current bill, he said, didn't prohibit intermarriage between nonwhite persons of different "races." He further pointed out—in a passage that, surprisingly, referred to Indians as "the American race," as distinct from members of "the white race"—that the antimiscegenation bill did not include measures "to restrict the intermingling of the white race or any other race with the American race." As Campbell and others well knew, given the skewed sex ratio of the white population and the uncounted but manifest presence of indigenous women in the territory, "there have been and probably will be more marriages in this territory between Indians and whites, than between persons of all other races combined."[44]

At the same time, virtually all European American and African American Wyomingites embraced the idea that they had a right and a duty to settle the territory, or in other words, to try to replace indigenous inhabitants with persons like themselves, preferably living in family groups. Wyoming Democrats had criticized federal Indian policy as too conciliatory from the beginning. Republicans soon followed suit. Their 1870 party platform declared that "we deprecate that policy of the general government which was established by our fathers in making treaties with the various Indian tribes, as independent nations."[45] The *Wyoming Tribune*, edited by Secretary Lee's brother-in-law, S. A. Bristol, lamented at the close of the first legislative session that the assembly had failed to pass a militia law, requested by the governor, thus "leaving the people to the red men's tender mercies, except where U.S. troops may happen to be stationed. The people desired to prepare themselves for future emergencies, and place themselves on a defensive *quasi* war footing."[46] Campbell, who hoped to avert Indian-white violence, tried to solve conflicts wherever he could by honoring treaty obligations, and when that proved impossible, by persuading Indians to cede more land to whites. Faced with evidence of miners' and settlers' encroachments on the Wind River Reservation, Campbell asked the commissioner of Indian Affairs for permission to deal with Shoshones to "secure to miners and settlers already on the land a right to what they have occupied, and open up to settlement the southern valleys of the reservation." He also pushed the federal government to open up Lakota country to prospectors.[47]

And so the displacement, defeat, and confinement of indigenous people, and the extension of United States dominance, identified with the sedentary presence of white families usually called "settlement," provided the common ground on which emigrant Americans argued about how power *within* the empire ought to be apportioned. This larger consensus led in 1869 to temporary, surprising, and paradoxical agreement between a majority of Democrats in the legislature and the Republican governor on one issue: woman suffrage.

Settlement required mobility. The railroad brought new ideas, as well as new people, into Wyoming Territory. Among those who passed through Cheyenne in 1869 were two women who had taken up a remarkable but increasingly common career for women, that of itinerant lecturer. Like many such female circuit orators, Missourian Redelia Bates and the far better known Anna Dickinson braved the annoyances and dangers of living on the road to deliver speeches on the controversial subject of woman suffrage in locales as unpromising as Cheyenne. When Susan B. Anthony, Elizabeth Cady Stanton, Bates, Dickinson, and others boarded trains and stagecoaches and wagons for remote places, they moved out of both the civilized province of the East and the protected confines of the woman's sphere to venture into the masculine wilds of the West and the bright light of public wrangling. Rambling from coast to coast, they reached a large new audience, including women who were not ready to speak or act publicly but who privately supported the idea of reforming women's position in American society.[48] Judging by Wyoming newspapers' frequent references in 1868 and 1869 to woman suffrage meetings, suffragist speakers' appearances, and suffragist publications across the nation, many Wyomingites were alert to questions of women's rights.[49]

Among those interested was William H. Bright, a Virginian who had joined the Union army, who had come to the Sweetwater with his wife, Julia, and their infant son. Like so many others in South Pass City, he kept a saloon and did some mining, neither with great success. He was, however, popular among his fellows, active in the Masonic lodge and the Democratic Party, and would represent his district when the legislature met for the first time. When Bright, who was chosen to be president of the new Territorial Council, announced on November 12, 1869, that he planned to introduce a bill for woman suffrage, many thought he was joking.

However, some of Bright's fellow politicians believed that he was serious indeed, and that his wife had convinced him to bring forward the measure. William and Julia Bright were the kind of Victorian couple who took their manliness and womanliness seriously, the kind of people charged with hauling the freight of empire westward to create an American province. William Bright was no angel, but his intentions were good. He played his part in the fraternal order, the party, and the territorial legislature, and if he sometimes fell short of the moral mark, it was not for lack of trying. Julia, for her part, took care of the baby and kept the house, prudently relying on private persuasion rather than public advocacy to influence her husband. Justice John W. Kingman later recalled that Bright "did his wife's bidding" and that Bright's "character was not above reproach, but he had an excellent, well-informed wife and he was a kind, indulgent husband. In fact, he venerated his wife and submitted to her judgment and influence more willingly than one could have supposed, and she was in favor of woman suffrage."[50]

Even those least favorably disposed toward woman suffrage believed that Julia Bright had quietly manipulated her husband into introducing the suffrage bill. Ben Sheeks, the South Pass City legislator who would lead the opposition, remembered that

> Mrs. Bright was a very womanly suffragist and I always understood and still believe that it was through her influence that the bill was introduced. I know that I supposed at the time that she was the author of the bill. What reason, if any, I had for thinking so I do not remember. Possibly it was only that she seemed intellectually and in education superior to Mr. Bright.[51]

But though woman suffrage was controversial, the female franchise was not the only women's rights matter to attract private and public support in Wyoming in 1869. The first session of the Wyoming territorial legislature considered, and passed with virtually no dispute, laws to give married women control over their property and earnings and to pay women teachers the same wages male teachers received.[52] This unusual package of rights and benefits begs explanation.

The answer is that influential Wyomingites saw women's rights as a device to advance the risky work of bringing the empire to the West. The *Cheyenne Leader* pointed out, indeed, that the law giving women the right to acquire, hold, and use property in their own name was "eminently just, and is one of those rights which should be vouchsafed to women as protection from shiftless and improvident husbands. It is perhaps more necessary in this Territory than in a more settled state of society in the East. Men risk oftener their means in venturesome speculation than elsewhere."[53] The vote, thus, was but one bead on a string of legislative reforms intended to entice white women to move to places like Cheyenne and Miner's Delight, to establish with their white female bodies the process of settlement. The legislature clearly hoped to recruit women to the project of empire by promising them more power.

But the agents of empire continued to wrangle over who was entitled to what kind of power. Democrats like William Bright believed that white American women had a greater claim to the right to vote than did the black American men who, according to the newly ratified Fourteenth Amendment to the Constitution, now enjoyed the franchise. Bright and his fellows expected that white women's votes would be instruments of racial control. They had reason to think such a thing, since Susan B. Anthony and Elizabeth Cady Stanton, the nation's best-known women's rights advocates, were furious at the unreliable Republican radicals who had abandoned woman suffrage. Having found a financial backer in the white supremacist Democrat George Francis Train, Anthony and Stanton were, in 1869, busily trumpeting the racist argument for women's votes on the lecture circuit and in the pages of their journal, the *Revolution.* The *Frontier Index* reported approvingly on the *Revolution*'s campaign against "the smelliferous skullduggery being played by the niggeropolists" in Washington. "Hip! hip! hip! hurrah for the telling efforts of the *Revolution,*" the *Index* exclaimed. "God bless the ladies, may their noble, patriotic, honest influence bring our poor distracted country back to peace and *white* prosperity, and crown their own adorable sex, with all the rights, immunities, privileges and marked honors the earth can bestow upon merit, purity, and shining christianity."[54]

Although Democrats, like Republicans, wished to publicize the territory in order to recruit more white settlers, not all Democrats thought that attracting national attention was worth giving women the vote. South Pass City's Ben Sheeks, for example, did all he could to defeat Bright's measure. While his colleagues argued that woman suffrage would mobilize morally upright eastern white women to "civilize" the territory, Sheeks mockingly reminded them that the term "woman" might be taken to refer to a variety of persons in Wyoming itself. When the House debated Bright's measure, Sheeks sought to amend it by adding "all colored women and squaws" to the ranks of the enfranchised.

Wyoming legislators brushed off Sheeks's suggestion as outrageous; in their eyes, any *true* woman was, of course, also white. Sheeks's amendment failed, and Bright's bill passed both houses of the legislature. Some who voted for woman suffrage claimed they'd done so as a joke, to embarrass the Republican governor, who would, they had no doubt, veto the measure. Others, Bright in particular, were sincere in their support of woman suffrage—for right-thinking white women like Bright's own wife, Julia. All who supported it, as well as those legislators who did not, shared the mission of attracting white emigration to Wyoming.[55]

But not many went as far as territorial secretary E. M. Lee in identifying the arrival of politically empowered white women with the expansion of the American Empire for Liberty. When, to the amazement of many, Governor Campbell signed the bill on December 10, Lee waxed ecstatic. Women, he believed, would exercise a "civilizing influence" in politics as they had in the home. The territory, he wrote in the *Wyoming Tribune,* had been

> placed far in advance of every other political community on the subject of human rights. That the policy of suffrage without regard to race or sex will ultimately be adopted by the entire nation may be regarded as no longer a matter of doubt, and to Wyoming belongs the proud privilege of pioneership in this grand modern reform. . . . Let fogyism, prejudice and caste find refuge among the *ghouls* of darkness and the dead past. Among the Rocky Mountains, seeking to establish an empire, we have inaugurated for the first time in history complete civil and political equality.[56]

Thus men like William Bright, John Campbell, and Edward Lee, who disagreed strongly on the issue of black rights but who shared a common imperial vision, came together in support of woman suffrage. It didn't, after all, take a huge constituency in that time or place to make the measure a law. The House approved by a vote of 7–4 with one abstention; the Council passed the bill 6–2, with one absent. The governor signed off. All that was required to break the male monopoly on formal politics in the United States, in this case, was the consent of fourteen men. The "experiment" with woman suffrage could begin.[57]

Wyoming women quickly seized and used their new public power. Some, clearly, had been reticent but strong supporters of woman suffrage, who greeted their good luck with action. They voted, served on juries, ran for office, and were appointed justices of the peace. The *Cheyenne Leader* reported on August 24, 1870, that at the local Republican convention "the ladies of Laramie County [Cheyenne], in convention assembled, make the following nominations for county officers: Amelia B. Post, Probate Judge; Mrs. Phebe Pickett, County Clerk." The party did nominate Mrs. Pickett for county clerk, as well as Mrs. M. A. Arnold for superintendent of public instruction, and made Mrs. W. D. Pease a member of the Republican County Committee for the year. On September 10 the *Leader* reported on territorial elections, stating that "the total vote of the Territory is about 3,200. The vote of Cheyenne is 776, of which 171 were ladies."[58]

Out in South Pass City, one woman succeeded in gaining political office. Fifty-six-year-old Esther Morris had arrived in South Pass City in the summer of 1869, joining her husband and three sons.[59] During the previous winter, Morris had been living in Peru, Illinois, not far from the town of Galena, where Susan B. Anthony had given a suffrage speech. Whether or not Morris attended the lecture, she would doubtless have been aware of the meeting, given extensive coverage of the suffragist's tour in midwestern newspapers.

The six-foot-tall Morris was precisely the type of woman Victorian Americans identified with successful settlement, strong-willed enough to survive hardship and dedicated to raising her sons to be upright citizens. "With her boys," one commentator noted, "what she said was law."[60] Morris and her son Robert had been "open advocates" of woman suffrage in South Pass City, and shortly after the passage of the bill they went to visit the Bright cabin to thank William Bright for his "services in their behalf." As Robert Morris wrote in a letter to Anthony and Stanton's *Revolution,* Bright held fast to a Victorian understanding of men's and women's separate spheres, insisting that he had not been "convinced by a woman's lecture or newspaper, for I never heard a woman speak from a rostrum."[61] Even so assertive a woman as Esther Morris made a point of reassuring men that "while she advocated the elevation of women, she does not wish the downfall of man."[62]

When South Pass City's justice of the peace resigned, Morris was appointed his successor, becoming the first American woman to hold that office. She served for some eight months, hearing both civil and criminal cases. According to that ardent supporter of woman suffrage, territorial secretary E. M. Lee, "She at once familiarized herself with the principles of common law and with the Territorial statutes. . . . Her court sessions were characterized by a degree of gravity and decorum rarely exhibited in the judicature of border precincts. . . . During her administration a decided improvement in the tone of public morals was noticeable."[63]

But even as Esther Morris worked to bring the influence of white middle-class womanhood to bear on the administration of territorial justice, she had her critics. Some who had felt the force of her moral will did not consider themselves to have been "improved" by the experience. She was said to have been "especially severe on drunkenness, remorselessly inflicting on every inebriate brought before her the full penalty of the law. Some are said to have tried the effect of tears upon her, but they afterward declared that it did no more good than pouring whiskey down a rathole."[64]

As white women like Esther Morris moved to engrave their mark on public life in Wyoming, the paper-thin prosuffrage consensus among white men began to shred. Republicans claimed that women voted with them, and the Democrats feared they might be right, since several Republicans were elected to the legislature and to local offices in 1870 and 1871. Women voters did seem to support Sunday saloon closings, a stance more agreeable to Republicans than to Democrats, although some commentators claimed that women were less partisan than men, voting for candidates more on character than on party affiliation.[65] The matter of "character" may also have been a matter of class. One man insisted that "most men who own property . . . have a wife, sisters and mother whose votes offset the votes of the reckless, worthless renegades who have no property, a kind of floating population that believes those who have property are their enemies, and who at every opportunity vote against the moral interests of the town."[66] Some impecunious male voters may well have suspected that the women who voted in Wyoming represented class interests other than their own.

But for every man who criticized women voters for their bourgeois morality, there were others who worried that the "wrong" kinds of women might take advantage of the chivalry of righteous men and exert a degrading influence at the polls. Rumors that "only 'disreputable women' vote; and that they always vote for the 'worst men'" moved Judge Kingman to defend the character of Wyoming's women voters in a letter from Laramie to the editors of the *Boston Herald*:

> I have made inquiry at our police courts and of our constables . . . as to
> the number of "disreputable women" in our city; and I am informed that
> there are not over forty such characters here, and that less than thirty of
> them are voters; and I am quite sure that no other town in the Territory
> has a larger proportion. . . . Our best and most cultivated women vote;
> and vote understandingly and independently and they cannot be bought
> with whiskey, or blinded by party prejudice.[67]

Women voters were not suspect simply on moral grounds. Democrats
must have been particularly angered at the spectacle of black women voting, an event that taxed white men's chivalry. Judge Kingman recalled
the first election in which women voted as an occasion that

> caused me much uneasiness. We had, at first, a large proportion of South-
> ern men and of Northern Copperheads. By that I mean men who advocated
> secession and came to Wyoming to escape being drafted. Carriages were
> employed by the candidates to bring ladies to the polls. At the hotels were
> a number of colored girls employed as servants. After a while a carriage
> drove up with four of these colored girls in it. They were helped out, and as
> they went up to the polls the crowd quietly parted; they voted and returned
> to the carriage without a word said. Then I breathed freely; I knew that all
> was safe.[68]

As Ben Sheeks's satirical amendment implied, Wyoming women voters, some of them black, others for one reason or another not quite
"true," might prove unreliable allies in the imperial crusade for white
dominance, let alone in the Democrats' avowed pursuit of white supremacy. White women who defected from that cause appeared to some
to forfeit their claim to moral superiority. One male suffrage opponent
explained that,

> as an instance of the demoralizing influence of politics on women, I re-
> member seeing a lady, the wife of a candidate for office, standing at the
> counter of a beer saloon drinking beer with a parcel of colored men. . . .
> She . . . was well-educated, and entirely respectable; but she was so in-
> tensely interested in her husband's success that she resorted to this means
> of getting votes for him. I saw this same lady and a school teacher of
> Cheyenne in their buggies driving colored men and women, and even
> known harlots, to and from the polls.[69]

What more *unsettling* image could a manly writer conjure than the specter
of a willful white woman wiping the foam from her lips, taking whip in
hand, gathering together the empire's least dependable recruits, and driving them off to exercise her, and their, regrettable rights?

Most disappointing of all, in the eyes of onetime supporters, woman suffrage did not bring a wave of white emigration to Wyoming. The South Pass gold boom busted; the railroad moved on. So too did some of the most ardent supporters of women's rights. Both William Bright and Edward Lee left the territory; ironically, those who most eagerly promoted permanent white settlement of Wyoming were among the first to seek out better opportunities elsewhere. The legislature met again in 1871, and with the numbers of suffrage supporters diminished, Democrats pushed to repeal women's right to vote.[70]

When Governor Campbell delivered his message to the legislature in 1871, he anticipated such an attempt, declaring that Wyoming women voters "have conducted themselves in every respect with as much tact, sound judgment, and good sense as men. . . . So long as none but good results are made manifest, the law should remain unrepealed."[71] Nonetheless, Democrats in the legislature, no longer without Republican opposition but still in the majority in both houses, were determined to do away with the law. Moreover, some Republicans, at swords' point with one another over the awarding of lucrative government contracts, had abandoned the suffrage ship. Nathan A. Baker, publisher of the *Cheyenne Leader,* had come to stand against anything ever supported by Edward Lee, including woman suffrage.[72] The *Leader* urged Republican legislators to vote for the repeal, in language strong enough to give the *Index* a run for its money:

> The abolition of the useless statute conferring suffrage upon women, will be regretted by none of the sex, save those in the ranks of the suffrage shriekers, the unsexed and uncultivated, we had almost said unchaste, of the Territory. The question has its advocates among those of lax socialistic ideas, the Woodhulls and the Tiltons of society. It has moreover the oder [*sic*] of free-loveism and depravity about it. An inseparable odium attaches, as subversive of nature, a foul and rotten thing.[73]

Heartily promoted by Ben Sheeks, the only man returned to the legislator from the 1869 session, the bill to repeal passed both houses, with all Democrats voting in favor and all Republicans opposed. A group of women from Laramie County had petitioned the legislature to preserve their rights; now only the governor stood in the way of disfranchisement.[74]

Governor John Campbell vetoed the bill. He clearly had a sense of the historical and political significance of his action, basing his argument on "certain universally admitted principles . . . which through the whole course of our national history have been powerfully and beneficially operative in making our institutions more and more popular, in framing laws more and more just." Campbell grounded his argument in the liberal principles of citizens' right to political representation, human equality before the law, and the guiding hand of experience in such matters. All such principles, he explained, led him to reason that woman suffrage was a fulfillment of, rather than a deviation from, the American ideal of "a government which 'derives all its just powers from the consent of the governed.'" In the end, he insisted, "a regard for the genius of our institutions—for the fundamental principles of American autonomy—and for the immutable principles of right and justice, will not permit me to sanction this change."[75]

The cause of liberty, then, sustained women's right to vote in Wyoming. But empire also provided a justification for upholding woman suffrage. The stirring American principles were, Campbell explained, products of a historical march of progress, embodied locally by the American state he and others carried into Wyoming Territory. Those who would take away women's votes, he argued, would "remand woman to that condition of tutelage and dependence which is her lot in all barbarous and uncivilized countries, and out of which she has been for eighteen centuries gradually but slowly emerging in all nations that have been blessed by the benign rays of a christian civilization."[76] One wonders what the neighboring Lakota or Shoshones might have thought of such a folktale.

This time, the Democrats fell one vote short of overriding the governor's veto. And so woman suffrage was preserved, never to be seriously threatened in Wyoming again. Wyoming women neither fomented revolution nor faded away, and their presence did abet American claims to Wyoming Territory, while their enfranchisement chipped a chink in the male monopoly on formal political power in the United States.

The success of woman suffrage in Wyoming, coinciding with the passage of a similar law in Utah, helped to stimulate the development of a new regional identity, of the West as a place where *women* could be free. By the time of the passage of the Nineteenth Amendment, the West had become, beyond dispute, recognizable as the region that enfranchised American women first.[77] If, by numerous measures, women in the American West enjoyed no more liberty or power than women in other places, the legend of liberated western womanhood did not need to be true to be powerful; it merely needed to be believed. By the end of the nineteenth century, a rising generation of women would seize the power of legend, of history, and of movement to shape the course of empire in the emerging West.

CHAPTER 4

MARKING WYOMING

Grace Raymond Hebard
and the West as Woman's Place

Women and wagons were not only suggestive
of our nation's development, but were a permanent factor in the earliest development of
the civilization of the nation.
Grace Raymond Hebard

The Trustees gave me a great deal of power,
and I used it. **Grace Raymond Hebard**

SOMEWHERE IN THE DECADES between Susan Magoffin's bridal journey and the 1890 census that deemed the West "settled," women who lived in the trans-Mississippi region began to insist on a public part and an audible voice in the story of the region. By the beginning of the twentieth century, they took an increasingly prominent place in the emerging region's public culture, participating openly in politics, interpreting western history, and seizing the power of public institutions with an eye to shaping the future of the terrain they called home. Beneficiaries of increasing educational opportunities, economic growth, the crusade for women's rights, and improvements in transportation systems, they were far less burdened by injunctions to female passivity, deference, and anonymity than the women I have written about so far. As "public intellectuals" they sought not only to interpret the immense changes they saw in the coming of modernity to the West, but to direct those changes to political ends, to leave a mark on the place. Wyoming's Grace Raymond Hebard was one such woman.

There was, perhaps, no more staunch advocate of the new regional legend, that the West was a place where men—and women!—could be free, than Grace Raymond Hebard. She was both product and advocate of the American empire, born in the town of Clinton, Iowa, in 1861, six months after that territory entered the union as a state. Throughout her life, Hebard insisted that the frontier had produced a region uniquely suited to the promulgation of liberty. She gloried in her own frontier roots, proclaiming that "perhaps my greatest heritage is that I am a pioneer daughter of pioneer parents. Poverty and hard work can give to one what luxury and leisure never can."[1]

At the same time, being a pioneer was, for Hebard, a matter of connecting a civilized, democratic past, embodied in family lineage, to a westward-moving present and future. Like her fellow historian (and sometimes adversary) Stella Drumm, Hebard took genealogy seriously. For her, family roots established both territorial and political claims, both the entitlement to occupy particular places and the affirmation of civil rights, for women as well as men. Hebard traced her ancestry not simply to passengers on the *Mayflower,* who had, of course, codified their rights and obligations in the famous Compact, but also insisted that she was descended from a signer of the document that prefigured democracy, the Magna Carta. Claiming such political legacies for women, Hebard took a leading role in establishing Wyoming chapters of national organizations like the Daughters of the American Revolution and the Colonial Dames.[2]

Grace Hebard thus saw her own family as the vehicle of Western civilization. Her parents, George Diah Alonzo Hebard, a Congregationalist minister, and Margaret Elizabeth Dominick Marven Hebard, left New York in 1858 to take up missionary work in Iowa. The Hebards got moving somewhere in the middle of a long wave of missionary activity that drew thousands of men and women westward in the name of true religion. George Hebard died when Grace was a child; Margaret carried on in Iowa, with her four children, alone. Like Huck Finn, Grace Hebard was a frontier child, schooled at home by a widow.

Also like Huck, Grace Hebard put more faith in her own sense of justice than in the true religion embraced by the benevolent widow. But unlike Huck, Hebard had a liking for her lessons. She went on to enter the State University of Iowa, majoring in engineering and gaining a reputation on campus as an athlete, scholar, and ardent supporter of women's rights. She graduated with a B.S. in 1882, the first woman to earn a bachelor's in science at that institution.

Like thousands of American women, Grace Raymond Hebard took advantage, for the first time, of the opportunity to attend college. She was, moreover, lucky enough to come along at the intersection of unprecedented moments in American women's history and the history of the American West. The Morrill Act of 1862, which set aside funds for agricultural and vocational colleges in western territories and states, offered higher education to women as well as men. Public colleges and universities became transmission stations of geographical as well as cultural transformation, as educated women and men fanned out across the country, taking on the work not simply of settlement but of civilization. Western institutions of higher learning would cast particularly broad nets on the developing hinterlands of new territories and states.

For women, lighting out for the territory in this fashion meant making life choices. Hebard's generation of college women generally rejected marriage in favor of pursuing a professional life. If they missed the rewards of marriage and motherhood, they nevertheless enjoyed a freedom to move independently not available to most wives and mothers.[3] To a greater degree than ever before, white women, claiming the mantle of expertise, served as independently mobile agents of change. College women like Hebard were making their mark throughout the United States, inventing new occupations, pioneering new social sciences, founding social service institutions, joining in reform crusades.[4] They found particularly urgent demand for their skills and energy in the states and territories of the enterprising but labor-starved American West.

Scarcely half a dozen years after the epoch-making Battle of the Little Bighorn, Grace Hebard was a twenty-one-year-old graduate of the engineering program at the State University of Iowa. She moved to Cheyenne with her mother, brothers, and sister in 1882, and with the help of an influential Republican politician secured a job as a draftsman in the surveyor general's office, an organization charged with locating, fixing, and charting the boundaries of the soon-to-be state. By 1891 Hebard had attained the rank of deputy state engineer under Elwood Mead, the man who would remake the West as head of the Bureau of Reclamation and dam builder par excellence.[5]

Hebard was a prodigiously ambitious young woman, but she knew that opportunities for females in engineering were, mildly put, limited. Thus gender diverted her career into more meandering channels than that of her famous boss. It is fitting, however, that Grace Hebard began her life in Wyoming as an agent of imperial geography, in a country so lately conquered by force of arms, still so thinly settled. In the half-century that followed, she would mobilize a variety of professional and personal credentials, tools, and resources on behalf of a complicated geographical project: to claim the Wyoming terrain for the United States, while marking her adopted home state as a distinct place, more western (and thus more American) than any other. Many Americans in many western locales carried on similar efforts, but in Hebard's hands these projects took on an additional political task. As she mapped, marked, and made meaning out of landscape, this self-described feminist also did everything she could to stake women's claim to space, to historical significance, and to political equality: to make the West woman's place.[6]

Grace Hebard was ever alert to opportunity. During her nine years working for Mead and living in Cheyenne, Hebard managed to get a master's degree in literature, largely by correspondence, from Iowa State. She had already begun to make a name for herself as one of the territory's wide-awake reformers; in 1889, the same year Hull House was founded in Chicago, Hebard spoke to the Wyoming State Constitutional Convention, urging the delegates to make sure that Wyoming entered the union as the nation's first state to fully enfranchise women. By 1891, approaching the age of thirty, unmarried by choice, and restless, Hebard determined to change careers and to make a move on her own, away from her family. Like many of her female contemporaries, she would use the academy as her base of operations.[7]

The town of Laramie was only fifty miles from Cheyenne, both close and far enough from mother and siblings to suit her purposes, a town newly established as home to the sole institution of higher learning in the territory. The University of Wyoming had opened its doors in 1887, after a legendary winter of dying cattle and busted ranches, as Wyoming moved to take advantage of the Morrill Act and other federal laws providing land and funding for colleges in western states and territories.[8] The population of the newly admitted state in 1890 was 64,405 (mostly white, but including an enumerated 1,850 Indians on the Wind River Reservation), scattered widely, here and there in small clusters, over 97,818 square miles. In 1891, when Hebard moved to Laramie, Wyoming was long on opportunity but desperately short on labor and expertise.

What better place for an educated, confident, energetic white woman to make a new start?[9] Mrs. Eva Downey, civic-minded wife of Laramie community leader Stephen A. Downey and mother of June Etta Downey, the University of Chicago Ph.D. psychologist who would become one of Hebard's most cherished colleagues, recalled Hebard's arrival in Laramie: "I shall always think with great pleasure of the first time you came to our home, on your way from the train, to take up your work as secretary to the Board of Trustees of the University. Quite a new feild [*sic*] of work at that time for a women. You were so filled with enthusiasm and delight at the new work."[10]

Hebard's first job at the university reflected the fluidity and relative openness of institutional development in the West, and of educational bureaucracy in embryo: she was appointed secretary to *and* member of the Board of Trustees of the University of Wyoming. In that odd dual position, she became an influential and controversial figure, and remains so, among Wyoming historians, to this day. While even her greatest adversary, the botanist Aven Nelson, conceded that Hebard possessed a "capacity for solving difficult business problems" and a "tact in dealing with the public" that served the university well, he and others deplored Hebard's unfeminine appetite for power.[11] Handling the university's finances as well as all official correspondence, Hebard admitted that "the Trustees gave me a great deal of power, and I used it."[12] While she may not precisely have had "a Svengali-like hold over generations of University of Wyoming trustees," it seems clear that when she could not directly control events, she did what she could to exert covert pressure.[13] As F. P. Graves, an early president of the university, recalled, "She zealously guarded all knowledge of the weaknesses I had exhibited and credited me with many successful projects which she herself had originated."[14]

Her detractors put a slightly different spin on such secretarial self-effacement. "Her power is recognized not only by the university people, but by many townspeople, yet her clerical position enables her to throw responsibility for any policy upon the executives," complained one professor.[15] When a university funds scandal in 1907 led to the resignation of several trustees, Hebard was found innocent of any wrongdoing but widely criticized for asserting herself. "It is a standing remark in Laramie," wrote the editor of the Douglas, Wyoming, Budget, in an editorial reprinted in Laramie's Boomerang, "that no professor or employee of the institution can hold his job without being branded 'ok' by Miss Secretary Hebard, and whenever she decrees it the president's head will fall in the basket." Lest Wyoming readers fail to recognize Hebard as a local version of Madame Defarge at the guillotine, the editorialist indulged in a more familiar metaphor, comparing Hebard to a renegade Indian: "The scalps of Presidents . . . may hang for many a moon in the Secretary's office as a practical demonstration of what a woman can do."[16]

Avid for work and for power, Hebard seized on the chance to do any job that cropped up, performing a variety of tasks encompassing everything from bookkeeping to acting as ad hoc dean of women. From 1894 to 1919 she also served, without pay, as university librarian, a position she used both to train young Wyoming women for professional work and to extend the university's political and intellectual presence throughout the state. There can be no doubt that Grace Raymond Hebard built the University of Wyoming library from scratch, and that in doing so she intended to change the lay of the land.

Hebard loved to tell the story of her first sight of the UW campus— "a vacant lot more accurately speaking," she said, "with a single, isolated, substantial building surrounded by the perpetually snow capped mountains of the Medicine Bow Range. The campus was without fence, without walks, or trees, shrubs, lawn, grass, or evidence of flowers during the past season, but the view in any way one might look was just . . . glorious." She decided to try to find the library, because "back in the East when one visited a University or College he always sought the Library and there read while waiting to fulfill an engagement." She saw a

man with a long string of keys, who turned out to be the university cus-
todian, and asked him where the library was. "The Library, the library,
the library," said the puzzled janitor, who at length led her to the room
that would later become her office. He opened the door on "a room without table, chair, desk, shelves, book-case, blackboard, curtain, only three
sacks of Government books piled in a pyramid in the center of the
floor!"[17]

Determined to equip, and then build, a library, Hebard embraced the
bricks-and-mortar approach to institutional development. She took it
upon herself to round up any other books that happened to be around
and to get some instruction in library administration at the Denver Public Library. She served as unofficial university librarian until 1908, when
she was appointed to the post. When she left the library in 1919, the cat-
alogued collection had grown to forty-two thousand books. From the
first, she had agitated for "a real, just a real library" in a building of its
own, a building that would become both center and icon of academic
culture transplanted to the remote high country, but the university had
other priorities. Despite Hebard's constant pressure, UW did not build
a library until 1924. When she spoke at the building's dedication,
Hebard was delighted to the heart. "Santa Claus," she said, "has finally
come."[18]

The library building was the citadel of her program. The women she
trained as librarians were its soldiers. Librarianship was an emerging career for educated women in the early twentieth century, and as many
scholars have pointed out, libraries were crucial sites of social and political education.[19] In Wyoming, libraries also acted as nodes of geographical transformation, tying far-flung clusters of settlement into a network embodied in buildings and books and paper and people, radiating
out from Laramie. In Hebard's view, public libraries would not only create good and loyal American citizens, but would modernize Wyoming,
in part by extending the university's influence across the state in the persons of mobile, educated women like herself.

The next step, she believed, was a professional library school at UW.
"With the formation of new counties and the increase of population in
Wyoming, which we trust may be constant and more numerous, there
will be more and more a demand for public libraries and trained people,
presumably women, to take charge of these," she wrote in her 1914 annual report to university president C. A. Duniway. "If the University of
Wyoming had a librarian in every county there would be a central source
of information for the University . . . for the public librarian meets a

greater variety and a greater number of citizens, students, and pupils than any office in this state." Not simply literary repositories, Hebard envisioned public libraries as centers of state-of-the-art political organizing. She proposed an ambitious library training curriculum, including a course in "legislative reference," which would, she said, "bear particularly upon legislative and municipal reform work and various sociological phases of library work." Indeed, she said, "I have a more extended plan in reference to this suggested school, about which I would find great pleasure in conferring with you."[20]

Hebard didn't get her library school, but by 1914 she had trained a number of young women who carried on the library work (and as their mentor, Hebard kept the pressure on the university's presidents for pay raises for her "college women" protégés).[21] Hebard herself had long since begun to direct most of her own energies to other projects. If public librarians could bind Wyoming together by claiming space in public buildings and, more abstractly, fostering citizenship and social progress in towns across the state, college professors at the state's only university were in a position to mold Wyoming's future leaders. Like the library, the college classroom offered a bully pulpit. It seemed like a good time to become a professor.

Hebard's campaign to get into the classroom began as early as 1893, when she earned a Ph.D. in political science from Illinois Wesleyan University, doing so once again largely by correspondence.[22] She began her career as a university professor substituting for the regular instructor of an economics class, and by 1906 had secured a faculty appointment in the department of political economy, being named head of the department little more than a year later. When her disgruntled predecessor accused her of buying a fake Ph.D. from a "notoriously loose" institution and scheming to replace him during a time when he had been taken ill, Hebard insisted that she had only been trying to help the university in an emergency situation.[23]

Correspondence doctorates seem suspicious to us now, though fast-changing information technologies may, sooner than we think, make "distance learning" Ph.D.s as commonplace as they were in the early years of the twentieth century. Academic structures in those days, particularly in the West, were considerably less formal than they are now, and at the time that Hebard received her Ph.D. few Wyoming faculty members held the degree.[24] At the small but growing University of Wyoming (by 1906, total enrollment had reached only 233 students), expediency trumped expertise. "The position of professor at the University of Wyoming in the early years," notes the historian Deborah Hardy, "demanded breadth, specialization, administrative ability, classroom discipline, a willingness to travel, research interests, talent in public relations, and generally, great good humor."[25] Hebard possessed all those attributes, along with plenty of hubris. She taught courses in state and national civics, federal constitutional law, Wyoming law (having been herself admitted to the state bar in 1898), international law, English constitutional law, sociology, money and banking, political parties, labor problems, railroad organization, children's literature and storytelling, and library science. She was particularly celebrated for her exciting renderings of western and Wyoming history (a subject to which we will shortly return). In time, she would also teach night classes in Americanization and patriotism for immigrants.[26] However unconventional her preparation for teaching, scores of notes from devoted students testify to Hebard's skill, enthusiasm, and magnetism in the classroom.

The university community regarded Hebard as an advocate for students, and a particularly adamant supporter of female undergraduates. One student who went on to teach English and history at Laramie High School expressed a widespread sentiment when she wrote: "I have had the opportunity to observe many instances in which you have rendered aid to young women which was really vital to them, and in which you spared neither trouble nor expense. . . . With the wish that Wyoming girls may long enjoy your help and sympathy, I extend to you my personal thanks for many favors rendered to me."[27] Agnes Wright Spring, a woman who would become state historian of both Colorado and Wyoming, studied history with Hebard and worked as her library assistant throughout her undergraduate years. Spring stated simply, "When folks ask why I became an historian, the answer is: Grace Raymond Hebard."[28] Another woman student put the matter more passionately: "I just love you so much, it almost hurts."[29]

For all her independence, Hebard lived her life in the midst of myriad female communities, local and extended, overlapping in space and time, maintained by the participants through daily socializing, letter writing (and infrequently, telegrams and telephone calls), publications, meetings and celebrations, and travel.[30] In Laramie, she was one of several women who held important administrative and academic positions in the first decades of the university's history, including the first three heads of the UW history department (Irene May Morse, Agnes Mathilde Wergeland, and Laura White), the psychologist June Downey, and the English literature scholar Clara France McIntyre. Like Hebard, these women played a crucial role in the transformation of Laramie, from a rough-and-ready railroad town to a college town professing culture and promoting beauty and comfort. They formed a close-knit (if sometimes contentious) women's network, embodied in the houses in the university neighborhood that women professors shared with one another, the gardens they nurtured, the dinner parties they gave for each other, and finally, in 1924, "The Professors' Club," an organization Hebard founded for women professors and administrators that continued to meet until 1961.[31]

Historians have demonstrated the significance of intimate emotional relations between professional women in the United States in Hebard's day, and such relationships shaped the geography of the United States, and of Wyoming, and of Laramie.[32] When Hebard first moved to Laramie, she lived with Irene Morse in lodgings they humorously called "Old Maids' Paradise." After Morse left for Massachusetts to study medicine, Hebard moved in with Morse's successor in the history department, Agnes Wergeland, at a house they called "The Doctors' Inn." Her twelve-year relationship with Wergeland, which ended only with Wergeland's death in 1914, was clearly the most significant attachment of her life. Wergeland had charted a distinguished academic course, leaving her native Norway to teach at Bryn Mawr and the University of Chicago before settling in Wyoming. A musician and poet as well as a historian, Wergeland shared with Hebard a love of outdoor sports and western landscape.[33]

Although women of their time and place would not have used the word "lesbian" to describe their relationship, Hebard and Wergeland were passionately involved. Wergeland wrote poetry, mostly in Norse, and Hebard saved a poem, translated from the Norse into English, titled "Thy Hand," a poem to a beloved who is also friend and colleague, to a woman of sensitivity and affection, talent and determination and courage:

> The music ceased.—I knew not—
> Thy hand was all my thought
> So small and fine and delicate it was
> The gentle throne for thy mild spirit,
> Thy strong and lovely profile's complement,
> Thy very self, thy soul, thy roguish smile.
>
> For all its whiteness, 'tis a working hand:
> Its clever fingers are the surest bond
> Between work and that wise clear will of yours
> Which is work's spirit.

Oh hand, of great and small the instrument,
Plaiting with kindly care the thousand strings
Which bind us,—it is thou
That with good counsel, as of friend to friend,
Helps us to find each other . . .

And I would gladly kiss these flower-stems,
So jealously half-hid by lace and silk
And in my own how gladly I would hold
Thy warm hand, index of thy noble mind.[34]

Thus deeply committed to one another, and supported by their accomplished women friends in Laramie, Hebard and Wergeland kept in touch with an international community of educated, reform-minded women. Both were ardent suffragists and proponents of women's education, and after Wergeland died, Hebard paid tribute to her memory by establishing two memorial scholarships, one a prize for history students at UW, the other a fellowship for women students in Norway to come to the United States to study history.[35] Hebard maintained the connection with that wider set of networks through her participation in the woman suffrage movement and through organizations ranging from the Daughters of the American Revolution and Colonial Dames to the American Association of University Women, the National Business and Professional Women's Club, and the National Association of Women Lawyers. These activities served Hebard's project of mapping Wyoming as a modern American place, of linking that remote and thinly populated locale with a forward-moving nation that had begun to recognize the potential of women like herself. As she did what she could to institutionalize the presence and prospects of independent, educated women within Wyoming, she worked to make her own national reputation as an emancipated woman of the West, the Wyoming incarnation of progressive womanhood and Progressive politics.

Since Hebard pushed so hard to keep Wyoming in step with the nation, it is hardly surprising that she championed the national movement for Americanization within Wyoming. Her doctoral dissertation, on the Americanization of immigrants, embodied a lifelong interest in the project of assimilation. As Wyoming's correspondent to the suffragist periodical *Woman Citizen,* as state regent for the Daughters of the American Revolution, as university professor in classes ranging from political economy, sociology, and law to children's literature, as night school teacher to citizenship classes, and in numerous public and private utterances, Hebard promoted Americanization. Historian Frank Van Nuys has shown how Hebard's career as an Americanizer followed a pattern common among the more conservative American Progressives, people who expressed "a qualified optimism" about the possibility of assimilating immigrants in the opening decades of the twentieth century but who ultimately succumbed to the xenophobia catalyzed by World War I. By the 1920s, many embraced immigration restriction.[36]

Hebard's first published work on the subject of Americanization appeared in 1896, in an article titled "Immigration and Needed Ballot Reform" in the *Illinois Wesleyan Magazine*.[37] But it was not until 1916, when the national Americanization movement began to centralize and to pick up speed, that she began to devote substantial time and energy to Americanization projects. At that point, she joined with advocates of Americanization both in Wyoming and in the national woman suffrage movement to promote assimilation through education, in particular through courses in American history, politics, and civics. "The aim," she told a meeting of the local chapter of the Federation of Women's Clubs in Sheridan in 1916, "is to turn out patriots with an abiding respect for American history and institutions."[38] She believed in Americanizing only those she deemed assimilable, northern and western Europeans, and advocated immigration restriction for everyone else, especially southern and eastern Europeans, whom she deemed a "heterogeneous mass, so blind to the duties of patriotism that they are unable to distinguish the red flag, typical of society unregulated by any principles of government, from the red, white, and blue—a perfect national emblem."[39]

But there was a decidedly local dimension to Hebard's nativist politics in this so recently conquered outpost of the United States. Remarkably, Wyoming offered Grace Hebard the power literally to Americanize. Since she had become a member of the Wyoming State Bar in 1898, she had credentials entitling her to act for the state, in special circumstances. When she taught a class of immigrants in 1917, the district court gave her the power to issue certificates of citizenship to students who passed her exams, without further examination in court. In the most literal sense, then, by unilaterally "naturalizing" resident aliens she became the agent of federal authority and legitimation over inhabitants of American territory within Wyoming. For those she made into citizens, Grace Raymond Hebard *was* the state.[40]

As Van Nuys has pointed out, Hebard's personal efforts on behalf of Americanization are laden with irony. Compared to other states, slow-growing, sparsely populated Wyoming had very few immigrants of any kind. Further, although Hebard railed against southern and eastern European immigrants, she met few of them, since not many such persons lived in Laramie, although the coal-mining regions of southwestern Wyoming did have significant numbers of immigrants from all parts of Europe, along with descendants of Chinese immigrants who had worked on the railroad. Most of the students in her own Americanization classes came from Britain, Germany, and Scandinavia. Perhaps even more ironically, this relentless campaigner for women's rights had, as early as her 1896 article, proposed educational and property qualifications for immigrant voters.[41]

What looks from one point of view like irony, from another looks like a puzzle. We might, for example, find it ironic, as Hebard's Wyoming contemporaries did, that she campaigned to outlaw child labor in Wyoming, a state that had virtually no industry and essentially no child labor aside from children's work on family ranches and farms. In that instance, Hebard maintained that "the policy of locking the door before the horse was stolen was always the best," a stance that suggested that she believed (or hoped) that it was only a matter of time before Wyoming developed a modern industrial economy.[42]

In Grace Hebard's time, Wyoming was in no danger of either industrializing or being swamped in a flood tide of immigration. Hebard's Americanization work, like her position on child labor, reflected the dream of a future in which Wyoming would be transformed from a mountain backwater into a modern American place. In Hebard's day, the pursuit of Americanization in Wyoming was far less about making citizens out of European immigrants and much more about making patriotism, civic participation, and American history seem second nature to the state's native-born people, Indian and white.

Hebard used her own mobility, her credentials as a scholar, her positions at the university, and her personal genealogy to carry forward this dream. She believed that if Wyomingites failed to participate in the most forward-looking crusades of their day, they risked being left behind, consigned to the margins of American politics and culture, ill-prepared for modern life. Year after year, Grace Hebard pursued a vision that connected a Wild West Wyoming past to a modern American future. She took to the road, touring the state and giving dozens of speeches on behalf of women's rights, Americanization, and historic preservation, and during World War I, Liberty Loans, food conservation, and patriotism. These activities were of a piece with her efforts to Americanize Wyoming's immigrants, directed as much at Americanizing Wyoming as at assimilating the immigrants themselves.

Those who seek irony in Hebard's career need look no further than the fact that Grace Raymond Hebard invested more of her time in the woman suffrage movement than in any other political cause with which she chose to affiliate herself.[43] Wyoming was, of course, the place where women had voted longest of anywhere in the United States: why expend energy fighting a battle long over? Without doubt, Hebard was devoted to the cause of women's rights, in the abstract. But her activism in the National American Woman Suffrage Association, her contributions to NAWSA's magazine, the *Woman Citizen,* and to the multivolume *History of Woman Suffrage,* her many speeches in and out of the state, indeed all of her efforts to promote the Nineteenth Amendment were directed at a combination of political and geographical ends.

As Wyoming point-woman for NAWSA president Carrie Chapman Catt's "Winning Plan," Hebard was responsible both for organizing her state's ratification campaign and for representing Wyoming suffragists at the national level. She used the position to present Wyoming to the nation not simply as an up-to-date place where women enjoyed the franchise, but as the *most* progressive state of the union so far as women's rights were concerned, the birthplace of an advanced form of liberty that spread, first of all, through the West. Marketing woman suffrage as the fruit of frontier individualism, she always reminded her audiences that Wyoming had led the way in enfranchising women.[44] She collected suffrage literature, including broadsides featuring maps of women's voting rights, state by state, that graphically illustrated the political message she sought to spread.[45]

In a speech delivered in Cheyenne in 1917, at the unveiling of a bronze memorial tablet commemorating woman suffrage in Wyoming, Hebard made her political geography explicit. The enfranchisement of women in the territory in 1869 was, she said, nothing less than "the embryo of a great democracy . . . [that] spread to the lands east of us and to our South, North and West." But Wyoming's influence was not limited to its neighbors; indeed, Hebard claimed, "the waves of light and liberty are being extended over these our United States, radiating with the sun on its journey around the world" from Australia and New Zealand to Canada and Britain and Sweden and even Russia. Proclaiming Wyoming's crucial role in worldwide liberation, she anchored the global movement once again to local imperatives. "What does it symbolize?" she asked. "Nothing more or less than that woman has proved beyond a question of doubt that she is equal to the responsibility of nation-building."[46]

Grace Hebard gave dozens of speeches throughout the state on behalf of women's rights over the course of her career. She appeared before both houses of the Wyoming legislature, bearing roses and carnations, when that body ratified the suffrage amendment in January 1920. Her labors in the state brought her a national role in the 1920 ratification campaign when she served as a member of the "Suffrage Emergency Brigade," a group that went to Connecticut to try to persuade that state's governor to call a special session of the state legislature so that Connecticut might become the crucial thirty-sixth state to ratify. Invoking her own New England roots (she claimed descent from two Connecticut governors), Hebard nonetheless presented herself as the living embodiment of western women's freedom. She insisted that "as the women of Wyoming have enjoyed suffrage since 1869, we have been able to give it a more thorough test than any other state. Suffrage has been a success in Wyoming."[47] Never one to shrink from bending the truth in a good cause, Hebard told Connecticut audiences: "This is the first time I was ever called upon to make suffrage speeches, for we don't have to make them out in Wyoming." She professed astonishment that the East had so tenaciously resisted giving women the vote, telling a reporter from the *New York Tribune,* "I never before saw an anti-suffragist. You know, out in Wyoming we have had woman suffrage for fifty years, and there is no such thing as an anti-suffrage man in our state—much less a woman."[48]

No height of hyperbole was too grand for Hebard to scale in the service of demonstrating Wyoming's centrality in the Anglo-American political tradition. She declared baldly that the 1869 territorial bill giving women the vote "has attracted more interest and comment than any other one article of civil affairs unless it be that of the Constitution of the United States, or the ancient Magna Charta of King John in 1215." It was only logical, she insisted, that such a benchmark of freedom should have come from "that great stretch of land, frontier in every fiber, then as now called Wyoming," a land inevitably American—more American, indeed, than anywhere else.[49]

Progressive politics, especially the campaign for woman suffrage, certainly occupied much of Hebard's time, but so too did the historical research and writing that was, perhaps, her most potent tool of nation building and feminist landscape-making. By the time of her death in 1936 she had published five books (including, in 1904, *A History and Government of Wyoming*) and numerous articles on a subject she helped to define as the history of an American West. For Grace Raymond Hebard, as for imperial American historians from Parson Weems and Washington Irving forward, the region so topographically and climatologically challenging, so lately the domain of resistant Indians, so spottily inhabited, shallowly governed, and riskily traversed, had to be understood as belonging, incontestably, to the United States. This American West was a place the United States was bound to conquer. The region was not simply manifestly destined, but positively and inevitably natural.

In addition to the Wyoming history text, which went into eleven editions, Hebard published four books with the Arthur H. Clark Company, a well-known publisher of works of western history. Her *Pathbreakers from River to Ocean* (1911) and *The Bozeman Trail* (co-authored with E. A. Brininstool, 1922) celebrated the exploits of white trappers, soldiers, and settlers, though Hebard reminded readers not to forget "the original native whose tragedy underlies the white man's triumph."[50] In *Pathbreakers* particularly, Hebard hoped "to enable the future citizens, particularly those who live in the states carved out of this story-making territory, to familiarize themselves with the brave deeds of the earliest inhabitants in an unsettled and unorganized territory."[51] A manuscript on the Pony Express, unfinished at her death, took up her familiar theme of mobile subjects making the way for empire in the West. Among those subjects she included Native Americans who recognized the inevitability of American conquest and furthered the course of empire. Throughout her scholarly career, Hebard insisted on the importance not only of Indian history, but also of indigenous oral traditions as historical sources. Her most significant scholarly projects were biographies of two Shoshones, *Washakie* (1930), the chief who led his people into the reservation era, and *Sacajawea* (1933), the woman who went west with Lewis and Clark.

Grace Raymond Hebard gave empire a feminist twist. Personal experience told her women walked at the heart of the march westward; feminist politics instructed her that their stories must not just be told, but celebrated. As she wrote in an article about Narcissa Whitman and Eliza Spaulding titled "The First White Women in Wyoming" and published in the *Washington Historical Quarterly* in 1917, "Women and wagons were not only suggestive of our nation's development, but were a permanent factor in the earliest development of the civilization of the nation."[52]

As a historian, Hebard has been best known for her hagiographic renditions of the history of woman suffrage in Wyoming and of the life of Sacagawea. Her attempts to create epic feminist heroes in the persons of

Esther Morris, "mother of woman suffrage," and Sacagawea have come under intense and, certainly, justifiable criticism over the years.[53] But even though Hebard's historical accounts must be read with great caution (quite frankly, she tended to make things up), we need to understand that her writings were influential in her time. Her versions of the story of woman suffrage and of the life of Sacagawea continue to influence historical debates. It is worth asking what kind of cultural and political work she meant her history to perform. When Grace Hebard wrote and spoke and marked Wyoming places in the name of history, she did so in an effort to engrave on the page and in real space the name of the American nation, and the values she believed it represented, including the cause of liberty for women.

Hebard clearly believed that historians had civic and geographical as well as intellectual obligations. History, for her, was a spatial as well as intellectual project. Her map "The History and Romance of Wyoming," still sold at the University of Wyoming bookstore, eloquently bespeaks her rosy vision of the spread of empire into the state she presented as the embodiment of an Empire for Liberty. When her women colleagues in the Professors' Club met to celebrate her seventieth birthday, the witty Clara McIntyre presented her with a homemade map depicting Hebard's own journeys, titled "Westward the Course of Hebard," a fascinating spatial representation of a life. Here we find not a literal time-geographic diagram of Hebard's biography, but instead a collage of the things Hebard was proud of, read east to west: her *Mayflower* ancestors and Colonial Dames affiliation, her suffrage speech in Chicago, her family roots and school life in Iowa, her passage west to Wyoming by train. McIntyre celebrated Hebard's activities in Wyoming as varied, peripatetic, and influential, depicting them with a wonderful profusion of icons, covering and finally bursting the borders of the state.

McIntyre had done a nice job of mapping her friend's heart and mind. Grace Hebard insisted that a woman who wanted to leave her mark on her country had to be mobile. Time and again, Hebard wrote about the travels she had been obliged to undertake in an effort to learn historical truth. As chief publicist for the idea that Sacagawea had lived until 1884, she had to expect controversy. She sought to authenticate her account by both rooting her story in Indians' words and invoking all the places she had gone in an effort to get things right. In 1930 she wrote her friend June Downey to tell her about a trip to the Wind River Reservation to research the life of Sacagawea, cataloguing the kind of landscape details that say to the reader, "You can believe me. I was there. I talked to the people who count. I saw it with my own eyes":

> I have stayed on the reservation in the school where the Shoshone Indians were. I have gone into the interior of the reservation with the U.S. government interpreter. I have interviewed Indians along their irrigation ditches where they were watering their alfalfa. I have sat on rocks in front of their wooden houses; I have gone into the passes and the sides of mountains, visiting Indians and getting interviews from them. . . . I have not only researched along these lines, but I have done considerable work in regard to trying to get a translation of the canyon and rock writings of the Indians.[54]

But the spatial enterprise of history was not simply the biographer's craft. It was also the public's business. In 1915 Hebard took a long-planned automobile trip around the state, sponsored by the Daughters of the American Revolution and the Wyoming Oregon Trail Commission. Accompanied by her sister, Alice, she stayed at ranches and hotels and friends' houses, entertained by DAR members and former students, giving speeches, sightseeing, collecting stories, visiting libraries, and following and marking historic trails and sites. In a lengthy journal, she carefully recorded both the comforts and the rigors of the long trip, including flat tires and accidents and good and bad meals. As part of the effort to mark imperial routes and fortifications, she stopped to dedicate a monument at the former site of Fort Bonneville, a fur trade post, where she and others spent three hours chiseling an inscription on a two-ton granite boulder that had been hauled to the spot to identify the site.[55] She also visited the Wind River Reservation to see the tablet she had caused to be installed as a grave marker for Sacagawea. Hebard also went to South Pass City, a place she would soon depict as a holy shrine to women's rights advocates, to locate the supposed site of the cabin of the redoubtable Esther H. Morris.

On the 1915 trip, Hebard identified Esther Morris simply as "the first woman justice of the peace in the world." She was much disappointed to discover that "the original building where she administered justice has disappeared," a rock barn standing in its stead.[56] But by 1920 Hebard had determined to give Morris credit for more than her judicial appointment. That year, she returned to South Pass City to erect a permanent marker for the "The Mother of Woman Suffrage." Piling up a rock cairn, Hebard also had a stone tablet carved to memorialize the "SITE OF OFFICE AND HOME OF ESTHER MORRIS, FIRST WOMAN JUSTICE OF THE PEACE, AUTHOR OF FEMALE SUFFRAGE IN WYOMING."

Grace Hebard liked western heroes, and she meant to see that more of them were women. As she was engraving women's history on Wyoming, she was equally determined to make Wyoming's mark on women's history by personifying women's rights in the figure of Esther Morris. In 1920, the year the Nineteenth Amendment was ratified, Hebard published "How Woman Suffrage Came to Wyoming," a pamphlet that argued that woman suffrage had first been introduced into the Wyoming territorial legislature in 1869 because Esther Morris had invited candidates standing for South Pass City's legislative seat to attend a women's tea party before the election. At the tea party, the strong-minded and savvy Morris had, Hebard said, asked both candidates to agree to introduce a woman suffrage bill into the legislature if elected. Not wanting to appear ungallant before the ladies, said Hebard, both men agreed to do so.[57]

Morris's advocacy of the suffrage cause was well known in South Pass, and legislator Bright did know Morris, and did speak with her right after he returned from the legislature, according to the documentary record. But Hebard's evidence for the historic tea party was thin at best. She had, indeed, only the testimony of H. G. Nickerson, the losing Republican candidate who was also a friend of hers, as foundation for the story.[58] Nevertheless, at the time that Hebard was waging her campaign for Esther Morris's and Wyoming's crucial importance to American democracy, no one contested Hebard's version of the story. Morris was an ardent suffragist from an old (according to Hebard) New York family. Morris had moved to Illinois and followed the western suffrage campaigns of Susan B. Anthony, then migrated to Wyoming, there to raise sons who became civic leaders in the state. For those who imagined the West as the land of the free, including emancipated women, Esther Morris was precisely the sort of woman to embody the westward course of empire. And there was no evidence to prove that the tea party did not actually take place.

In strong-minded, tea-pouring Esther Morris, Hebard created a hero in her own image. The two women resembled each other in assertive temperament, feminist politics, and even (Hebard claimed) elegant genealogy. Hebard probably gave Morris too much credit for the passage of the suffrage bill, though I would argue that, at the very least, Morris embodied the presence of the suffrage movement in the territory at a time when political power in Wyoming was remarkably fluid. But if Hebard's Morris was too much the product of the historian's present rather than the subject's past, Hebard's Sacagawea was even more the creation of research guided by political instinct.

For Grace Hebard, history was a vehicle for crusades on behalf of both women and Indians. She wrote that she intended to "rescue Saca-jawea . . . from semi-oblivion . . . to right previous historical wrongs."[59] Hebard, indeed, would devote most of her scholarly life to writing a bi-ography of the Shoshone woman, whom she portrayed as valiant guide to white men and respected wise woman to the Shoshone people. Hebard's Sacagawea was a symbol of successful Americanization, stand-ing for the nobility of the uncorrupted Indian character and the innate dignity and heroism of women. Like Esther Morris, this Sacagawea was, for Hebard, a western pathbreaker, a major, if neglected, figure in the frontier epic. Much of the history of the American West has been writ-ten more in the spirit of forging cultural identity than in the interest of meticulously reconstructing the past. Like many western historians of her day, Hebard was a mythmaker. Her sagas were intended to immor-talize heroes who had been ignored. Hebard's protégé, Wyoming histo-rian Agnes Wright Spring, would say that "Dr. Hebard's historical work . . . [came] as the direct result of her interest in women." Hebard's friend June Downey put the matter more simply, calling the biography of Sacagawea "a task of love."[60]

At the same time, Hebard's rescue mission was inspired by another consideration: to assert Wyoming's significance to the march of western conquest, and to women's history, by claiming Sacagawea as Wyoming's own. Sacagawea hardly needed saving; she had long been a legendary figure in the history of western conquest. By the opening of the twenti-eth century, when Hebard first learned that people at the Wind River Reservation believed that Sacagawea had ended her life in Wyoming in 1884, the Shoshone woman had, in various ways, already been claimed as historical property by the states of North and South Dakota, which honored her memory at a grave at the site of old Fort Manuel on the Missouri River in South Dakota.

The more research Hebard did, the more persuaded she became that Sacagawea had lived to an old age and died in Wyoming. So determined was Hebard to mark that fact in space that her campaign to make Saca-gawea Wyoming's own led to the Bureau of Indian Affairs inquiry con-ducted by Charles Eastman in 1925 (see chapter 1). In 1926, armed with the Eastman report, Grace Hebard pressured U.S. senator John Kendrick to introduce a resolution into Congress to sponsor a memorial for Saca-gawea at Fort Washakie on the Wind River Reservation. When Kendrick introduced the measure, a firestorm of controversy erupted.[61] South Dakota historian Doane Robinson enlisted his own senators to fight the

Wyoming memorial and began to round up scholarly allies, including North Dakota historian Lewis Crawford and the Missouri Historical Society's fur trade expert Stella Drumm, who had found and edited the journal of trader John Luttig, the document that was most often used to establish Sacagawea's death in 1812.[62]

Hebard countered with her own organizing efforts, writing to historians from Oregon and Utah to Wisconsin to try to buttress her claims, hiring a research assistant to delve into collections in Oklahoma and Kansas, pursuing the matter for years on end, without conclusion. The conflict became heated and highly personal. And yet, though the most vitriolic attacks on her came from a historian in Montana, and despite the fact that her own dogged research had led to the discovery of not a few historical documents interesting in their own right, Hebard chose to view the conflict as a question of eastern nit-picking versus the intuitive judgment of westerners. When, in 1928, she received a cordial letter from the historian Louise Phelps Kellogg of the Wisconsin Historical Society, Hebard's reply was almost tearful in tone: "The controversy has been so intense and has become so personal by some of the historians," she wrote, "that I have heretofore approached all historians east of the Missouri River with a great deal of caution."[63]

But the criticism had left even the stubborn Hebard with doubts. "I cannot get it out of my mind that I am not wrong," she wrote to Kellogg, citing "so much circumstantial evidence and coincidences that corroborate the facts which I have been able to get. . . . I must in the main part be right. Yet with all of this, I may be wrong."[64] Relying extensively on Native people's oral testimony, Hebard was far ahead of her time in taking seriously the kind of evidence Stella Drumm dismissed as "traditions, or winter tales, of some old Indians."[65] Like other historians, however, she hoped that the archive would ultimately bear out her own version of the truth.

There is good reason to doubt Grace Hebard's account of Sacagawea's story, but no cause to doubt her impact upon her time and place. Hebard hoped to establish her own, and women's, and Wyoming's claim to an American heritage of progress and liberty, carried across a continent by people like her. On that 1915 trip across Wyoming, marking trails and monuments, she added her own name to the hundreds of signatures on Independence Rock, that milestone of migration on the Oregon Trail. Thinking of herself as a pioneer, she didn't imagine her signature as graffiti, as a crime of vandalism. For Hebard, writing western history was of a piece with making the West itself: she was a woman making history. Here was ritual, reminder, remaking of a nation, scrawled across a space hard as rock, distant from human settlement, big and high enough to afford a view for miles around. Both the movements of Americans, and the stories of their movements, claimed a wilderness for civilization. "There is great happiness," Hebard wrote, "in knowing that you have saved something of value from obscurity. Perhaps that is the chief reward of the pathbreaker, because, of course, he is a discoverer."[66]

The woman whose name Hebard rendered as Sacajawea didn't "need" saving, any more than Fort Bonneville, or any other site of empire in Wyoming, "needed" rediscovering. But then, Grace Raymond Hebard had a habit of presenting her intentional actions as necessities: creating a library system in a new territory, educating college students, Americanizing immigrants, fighting to enfranchise women, narrating the history of Wyoming and the West. Each activity, in the hands of an independent woman, served both nation and womanhood.

On that 1915 trail-marking trip in Wyoming, Hebard and her sister visited the Holm Lodge near Jackson, a popular tourist hotel. There, Hebard recalled, "The matron says the country is full of young women looking for the 'Virginian.'"[67] Grace Hebard was, of course, not one to search for a cowboy to take her away. Imagine the foolishness of thinking that the purpose of the western woman was to attach herself to a man of any kind, even a great western hero. With a Ph.D., a lot of energy, a sense of mission, and room to move, a woman, in her view, didn't need a man to have an empire.

CHAPTER 5

"SO MANY MILES TO A PERSON"

Fabiola Cabeza de Baca Makes New Mexico

In the rocks were deep grooves where the women ground the maize into meal.
Fabiola Cabeza de Baca

I always envied any woman who could ride a bronco. **Fabiola Cabeza de Baca**

OR NEARLY FIVE HUNDRED YEARS, an expanse of terrain that eventually became part of the American West has been identified as "Nuevo México," a place at once prior to, part of, and at odds with the American West. In the eyes of those who built New Spain, New Mexico was the remote edge of the northern frontier, so poor and backward and tenuously attached to the mother country that the signatures of empire would be inscribed in a distinctly local hand. When Americans came to conquer in the middle of the nineteenth century, the newcomers' ways of bounding their territory, holding and using their land, worshiping their gods, and speaking to one another challenged long-established knowledge.

In 1850 New Mexico achieved United States territorial status. Its new-drawn borders overlapped communal and other private land grants dating back to Spanish colonial times, Indian country from the pueblos of the Rio Grande to the high mesas of Navajo terrain, vast dry places where travel and settlement had been—and would remain—contentious ventures.[1] In 1912, when it was admitted as the forty-seventh state of the union, New Mexico became a fully incorporated part of the United States. From the vantage point of the twenty-first century, we look back at the history of this place and name heroic moments that seem to belong to the story of the West: the death of Billy the Kid, the coming of the Santa Fe Railroad, the morning at Alamagordo when scientists and soldiers made the sun rise twice. New Mexico has become an American place that marks its western past in a manner Grace Raymond Hebard would have well understood.

And yet, preceding the West, New Mexico long cultivated its own difference from the rest of the western United States, a difference sometimes romantically expressed, as an identity, as "the Land of Enchantment," a magical other-place, a fairyland never quite transformed into Marlboro country.[2] Less romantically, as the historian George I. Sánchez pointed out in 1940, the story of New Mexico has been a narrative of "the struggle for existence of those men, women, and children who have clung tenaciously to a precarious foothold" in hard country, a tale of "a people who have spanned the gap of centuries in an humble, yet relentless, day-by-day mode of survival."[3] In Susan Magoffin's day, these hardy survivors would have identified themselves as Spanish or Mexican, or as belonging to myriad categories reflecting racial mixtures and gradations—*mestisaje*. In the American period, many have come to refer to themselves as "Hispanic," a term of identity rooted in both place and time. Women have played a crucial role in preserving, reproducing, and projecting Mexican American, Hispanic, and Chicano identity over time.[4] Some of those women have insisted on playing a speaking part in the drama of binding time and space into history and place in the many moments and locales that compose New Mexico.[5]

Those who attempted to claim a public voice had an uphill battle. Historian Sarah Deutsch has shown how modernization and Americanization marginalized Hispanic women in the newly American Southwest. The railroad spurred industrialization, and men left the villages in search of wage jobs, families grew more and more dependent on the cash that men earned, and women and their children had more and more trouble hanging on to self-sufficient small farms and village households. "As Hispanic women moved away from the villages," Deutsch explains, "they, like the men, moved away from their center of power":

> without their property and their garden to give them a right to an independent place in the community as land owner and producer, their roles were increasingly limited to consumer and reproducer. . . . As non-migrants, women had been the principal creators as well as sustainers of community and neighborhood in the villages, a stable central force of village society. Outside the villages, they were, instead, mobile and marginal.[6]

But however heavy the odds, modernity did offer new opportunities to some New Mexico Hispanas. The generation that spawned Grace Raymond Hebard and her colleagues in the Professors' Club also brought forth a remarkable group of New Mexico women. Like Hebard's circle, they were relatively privileged, often unmarried. They claimed the right to education, to a public voice and presence, to the power to shape their time and place.[7] Such elite New Mexico women drew on the long history of settled communities, on continuing conflicts over land, labor, and social life, and on a determination to preserve a Spanish past and a distinctive place.[8]

Amid this group of gifted and ambitious women, the writer, home economist, antiquarian, and historian Fabiola Cabeza de Baca stands out as a practitioner of the arts of remembering, storing, moving, preparing, persuading, and extending, in her effort to construct and preserve the place she knew as New Mexico. Over the centuries, New Mexico had been repeatedly resurveyed and rebounded, multiply traversed and inhabited. In the course of Cabeza de Baca's ninety-seven years the place would become more and more geographically regularized, commodified, and accessible, more closely and quickly linked with distant places to the east, and more thoroughly embedded in the grand geography of the United States.[9]

In the face of this rapid and historic transformation, Fabiola Cabeza de Baca, like many others, embraced a powerful and problematic determination to preserve a "Spanish" past. Critics have derided Cabeza de Baca and those like her as sentimental snobs whose insistence on the purity of their Spanish blood romanticizes and distorts a history marked by invasion, expropriation, and oppression, on the one hand, and centuries of cultural and racial mixing and connection on the other.[10] To be sure, Cabeza de Baca's and others' insistence on a "pure" Spanish heritage did much to obscure and repress a far more pervasive mestizo past and present.[11]

But as the historian John Nieto-Phillips has explained, it is less important to determine whether Spanish American identity is "true" or "false" than "to examine how that identity evolved and was shaped in various contexts," and to understand the consequences of what Nieto-Phillips calls *hispanidad.*[12] Cabeza de Baca held fast to *hispanidad,* to its roots not only in the past but also in place. At the same time, she worked to venerate and preserve a more mixed and dynamic New Mexico heritage, the product of centuries of interaction between Hispanics, Indians, and Anglos. Acutely alive to the possibilities and constraints of gender, of ethnicity, of place, Cabeza de Baca reworked the world in which she moved, with an eye on both the past and the future.

To no small extent, new geographies shaped her purposes. New Mexico was a territory of the United States when she was born, and attained statehood in her lifetime. As Cabeza de Baca moved within the new geopolitical order, she devoted her life to ensuring that the state would never be imagined as just another western place, a site of capital and conquest like Washington or Wyoming or, for that matter, neighboring Arizona. She believed that as an educated, energetic, and well-placed woman she could employ culture, technology, and communication to shape the changes she regarded as inevitable. She intended to mark New Mexico's future with its history, and relentlessly portrayed the place she called home as the living product of a continuing but complex "Spanish," Hispanic, and Indian history, a multivalent "American" present, and a tomorrow yet to be determined.

Fascinated by the possibilities of both old and new techniques and technologies, Cabeza de Baca hoped that the future would make room for multiple cultural worlds, and that those worlds would be fertile and fruitful and respectful and shared, despite devastating past experience. Her vision for New Mexico embraced a "Good Life" rooted, as she said, "in the soil," crafted from and preserved in long-standing everyday experience among ordinary people, transported across space and transmitted through time by the repeated actions and faithfulness of those same people. Realistic about the modern inventions and American practices that were transforming the world around her, she insisted that the New Mexico "Good Life" of the future lay precisely in knowing how to make strong connections among scattered places, to tell stories, to make and share good food, to preserve family identities. In short, the Good Life endured in all the little things women did, every day.[13]

Over nearly a century of life on the go, Fabiola Cabeza de Baca combined an attachment to "traditional" ways with a recognition that human action and the passage of time compelled movement and change. In unpublished writings, in public speeches, and most notably in her popular memoir, *We Fed Them Cactus,* she portrayed New Mexico not only as a timeless pastoral utopia but also as a lively place with a history of its own, inhabited by men and women who claimed their territory by moving across and through it as well as hanging on in isolated settlements. New Mexico's sparse population meant that community could only be maintained through movement. "New Mexico has not reached a million in population—some of our counties are larger in area than many of our eastern states—we say so many miles to a person rather than persons to the mile. Everybody knows everybody else," she wrote in an undated speech titled "This Is New Mexico." This territory was neither empty nor static, eastern American impressions notwithstanding, though it was an immense place that required extraordinary mobility of at least some of its inhabitants in order to be understood as a place at all.[14]

Other well-connected Hispanas of her time embraced a similar social vision, and some of them, most notably Nina Otero-Warren, pursued careers in politics.[15] A lifelong Democrat, Cabeza de Baca never sought office, insisting that the most effective means to resist cultural domination did not lay in formal politics. "I have been told by outsiders that New Mexico has rotten politics but since we know everybody we are aware of their good and bad traits. . . . Politics is a great game in our state," she wrote.[16] Instead, believing in the efficacy of the ordinary rather than the grandiose, she trusted in the mobilization of small gestures of persistence.

Fabiola Cabeza de Baca was born to move, in 1894, on her grandfather's farm near Las Vegas, New Mexico. Her mother died when she was four years old, and by the time she was twelve she divided her life between her father's Spear Bar Ranch at La Liendre by the Llano Estacado (Staked Plains) of eastern New Mexico and a comfortable two-story stone house in the town of Las Vegas. Although she would later maintain that "my background is a mixture of the Spanish and American cultures," she also insisted that "I am of the People and of Spanish ancestry."[17] She was brought up by her father and her paternal grandmother in a family deeply imbued with a sense of Spanish identity, cemented through blood ties.[18]

As much as that Spanish identity depended on maintaining a documented connection to the earth—to the wide, dry, austere place they worked cattle and sheep—and to family—a vast and scattered social network established as much through visiting as genealogy—it also depended on moving around. Cabeza de Baca stitched one place to another as she traveled on horseback and in buggies and carriages, reading the landscape for signs of human presence, acquiring knowledge stored and communicated first in memory and in conversation, and later in the written, English-language pages of her memoir, *We Fed Them Cactus*.

As Cabeza de Baca told the story, the *finca* where she was born was not an ancient homestead, but a place her grandfather, a Las Vegas merchant, had purchased as a "gentleman's farm." Still, it was a working farm, where her family and their hired help raised animals and took care of fields and orchards. Farming the dry country meant building and rebuilding a dam on the Gallinas River, a structure made of rocks, trees, and willow branches, held together with mud. "Papa Tomasito spent a lifetime and a fortune building the dam," Fabiola recalled, and from early spring to the end of fall, some workers had to put time into shoring it up every day.[19]

As Fabiola described her first years of life on the farm, writing both from her own memories and family stories, she charted overlapping patterns of movement. Every day, her grandfather drove his buggy out to supervise work on the farm (and on the dam), and made frequent trips to Las Vegas in a large carriage drawn by two horses. Hired men had at one time lived on the place, but they became commuters, coming from the village across the river, after her grandfather built a modern house.

Women, too, made the rounds. On Sundays, the children rode with their grandmother, Doña Estefana Delgado, into the village to visit with the grandmother's *comadres* and to look after the sick and the indigent. On other Sundays, her grandmother took them to the hills to gather medicinal herbs. Cabeza de Baca learned early to respect the various uses of the traditional and the modern. Doña Estefana was well versed in folk medicine, but willing to employ scientific measures. When a smallpox epidemic broke out, Fabiola's grandmother tried to convince villagers that vaccination could prevent the disease. Doña Estefana managed to obtain vaccine from a cousin who was a doctor in El Paso, but she had to rely on her local claim to religious authority to bring the power of scientific medicine to the village. "Not until my grandparents had god children in the villages was grandmother able to control the epidemic," Fabiola wrote. Thereafter she vaccinated "her children, grandchildren, and others."[20]

The work of maintaining the ranch and its ties to the surrounding community wore on both of Fabiola's grandparents, but particularly on her grandmother, whose dowry, Fabiola took pains to report, had furnished the means for her husband to buy his gentleman's farm. Cabeza de Baca watched as her grandfather, "a real aristocrat," lost "more than one fortune. He had built his fortune with grandmother's dowry and inheritance but, according to tradition, once married, the husband managed the fortune." A constant stream of relatives and friends from all over eastern New Mexico and northwest Texas stopped by on their way to and from Las Vegas. The company was a "great drain" on her grandparents' resources, according to Cabeza de Baca: "If the families were not making the trips, their employees stopped by for the night. Their horses had to be fed also."[21] The family determined to move back to Las Vegas, and her grandmother welcomed the decision. "Grandmother had never been happy at the hacienda . . . she was a very tired person. . . . For grandfather it was a hard decision but grandmother did not give him time to change his mind. She started disposing of furniture and other possessions," leaving the ranching to Fabiola's father.[22]

They moved to town, but the Cabeza de Bacas maintained strong ties in the countryside. However much her grandmother had learned to see the ranch as a place of draining drudgery, Fabiola Cabeza de Baca loved her childhood trips back and forth over the miles between Las Vegas and the ranch, loved the very process of travel. In *We Fed Them Cac-*

tus, she would describe those journeys as "delightful," remembering peaceful nights under the stars and local ranchers who "welcomed us with open arms, for they seemed hungry for outside intercourse." Extending hospitality may have borne heavily on her own family, but keeping an open house for rural neighbors had earned them the privilege of reciprocity.[23]

During the summers on her father's *rancho,* Fabiola was on vacation. No one expected her to do farm work, and neither was she trained in the ways of women's work. She remembered instead the joy and freedom she felt out in the country. While she was still expected to "lead a ladylike life," she looked enviously at "uncouth neighbors" who permitted "women to do men's work." She confessed that "I always envied any woman who could ride a bronco. . . . How skillfully they saddled a horse! I often watched them catch a pony out in the pasture, just as the men did on our range, but it never was my privilege to have to do it. When I arose each morning, my horse was already saddled and tied to a hitching post waiting for me if I cared to ride." Cabeza de Baca nevertheless managed to stretch the boundaries of femininity. As a young girl riding out with her father and brother to mend fences on the ranch, she recalled being "delighted, for I would ride out and explore new country. Contrary to Spanish custom, Papa always allowed me to go wherever he or [her brother] Luis went."[24] Her fertile imagination led her to see seemingly uninhabited landscapes as places teeming with a human past:

> There was so much unwritten history of the Llano, and as I rode out in the pastures, ruins of houses and chapels made me wish they could speak so that they might tell of the life of the inhabitants who had dwelled within. But they were silent and I had to create in my mind imaginary characters living in these lonely ranchos. Yet they may not have been lonely; there may have been much gaiety and real living with nothing to disturb their tranquillity.[25]

From an early age, then, traveling had schooled her in the particular history of New Mexico, a place where remembering the past was a technique to resist the unsettling forces of Americanization. She was a close observer of the landscape she traversed, looking for signs of history in the rocks themselves:

> The country not only held in secret the lives of the Spanish colonists, but of the Indians who thousands of years before had inhabited the land. There were the petroglyphs depicting human figures, animals, and other signs. What did they mean? In my mind, I would decipher the figures. . . . I lived

in the past as I roamed the range and studied the petroglyphs. These may have been relatively recent, for in the rocks were deep grooves where the women ground the maize into meal.[26]

Even as a child, Cabeza de Baca believed that history included ordinary women. Having watched how work wore down her own grandmother, she understood that grooves in the rocks were inscriptions of women's repetitive, arduous, trivial, and eminently consumable knowledge of place, as well as indelible marks on that place.[27] Here was an intimate, boring, altogether forgettable kind of laboring movement that etched presence and perseverance deep in something hard. Cabeza de Baca would remember, and she would write about it.

If a horse had been the vehicle that had brought her to those places and thoughts, the written word would become, for Fabiola Cabeza de Baca, an indispensable technology. Town life also offered certain benefits. By the time Cabeza de Baca was riding the range, she was well along in her education. Her grandmother had argued for the move to Las Vegas on the grounds that "it was time for [the children] to go to school," and Fabiola was an apt pupil. But writing things down was also a family tradition. Her recollections of life on the Llano Estacado came not only from her own and others' memories, but also from her brother Luis's scrapbook of stories told to them by an old servant and "a notebook kept by my father as far back as 1885." Fascinated with New Mexico's history and her own genealogy, she would come to treasure, preserve, and translate colonial Spanish documents, including the 1535 journals of her ancestor, Alvar Nuñez Cabeza de Baca, chronicles she credited with beginning the written history of New Mexico.[28] To publish in English her early recognition of women's laborious inscriptions on the land was to seize the power of both movement and storage, to make a lasting record in a powerful medium, and to carry forward a family practice that stretched back, in New Mexico, before permanent Spanish colonization.[29]

As New Mexico moved toward statehood, Fabiola Cabeza de Baca claimed New Mexico as a place of her own, by moving to and getting to know a number of places in that land. But her trips away from the territory (and later the state) also shaped her sense of place. Her first foray took her to Spain in 1906, at the age of twelve, to study language, art, and history. Spain would become a compass point in her mental geography, and she was to return to that country again and again.[30]

Armed with curiosity, the experience of travel, and historical knowledge, Cabeza de Baca set out to make an impact on her world as hundreds of thousands of American women have, from the early nineteenth century to the present day: as a schoolteacher. Western national expansion provided the catalyst for women's move into elementary and secondary education. In the years surrounding the Civil War, women took over the teaching profession, once the province of men, partly because they were determined and imaginative in their efforts to find new venues for their talents, and partly because the nation demanded a mobile, skilled, and cheap labor force to staff schoolhouses spreading across the continent like small, square engines of national incorporation. In this way, each remote outpost of empire became also a place where some woman asserted authority.[31]

After graduating from high school, Cabeza de Baca went to teach in a rural school six miles from her family's ranch. At that time, the roads were so bad that "only the Model T. Ford could make the high centers which were still prevalent." So, like Western teachers before and after, she had to find a place to board.[32] In some regards, her stories about rural school-keeping resembled those of teachers across the West in the early twentieth century. Children were workers as well as learners, carting wood and hauling water and cleaning the schoolhouse. The hazards of the job included brushes with rattlesnakes and blizzards that stranded the children at school all night. The rewards included seeing the children learn, making the school into a community center, winning the support and hospitality of the local people.[33]

In other ways, the particularities of New Mexico and Cabeza de Baca's own agendas shaped her rural teaching. In the United States, public schools have been expected to serve as forces for assimilating immigrants, erasing social inequalities, and forging a common civic culture. Whatever their intentions, teachers have often acted to repress "foreign" ways, most notably by forbidding students to speak the languages they spoke at home. But Cabeza de Baca saw her job differently, and sought to tailor her efforts to local conditions. "It was a mixed school," she recalled. "There were the children of the homesteaders, the children of parents of Spanish extraction and children with Indian blood but of the Spanish tongue."[34]

To teach this diverse group, Cabeza de Baca developed bilingual textbooks so that the English-speaking and Spanish-speaking students would learn one another's languages. She regarded bilingualism, properly pronounced and carefully written, as a powerful means both of preserving New Mexican distinctiveness and of maintaining a "good life" in a worthy world. Her students sang folk songs in Spanish, cowboy ballads and hillbilly songs, "The Star Spangled Banner."[35] They were Americans, but in their own words, on their own terms.

Cabeza de Baca seized on the common frontier histories of Spanish and English America to make connections. Those histories, she believed, had shaped the families whose children she taught, people from "different national groups," but all "simple, wholesome people living from the soil. They certainly were a hardy lot, for otherwise they could not have survived the cruelty of the wind, the droughts and the poverty which surrounded most of them."[36] Abraham Lincoln became, for her, an icon of an equality born of frontier hardship, and a picture of Lincoln hung in her schoolroom.[37] Much later, looking back at the history of New Mexico, she would use Lincoln as a touchstone of common virtue in a world of ethnic prejudice. Describing the state's adobe architecture, she remarked that "Americans coming during [the] Spanish or Mexican eras were critical of the mud houses." But, she reminded her audience pragmatically, "It was a frontier country, with less advantages than the eastern shores of the United States, which were close to sea travel." The resourceful Spanish colonists had, she pointed out, "made use of native materials for building as well as for subsisting." And with no little irony, she added that "some of our great Americans were born in log cabins, crudely built. Many of these have been preserved in tribute to the pioneers who helped to build our nation."[38]

As a rural schoolteacher, Cabeza de Baca insisted that the farm kids who walked miles to school each day must know not only their histories but also their geographies—the U.S. states and territories and capitals; industries and products of all the states; rivers, lakes, oceans, and mountain ranges. Countries and capitals of Europe and Asia. Landscapes reaching back to the Bible—the Dead, the Red, the Mediterranean Seas. But Cabeza de Baca was determined to locate that remote schoolhouse not only in American and Western cultural traditions, but also in a distinctive regionalization invoking the historical connection to Spain. "I am sure," she wrote, "that those sixth graders knew more about Mexico, Central and South America than the average high school graduate knows today."[39]

The rural schoolroom provided a base for Cabeza de Baca's aspirations, but not wide enough scope. Continuing to teach, she returned to Las Vegas to earn a degree in pedagogy from New Mexico Normal (later New Mexico Highlands University) in 1921. Few American women of the time, of any ethnic group, graduated from college. And as we have seen, women with college degrees were rare throughout the West.[40]

Cabeza de Baca admitted that her father had at first opposed her plan to teach only six miles from the ranch, saying that he "was not so sure that it was the proper thing for me to do."[41] Thus it is all the more remarkable that Cabeza de Baca traveled on, to get a professional degree in home economics from New Mexico State in Las Cruces, nearly 350 miles away, and then to take up a thirty-year career as an itinerant home extension agent working a vast seven-county region of northern New Mexico for the United States Agricultural Extension Service.

Clearly Fabiola Cabeza de Baca, a devout Catholic, a dutiful family woman, a devotee of tradition, was in some ways fiercely independent, perhaps even defiant. Sometime later in life, she would write that in Spanish New Mexican circles marriage was as much a matter of filial piety as of personal preference. "Although by the time I was of marriageable age, the custom of arranging marriages was no longer observed," she explained, "no one of my generation would think of marrying anyone objectionable to our parents." In fact, however, Cabeza de Baca did precisely that. In 1929, already an ostensible spinster of thirty-five, she eloped to Mexico with an insurance broker named Carlos Gilbert, a man her family never accepted. The marriage, which may have lasted a decade, remains a murky part of her life, shrouded by family reticence and her own later silence. According to Cynthia Orozco, historian of the League of United Latin American Citizens, Carlos Gilbert was a LULAC activist whose politics, emphasizing Mexican American identity, may have been anathema to a family that took such pride in its distinguished Spanish heritage.[42]

Whatever her own domestic trials (or, for that matter, pleasures), Cabeza de Baca continued to work on the road throughout and beyond her marriage. Her professional life, spent chiefly in other people's households, was remarkably productive. As a federal home extension agent, Cabeza de Baca used her exceptional education, fluency, expertise, and geographical and occupational mobility to honor, ease, preserve, and celebrate New Mexicans' long heritage of making a life that was "good, but not always easy."[43] When she first joined the New Mexico Agricultural Extension Service in 1929, she took a two-month orientation course traveling with veteran agents in San Miguel County. The experience "gave me a concept of the vastness of the territory to be covered in the work, and how little could be accomplished, even in ten years."[44]

Working for the Extension Service meant seeing the New Mexico landscape in a new way. Accustomed to thinking in terms of journeys from one place to another, she now learned to speak of the immense ground she had to cover in reference to how much she could accomplish in a given time span. She also learned to navigate according to American political boundaries. Given the choice of working in Socorro and Valencia Counties or in Santa Fe, Rio Arriba, and part of Taos County, she chose the latter, "since I knew northern New Mexico better." Over many years in the Extension Service, as her work encompassed more and more territory, she would develop the habit of locating places in New Mexico as much according to county boundaries as to other markers.[45]

In Cabeza de Baca's view, the job of an extension agent was to bring to distant villages and rural households the benefits of new ideas and goods, while respecting the value of old ways of doing things. She was far more sensitive to local traditions and more realistic about rural people's choices than most extension agents in New Mexico had previously been.[46] Armed with the latest in kitchen equipment (the canning kettle, the pressure cooker), government bulletins, and her college training in home economics, Cabeza de Baca set out for thirty years of life on the road.

Before she could embark, she had a lot to learn. Country schoolteaching had given her some pedagogical skills, but she had lived most of her life in other people's houses. When it came to knowing how to manage a New Mexican household, she was woefully ignorant. Looking back, in a speech to students graduating in home economics from New Mexico Highlands University, she described her initiation into the field ("domestic science then") in almost laughable terms: "What did we learn—fancy hand sewing. I remember making a tea apron of fine cambric trimmed in lace. . . . We also learned to make candies and cookies." At Highlands, however, the training had been rigorous and comprehensive, encompassing "foods, clothing, home management, art appreciation, house planning, home nursing, child care, interior decoration, chemistry of food and nutrition, textiles, and perhaps some others."[47]

Fabiola Cabeza de Baca had accrued a sizable measure of booklearning and laboratory instruction in the arts and sciences of domesticity, an occupation supposed to come naturally to women. But she was completely without experience in the daily press of women's work. "My qualifications as a home demonstration agent were anything but adequate," she recollected. "My father had always had a home garden, yet I had never as much as gathered a vegetable. I learned ranch cooking from the men, but horse back riding was more interesting." At one time in her youth, the ranch hands had left her to do the breakfast dishes, and she had decided instead to go for a ride. When she returned, someone had set the dirty plates and flatware and cooking utensils in a line, lead-

ing through the yard out to the well. "The poor dishes were thirsty and
started out for relief," her brother told her.[48]

In time, Cabeza de Baca mastered the arts and sciences of cooking and
housekeeping. Still, before she could even head off to the places where
she would do her teaching, she had yet another skill to learn. "It may
seem strange," she recalled, "but I never had been interested in learning
how to drive an automobile. In my new job, I had to own and drive a
car." Her father bought her an auto and taught her to drive, but the rough
terrain and wretched roads of New Mexico made driving the home extension circuit a real ordeal.

> The roads which I had to travel were country wagon trails. There were
> arroyos to cross, no bridges. When it rained, often I had to wait hours for
> the water to subside in order to cross them. Many times I had to walk miles
> to get help when my car had stuck in the mud or slipped on ice into a rut.
> Cars could not travel over thirty-five miles an hour, which meant start-
> ing at sun up to make the communities in which work had been planned.[49]

The hours alone could be brutal: "A home demonstration agent started
her day no later than six o'clock in the morning and returning home as
late as midnight at times."[50]

Under such circumstances, most people would probably have preferred
to stay at home, but Cabeza de Baca kept moving, even in the face of ca-
tastrophe. In 1932 her car was struck by a train, and as a result of injuries from the accident she had to have a leg amputated. It took her nearly
two years to recover, but her programs had been so successful that her
rural clients continued them even during her long convalescence. From
1934 until 1959 she was back on the road, bringing groups of women,
men, and children together in their neighbors' homes to learn canning,
work on sewing projects, explore new gardening and poultry-raising
techniques, learn home repair. After eighteen years working chiefly in
Santa Fe County, she had been so effective that she was assigned as agent
at large in counties that had no staff of their own. Now she ranged over
an immense area encompassing much of northern New Mexico. "I have
not been interested in statistics, I did not keep count of the homes which
I visited," she wrote. "There were thousands."[51]

Cabeza de Baca held that extension work was an exchange in which
she learned as well as taught. She helped hard-pressed families get access to canning equipment and sewing machines, and made information
available to families not comfortable with English by speaking Spanish
(and later Tewa and Towa), translating government bulletins from En-

glish into Spanish, writing her own bilingual materials.[52] Cabeza de Baca
in turn heard stories she would treasure, collected folklore about herbal
medicine, planting practices, and religious rituals, and learned much of
what she would later recount about New Mexican cooking from the
women of the villages she served. She kept voluminous notes about remedies, rituals, and recipes, taking palpable pleasure in cataloguing local
knowledge, techniques, and skills, observing the mingling of faith and
science. In a speech given on San Isidro's Day, March 12, she told her
audience to "plant peas on St. Patrick's Day, March 17th, to be assured
of a good crop. . . . Chile seed if planted outdoors is put in on May 3rd,
Feast of the Holy Cross, and if you wish to have pumpkins ripen, plant
them on this day." Some of this knowledge appeared the product of long
practical experience; other suggestions, however, seemed less subject to
scientific testing: "When onion sets start to come up, cut the tops during the full moon so that they will make a good growth." Cabeza de Baca
did not credit all village homilies equally, but she learned not to patron-
ize. "We all, more or less, follow folklore patterns, enjoy folk tales and
perhaps, unconsciously live folklore," she concluded.[53]

In turn, she hated it when those she deemed outsiders and "misinformed New Mexicans" treated New Mexico as a backward, mean, and
miserable place. She was infuriated, in the 1960s, when the *New York
Times* and other newspapers ran stories identifying northern New Mexico as a place where poverty, hunger, and ignorance ruled. "There is
poverty in these counties," she wrote in an uncharacteristically angry essay titled "Hunger," "but no hunger." The families that lived in the villages, she pointed out, owned their own homes and the surrounding lands.
Because reporters and politicians who had visited the villages "did not
go inside the homes," they didn't, in Cabeza de Baca's view, really know
what they were talking about. She had spent a lifetime, including the years
of the depression, "working in the homes in the kitchens." When she
had started out in 1929, her clients had long produced fruit, vegetables,
and meats and preserved food by drying. New Mexico farmers grew nutritious beans and chiles, and New Mexicans went to the hillsides, early
in the spring, when crops and gardens were not yet producing, to gather
edible plants like "lambsquarters, pigweed, waco, chimaja and . . .
purslanes" that, under laboratory experimentation, had been proven to
be rich in vitamin C.

Cabeza de Baca was no stranger to the hardships of trying to live off
the land in New Mexico; after all, her father had lost his ranch in the
drought of 1918, a hideous experience poignantly detailed in *We Fed*

Them Cactus. She admitted in "Hunger" that New Mexico villagers had lost some of the capacity to provide for themselves, citing U.S. Forest Service takeovers of grazing land and the division and subdivision of farms through inheritance. Yet she insisted that for those whose crops failed, extended families provided a safety net. And with the help of government agencies like the one she represented, the indigent, she said, could rely on school lunch programs, food stamps, and welfare checks to get what they could not produce themselves. Poverty, she believed, was a fact of life, but hunger was, for her, a moral problem. "If there is hunger anywhere in our country," she concluded, "it is due to parents spending their money on liquor, gambling, or other misuse of money."[54]

Cabeza de Baca was assuredly an agent of the state and of modernization, but clearly she also considered herself part of a deeply rooted social order based on principles of mutual aid. The materiality of movement, of shared experience, of work done, was itself a way to bind together a New Mexican time and space. "Extension means just that," she explained: "To extend the work by way of passing it to friends, neighbors and relatives."[55] Her personal extension project entailed traveling to thousands of remote households, watching and cooking and making suggestions, sharing "scientific" nutritional knowledge with women she considered the "real" experts, writing down the recipes, preparing endless bilingual and translated newsletters, pamphlets, and bulletins, composing in Spanish a weekly homemakers' column for Santa Fe's *El Nuevo Mexicano,* doing weekly radio broadcasts, and finally, publishing cookbooks and an extended memoir.[56] All these endeavors extended across the potentially endless space and time of publication a distinctive place, as much the product of her imagination and intent as of history.

But Cabeza de Baca always believed that history and culture were built up in daily increments. When she wrote about home extension in a fictional memoir and recipe book titled *The Good Life,* she called on future readers to use the recipes and "think of my people and the occasions in the lives of those people who added '*un poquito de . . . y un poquito de . . .*' to produce savorous and nutritious New Mexico foods."[57] Life was like that, the product of a little of this and a little of that.

After her retirement from the Extension Service, Cabeza de Baca continued to offer her services as a trainer and consultant to the United Nations and the Peace Corps.[58] In the meantime, she devoted herself to La Sociedad Folklórica of Santa Fe, an organization of some forty Hispanic women involved in preserving Spanish culture, traditions, and folklore. Their archives included "a large collection of old songs, *cuentos,* fairy

tales, adages, sayings, *versos,* food recipes handed down through generations, material on customs, training, superstitions, folk remedies and
many other lore."[59]

The Sociedad also had its own rituals, conducting meetings in Spanish and hosting events including an annual *velorio,* a gathering "in a home
to pay homage to a Saint . . . an offer of thanksgiving for favors received
or to ask for favors." On July 25, the members of the Sociedad gathered
to pay homage to their patron saint, St. Anne, on the eve of her feast.
One member offered her home and three others also acted as "hostesses."
Generally the event was held outdoors ("Most of the homes have lovely
patios"), and each member was permitted to bring her husband or, for
"those unattached," a guest. All members were expected to bring "a covered dish which must be a traditional food," but Cabeza de Baca also
noted that "today at *velorios,* coca cola, cakes, and store cookies are commonly served." The hostesses provided the meat, either barbecued lamb
or kid, but kids, Cabeza de Baca pointed out, were becoming rarer and
more expensive. And there were other signs of change. "The meal is
served early," she wryly explained, "since modern men are not as fond
of praying as our ancestors were." Evidently, after the meal, the women
gathered in the house for prayers and hymns; what the men did, she did
not say.[60]

For Fabiola Cabeza de Baca, folklore was alive, and it was collective.
What began as "traditional expressions of unsophisticated groups of
people . . . oral or informal in transmission, that are of unknown or forgotten origin, that are personal property of no one," were, nonetheless,
"subject to modification while being communicated." In New Mexico,
Indian, Spanish, and Anglo traditions overlapped even as they remained
identifiably distinct. The state (and Cabeza de Baca herself) trumpeted
its purported "tricultural heritage," but new circumstances and people
were creating new lore all the time. "The Beatles have created a modern
folklore," Cabeza de Baca pointed out, and "as the Space Age grows,
our folklore will experience a new era of heroes, customs, traditions, and
a new way of life."[61]

Devoted as she was to preserving and passing on tradition, Fabiola
Cabeza de Baca took evident delight in seeing the ways in which modern New Mexicans used new means to preserve old practices. There were
the Coca Cola and "covered dishes" at the *velorio* for St. Anne. And at
Indian feasts like the annual Mattachines dance at San Ildefonso on January 23, celebrants from surrounding pueblos did not travel in wagons,
but "lately most arrive in cars or pickups."[62]

But nowhere was the mingling of preservation and transformation more evident than in Cabeza de Baca's genealogical work. Just as Grace Raymond Hebard and organizations like the Daughters of the American Revolution mobilized genealogy on behalf not only of their own prestige but of nationalist geography as well, Fabiola Cabeza de Baca and her colleagues in the Sociedad Folklórica rooted current claims in both family and cultural pasts. Partly in connection with her work for the Sociedad, Cabeza de Baca researched New Mexico's Spanish colonial history and pursued the study of her genealogy. As she explained, "The members [of the Sociedad] must be of Hispanic descent, either from the father or the mother or both." Cabeza de Baca, at least, would use genealogy to make the category of "Hispanic descent" as expansive as possible. As she endeavored to track and preserve the descendants of early Spanish settlers in New Mexico, she produced copious and at times immense genealogical charts, along with writing narrative histories of a proliferating network of people who traced their intertwined lineages to Delgados, Romeros, Bacas, Cabeza de Bacas, Salazars, Gonzaleses, Armijos, and others. Along the way, she copied and translated numerous documents, particularly wills and testaments. She was determined to prove that New Mexico had in colonial times been not an impoverished backwater but a civilized country in which an elite class did control and manage wealth. And she was particularly interested in Spanish colonial women's legal and property rights (especially dower rights), their economic agency, and their determination to provide for their children, daughters included.[63]

Just as assuredly, Cabeza de Baca hoped to use genealogical research to revivify connections among New Mexicans scattered by the forces of modernity. She carried on extensive correspondence with far-flung relatives who shared her interest in tracing family lineage. The letters exchanged revealed as much about contemporary life as about past descent. When a relative named Frank McCullock (or McCulloch) wrote from Albuquerque to ask her to clear up a point of genealogy, he also mentioned that he'd attended a dinner for "Bernard and Dolores," a couple who were moving to Denver. "Bernard's job," he wrote, "is with Dow Chemical which is located at Rockey Flats," which McCullock located very precisely for the geographically minded Cabeza de Baca: "12 miles west of Denver, 12 miles south of Boulder and 12 miles north of Golden." The couple hoped that the job with Dow Chemical might offer travel opportunities—"Bernard and Dolores have sort of a secret yen to go to some Latin American country and maybe through Dow Chemical, they can do it." McCullock thought they would prosper in any new setting. Bernard, he said, was "a good worker and Doloris [sic] is one of the most wonderful wives, housekeepers, I've ever known." As proof of the couple's versatility, McCullock offered the kind of evidence he knew Cabeza de Baca would value, explaining that Dolores had taken "a course in continental cookery at the University and as a result of this, their meals may include any sort of an exotic surprise." These New Mexicans, he said, were "also very gay and sociable, so we do not worry about their being lonely in new and strange surroundings."[64]

Such reassurances were not idle. The centrifugal pressures of postindustrial life could indeed make a person lonely. Among those most keenly interested in the Baca family heritage was John Landon, a supervisor of employee trainers at the Lockheed Aircraft plant in Lancaster, California, and a man who clearly felt close enough to Fabiola Cabeza de Baca to share his heartaches as well as his genealogical avocation. On May 6, 1972, Landon wrote to Cabeza de Baca describing a genealogical chart he had constructed, identifying "*all* the Bacas . . . plus the genealogies you have given me, plus Chavez's, Montoyas"; the chart, he said, measured eight feet by seven feet and covered most of his bedroom wall. Landon confessed in that letter that he and another relative were suffering from depression and asked Cabeza de Baca, "Isn't there one of those weeds New Mexicans are so fond of brewing into 'tea' that you can prescribe for us?" Absent an herbal cure, he wished there were at least "some way you could enclose some sopaipillas in your letter (I may just take your cookbook off the shelf and tell Lidia [la esposa] to get busy)."[65] Although Landon had pronounced himself "partially cured" that May, he confessed the next February 14 that he'd been through another bad bout of depression, which he called "the Senator Tom Eagleston [sic] syndrome." But he gamely assured Cabeza de Baca, "I'll just have to capitalize on my *up* periods," and invoked a common hero to try to convince her that he was all right: "Abraham Lincoln functioned very effectively despite black periods of melancholia. I'll get by too."[66]

Fabiola Cabeza de Baca carefully nurtured family attachments across the reaches of the West, and treated those connections as a renewal of a grand New Mexico geography that had been temporarily reduced and suppressed. "New Mexico has been a land of transition," she explained with seeming diffidence, but went on to make bold claims. "At one time," she asserted, "it embraced the states of Arizona, California, Utah, Nevada, Texas and part of Colorado."[67] That statement was, at a minimum, historically questionable, but it invoked an imagined territory stretching across the centuries, culturally powerful enough to contest seemingly settled questions of ethnic identity and dominance. Modern-day New Mexico might be a shrunken remnant of its former mighty self, but it remained for Cabeza de Baca the territory of "three distinctive ethnic groups . . . the Indians, who were here from pre-historic times; those who are descended from the first Spanish colonizers and who I shall call Hispanos; and those erroneously called Anglos, who I shall call Other Americans."[68] She was, assuredly, reinforcing the myth of triculturalism in a historically mestizo terrain. But she was also insisting on a multicultural presence in a West too often bleached white.

In holding out hope for small actions, for ingredients and tools and techniques, for cars and chiles and the names of places and words on a page, Cabeza de Baca's romantic belief in a "good life," sustained through deliberate motion, offered at least the consolation of hope. Doubtless she indulged in nostalgia and sentimentalism. But sentiment and emancipatory politics are not necessarily contradictory, especially when the liberty to move is a badge of power. Fabiola Cabeza de Baca traced her roots to a sixteenth-century Spanish explorer and exchanged genealogical research with extended family members across a vast region. She traveled in Spain and in Mexico, saw the atomic age come to the country she had criss-crossed on horseback, watched "people from as far north as Tierra Amarilla, Abiquiu, Penasco, Truchas, Cordoba, Trampas, Chimayo, Espanola, the Pojoaque and Nambe Valleys and others commute to their jobs at Los Alamos in all kinds of weather."[69] She had anticipated other New Mexicans' modern movements, a phenomenon she weighed carefully, and hopefully. She put her trust in the ordinary people whose lives had changed but whose daily actions, thoughts, and work would cherish and perpetuate a familiar, different place, as long as the smell of roasting chiles called New Mexicans home:

> Farm families in most communities can now afford electricity and modern plumbing in their homes. . . . Boys through the G I Bill have gone to college, many already have master [*sic*] degrees and some P H D's. More girls are going to college every year and it is gratifying that education is available to all who desire it.
>
> [Yet] the call of the land still persists in the Hispano's life. Let there be a fiesta in their villages and they manage to get there, P H D's and all.
>
> It had to come about that these boys and girls had to leave their farms. There was not enough land for them to make a living, but, curiously enough, some of them are saving money or already have saved enough to buy a piece of land near their old homestead or if available, their old home place.

The old traditions, folk ways perhaps may be on the way out, but the New Mexican food habits will persist as long as chile, beans, corn and favorite foods can be grown or obtained in the markets.[70]

Fabiola Cabeza de Baca proved, on this occasion as before, an astute observer of social transformation in New Mexico, and in the American West. Between her birth in 1894 and her death in 1991, the expanding market had remade the western landscape. From World War II to the end of the twentieth century, global capital, ever more liquid, wielded the capacity to disrupt, disperse, display, and distribute the trappings of settled place, to penetrate and fragment regional geography, to remake places over and over, to move people and things where the money went.[71] By the turn of the millennium, homesick New Mexicans in New York or, for that matter, New South Wales could order chiles over the internet one day and be fixing up *enchiladas verdes* the next, thousands of miles from the fields but only a matter of hours by air. In a world of flux, of perpetual creation and destruction of spaces, the power to name and claim a place, and perhaps a "good life," belonged to people who asserted the will, the capacity, and the right to mobilize.

PART THREE: BEYOND THE WEST

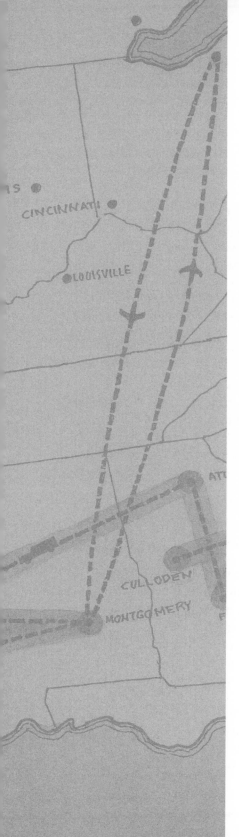

CHAPTER 6

RESISTING ARREST

Jo Ann Robinson and the Power to Move

Either fortuitously or with a purpose, Montgomery, the first Capital of the Confederacy, has been a guinea pig for the great sociological experiment. **Alabama Journal**

African American western history . . . intrudes itself onto our sensibilities and forces a reexamination of the imagined West. **Quintard Taylor, *In Search of the Racial Frontier***

The city was their home, the place of their hopes and dreams, their future. **Jo Ann Gibson Robinson, *The Montgomery Bus Boycott and the Women Who Started It***

MARKETS AND NATIONS ARE CREATURES of motion. They require the circulation of people and money, goods and ideas. In the years between World War II and the 1970s, Americans in widely dispersed places lived more and more within the web of the nation and did their business more and more often with entities that operated on a national scale. Mass media, nationwide advertising and distribution of consumer goods, and, soon, multinational corporations reshaped Americans' daily lives even as the federal government linked distant places with federally sponsored highways and military installations, entitlement programs and regulations, incitements to patriotism, and dire warnings about the nation's enemies.

New political and economic connections penetrated and disrupted settled patterns of locale and of region, offering unprecedented opportunities and risks. People and places often suffered in the change, but the breaching of local isolation by nationalizing forces also carried the power to upset local tyrannies and offer open horizons to people eager to seize their dignity and their dreams.

One such person was Jo Ann Gibson Robinson. The story of her courageous journey remained largely unknown until 1984, when historian David Garrow contacted the sixty-eight-year-old Robinson at her home in Los Angeles. She was by then a retired college professor and English teacher, a community activist in civic, political, and religious groups, and an owner of apartment buildings. She had lived in L.A. for nearly twenty-four years. Garrow traveled to California in April, called Robinson on the telephone, and offered to come see her. She, however, insisted on driving to the place he was staying, picking him up, and taking him to her home. There, she showed him a typescript, more than two hundred pages long, detailing her recollections of momentous events some thirty years earlier and thousands of miles away. As president of the Montgomery, Alabama, Women's Political Council, Robinson had, in 1955, played a crucial part in the public transportation struggle that sparked the black freedom movement in the American South.[1]

Jo Ann Robinson had left the South for the West in 1961. She crossed

the Mississippi and moved out of one region and into another at precisely the time that American regionalism was breaking down. But American regions are as much states of mind (or myths, perhaps) as bounded
territories, and in many ways, the distinctive regions of the United States
have constituted one another.[2] In American history, the concept of the
West has always been hitched to the possibility of mobility, of transformation, of progress. By contrast, the regional identity of the South has
relied heavily on the premise that people know their places, and places
can be fixed in time and space. The partisans of southern identity, a concept inextricable from white supremacy, staked their claims to be able
to fix place *and* race on the notion that social and political boundaries
are real, obvious, formidable, and permanent. The South long maintained
its regional distinctiveness not by moving, but by standing firm against
motion and change and fluidity.

Jo Ann Robinson was born, educated, and raised in the South, but
the South could not contain her. Long before she was a western woman
by virtue of residence, Robinson embraced a determination to move at
her own pace that was squarely at odds with white southern ideas about
where African Americans belonged, where they went, how far they might
go. Her memoirs can be read as an expansion into the South of the possibility of the western myth, of the ever-open potential for a new start.

Of course, Jo Ann Robinson was not merely an embodiment of a western ideal; to call her simply a "western woman" would be like starting
Huckleberry Finn's story after he lit out for the territory. Too much would
be left out. The significance of her life outside the West shows us how
her story stretches the western frame.[3] In his recent masterful synthesis
of African American history in the American West, Quintard Taylor has
shown how African American history in particular "forces a re-exami-
nation of the imagined West."[4] As Taylor's work and that of other historians demonstrate, recognizing African American presence in the West
means seeing a different historical landscape, one spanning five centuries
of transformation, in which the United States built itself as a nation and,
within that nation, more or less urbanized areas take pride of narrative
place.[5] If, as historian Gerald Nash wrote, the post–World War II West
should be understood as an "urban archipelago," no group of people
better embodies the human movements that have linked those islands
of life than African Americans.[6] I want to take Taylor's and Nash's con-
tention a step further. Following Jo Ann Robinson on her epic journey,
we will see how African American activists brought a revitalized national
commitment to freedom and democracy, an urban set of social and po-

litical resources, and a curiously western sense of possibility to bear on a resistant South.

The story of African American political geography in the 1950s is a story of nation exploding region, of humans moving around, seizing new ideas, creating new ways to live. African Americans' lives after World War II underwent nothing less than a revolution. Galvanized by the nationalizing forces unleashed by the war, African Americans moved out of the South, heading north and west, and departed the countryside and small towns for cities throughout the nation. Meanwhile, new ideas, expectations, and hopes breached the ramparts of southern segregation as the federal government, slowly, reluctantly, but tangibly, began to shift its weight behind the cause of racial justice everywhere in the land.

Jo Ann Robinson was an African American woman who acted locally but situated her actions in a national framework. Her life and her beliefs were forged in national processes from the civil rights movement to the great urban migration of African Americans. Robinson was a force in local communities in five different states. She was also a catalyst for and lifelong activist in a national, even global, crusade for justice. Her words and work can show us how people who aren't supposed to move—women and African Americans—shaped American history in general, and the American West in particular, in the period following World War II.

At the same time, her life was framed by the Cold War: by political, economic, and cultural forces that mobilized Americans on behalf of a struggle against international communism but also worked to contain, constrain, and control Americans' thoughts and actions. For nearly half a century, opinion makers marketed an ideology of containment intended to keep potentially disruptive Americans—women, people of color, workers—in line and in place.[7] The tension between "containment and emancipation," as the historian A. Yvette Huginnie has observed, took shape both in everyday frictions and in epic struggle.[8] Jo Ann Robinson made her mark in an era in which women's and African Americans' right and capacity to move themselves from place to place expanded, and in so expanding began to burst the borders of race, gender, and region and revolutionize a nation.

By the time Jo Ann Robinson moved to Los Angeles, the American West was also at a crossroads. Between 1882, when Grace Hebard moved to Wyoming, and 1954, which saw the publication of Cabeza de Baca's *We Fed Them Cactus,* the West became an indisputably American place, even, in Gerald Nash's term, a rapidly urbanizing "pacesetter" for the

United States.[9] The modern, industrial nation at midcentury teemed with mobile inhabitants coping with the consequences of their movements, an unsettled country, by no means finished. Burgeoning transportation and communication technologies, expanding economic systems and opportunities, and the growing presence of the federal government in far-flung locales transfigured the landscape.

The Cold War took its most notorious shape, in the West as elsewhere, in the proliferation of military, scientific, and industrial enclaves of fear, enclosure, secrecy, and potential violence.[10] But other systems, stimulated to no small degree by Cold War development, had the potential to open, empower, illuminate, and nurture. Perhaps foremost among these was the system of state-supported higher education, which had provided talented and ambitious women like Hebard and Cabeza de Baca with opportunities unavailable earlier, even to privileged white women like Susan Magoffin. As more and more young women throughout the country left home to learn and, in turn, to teach, they claimed a wider field of action. Even women like Hebard and Cabeza de Baca—single, materially comfortable, unusually self-confident—had to struggle against the assumption that the power to move ought, by right and reason, to belong to men. But move they did, in ways and with consequences I have already related.

For other women, no matter how educated or enterprising, claiming the power of education meant contesting not only the bounds of womanhood but also the bonds of a race system that was mapped onto the very landscape they traversed. For African American women in the middle of the twentieth century, making one's daily rounds meant repeated encounters with the crushing indignities of racial boundaries. The geography of race was particularly Manichaean in the part of the United States where white secessionists had once declared themselves founders of a separate entity, the Confederate States of America, a stillborn nation preserved a hundred years later in vestigial form and stubborn memory as the South.

The landscape of racism in the South was a geography of thwarted action, of arrested motion. The civil rights movement that caught fire in the 1950s, spreading out across the country from the South, was thus premised on claiming the power to move, and in so doing to remap space. For many African Americans, women as well as men, freedom and dignity meant seizing new means to move; not drawing lines, but crossing them. Jo Ann Robinson worked to replace the incarcerating geography of the southern region with a personal and collective capacity to move, physically, intellectually, and rhetorically, through and among different spaces: cities, the nation, the world. Her words and actions defied regional containment.

Jo Ann Gibson Robinson's life began in the country but before long took passage to town. She was born to landowning black farmers in Culloden, Georgia, in 1916, the youngest of twelve children. When one of her brothers bought a house in Macon, the family sold the farm and moved to the city. There, Robinson took advantage of the public education available to her, being honored as valedictorian of her high school class. She attended Georgia State College at Fort Valley, and stayed in Macon to take a teaching job. She married a man named Wilbur Robinson, but "the loss of a child made me very bitter, and the marriage did not last." So the next year, she moved by herself to Atlanta to enter the graduate program in English at Atlanta University, and upon earning her M.A. took another job at Mary Allen College in Crockett, Texas. A year later, she received a better offer from Alabama State, a historically black public college, and moved to Montgomery in 1949, at the age of thirty-three.[11]

In Montgomery, Robinson found a well-established African American community, in which educated women like herself played a prominent role. Middle-class blacks in Montgomery tended, at that point, to suppress their anger at race segregation and oppression. They nonetheless joined and led a number of civil rights organizations, including the National Association for the Advancement of Colored People.

The group that would become Robinson's institutional home and springboard was the Women's Political Council, an organization led by women whom scholars have described as "activist," "militant," even "social agitators."[12] The WPC had been founded in 1946 by Mary Fair Burks, a woman well aware of racial boundary lines and determined to erase them. A native of Montgomery, Burks had, from the time she began to understand "the scars I suffered as a result of racism," waged "my own private guerilla warfare" against race-divided space. She walked through segregated parks, used "WHITES ONLY" elevators and rest rooms marked "FOR WHITE LADIES ONLY." "I became a sprinter," Burks wrote, "by getting to doors before whites had a chance to slam them in my face."[13]

Burks, like Robinson, had left her hometown to attend graduate school, in this case, the University of Michigan. "Ann Arbor was almost Eden," she wrote. "For the first time since I had learned about segre-

gation, I knew what it meant to feel and live like a whole human being." She returned to segregated Montgomery, to teach at the Laboratory
High School at Alabama State, more angry than ever about southern
segregation.[14]

An incident on the streets of Montgomery, the kind of everyday has-
sle that has come to seem part of the cost of modern city life but that
takes on larger significance when race is at issue, spurred Burks to act
publicly. "I was in my car behind a bus when the traffic light turned
green," she recalled. "As I started to accelerate, I saw a white woman attempting to get to the curb. The short of it was that after the woman
stopped cursing me, I was arrested."[15]

Threatened by a club-wielding police officer and thrown in jail on
trumped-up charges, Burks called her husband, who showed up with a
white attorney who "read the charge, tore it up and demanded my re-
lease." The furious Burks determined to do something, and the following Sunday, hearing the Reverend Vernon Johns admonish his compla-
cent congregation at the Dexter Avenue Baptist Church, Burks decided
to try to organize women "to address some of the glaring racial problems." She contacted fifty women; forty showed up for the first meeting,
where nearly everyone present told about an incident similar to Burks's
recent experience. They agreed on a multifaceted program of action, including voter registration, protest about abuses on city buses and the segregation of city parks, and educational programs aimed at high school
students and at adult voters. At Burks's urging, the group chose the name
Women's Political Council. In a few short years, their efforts to remake
the social and political landscape of Montgomery would reverberate
across Alabama, the South, and the nation.[16]

Working to empower Montgomery's African American community,
WPC members staked out an activist position and covered a lot of ground.
They pledged themselves to become registered voters, a daunting un-
dertaking that meant conquering racist literacy tests and poll taxes, not
to mention intimidation. And once they were registered, they fanned out
to open voter education schools in the churches, took new voters to the
courthouse to register, "even accompanied them when they returned to
the courthouse to check on the results of the applications (which should
have been mailed to them). This last strategy," Burks wrote, "increased
the success rate."[17]

But the WPC also managed to get other political groups onto its own
turf. African American women were barred from joining Montgomery's
League of Women Voters, but the WPC invited league members to its

meetings to discuss upcoming candidates and elections. The council also pressured other black political groups to vote as a bloc for candidates they deemed "least objectionable." Burks was particularly proud of the WPC's use of political education programs for high school students, which she called "subversive tactics to serve our own ends."[18]

In the midst of all this activity, WPC members were also heading off to City Hall to lodge complaints about abuses on the buses. "True," wrote Burks, "we succeeded only in annoying the commission, but this was better than doing nothing." By the time Jo Ann Robinson arrived in Montgomery in 1949, WPC activities were gaining momentum. Robinson joined the Dexter Avenue Baptist Church and, in 1950, the WPC. She became Burks's friend as well as her colleague. "Although Montgomery had the reputation of being cool to strangers," Burks wrote, Robinson "was invited to join several civic and social clubs and became a much sought after dinner guest." Robinson was, moreover, "a dedicated and committed person, committed to friends, committed to work, committed to causes." As a member of the WPC, Burks recalled, Robinson "did the work of ten women."[19]

When Robinson signed on with the WPC, she had another story to add to those the members had recalled at their organizational meeting, the story of her own encounter with the arresting geography of race. Like many academics with out-of-town family, Robinson had planned to spend her first Christmas break with relatives, in this case in Cleveland, Ohio. Few Americans traveled by air in 1949, but Robinson was a notably mobile woman. Like Mary Fair Burks but unlike most African Americans of the time, moreover, she owned her own car—and was willing to go to rather elaborate lengths to make sure it was safely stored while managing to get herself and her baggage to the airport on time. "One of the men students loaded my suitcases in my car for me," she recalled, "and I drove at a leisurely pace out to the airport, checked my luggage for a trip to the East, then returned to the college campus, locked my car in a garage, made my way to the nearest bus stop, and waited for the short ride to a friend's home. We were all going to the airport together. I had never felt freer or happier."[20]

Most African Americans did not then, and still do not, take for granted the freedom to move unimpeded through space, let alone the right to enjoy public support of personal mobility. But even as racism has always structured American space, space has never imbibed race in a rational or orderly way. Learning the racial ways of space requires local knowledge. The more African Americans moved from one place to another in the United States, the more arbitrary, esoteric, and varied the forms of racial rules they encountered. Segregation practices also changed over time. In Mobile, Alabama, during the 1940s and 1950s, passengers were seated on a first come, first served basis. In Macon, Georgia, and elsewhere, blacks were expected to seat themselves from the rear of the bus forward, while whites were to sit from the front toward the rear until all seats were taken. At one point in the Montgomery struggle, white leaders proposed that buses have "flexible" whites-only sections, to be designated by a movable sign saying "white" on one side and "colored" on the other, a practice abandoned in the city decades earlier.[21]

That winter morning in 1949, Montgomery newcomer Jo Ann Gibson Robinson got a rude awakening. The city bus she planned to ride had only two passengers on it when she boarded: a white woman sitting in the third row from the front, and a black man near the back. Lost in thoughts of the holiday to come, and unaware that local conventions of transit segregation in Montgomery called for the first ten rows to be reserved for whites, Robinson took a seat in the fifth row.[22] The driver leaped to his feet and hustled back to confront Robinson. "He was standing over me saying, 'Get up from there! Get up from there!' with his hand drawn back. . . . I felt like a dog," she wrote. She stumbled off the bus in tears, and cried, she said, "all the way to Cleveland." Then she got mad. When she returned from her vacation, she called a meeting of the Women's Political Council.[23]

Historians have demonstrated that African American women faced down discrimination on public transportation from the moment such transit systems first appeared in the United States. Quintard Taylor noted that during the Civil War African Americans in California sued to challenge segregated public transportation on several occasions. Charlotte Brown of San Francisco twice brought suit against the city's Omnibus Company, in 1863 and 1865, winning both times. In San Francisco in 1866, the wealthy abolitionist Mary Ellen Pleasant sued the North Beach and Mission Railroad after she had been denied a ride.[24] The WPC was already well aware of local incidents of harassment by Montgomery bus drivers against black passengers, especially women. By 1953, the WPC had collected some thirty complaints against the bus company. Between 1950 and 1955, Robinson and other WPC members met regularly with the mayor of Montgomery, persistently protesting a pattern of abusive behavior ranging from obscene language and general rudeness on drivers' parts toward black patrons, to buses that stopped at every block in white neighborhoods but only every two blocks in black areas, to drivers who made blacks pay at the front then get off the bus to reenter at the back door—and often left before the black passenger was back on board. Worst of all, since seventy percent of passengers were black, reserving some ten double seats for whites often meant that black passengers were standing over empty seats. Over several years, a host of black civil rights and civic groups repeatedly brought their concerns to the mayor and city government, but got nowhere.[25]

By 1955, tensions were high. On March 2, Claudette Colvin, a student at Booker T. Washington High School, boarded a crowded bus and took a seat in the section customarily reserved for African Americans. When the bus driver insisted that she give up her seat to a white passenger, Colvin refused. The police were called and she was dragged from the bus, handcuffed, and thrown into jail, charged with misconduct, resisting arrest, and violating city segregation laws. The incident aroused anger in the community, and Robinson and Burks, among others, raised the possibility of a boycott. "On paper," Robinson recalled, "the WPC had already planned for fifty thousand notices calling people to boycott the buses, only the specifics of time and place had to be added. And as tempers flared and emotions ran high, the women became active."[26]

Colvin was a member of the congregation at the Bell Street Baptist Church, an A student, a deeply religious person. Her minister, U. J. Fields, stated that "she had been encouraged by her parents to 'be a real person,' although her parents probably did not encourage her to defy the Alabama State segregation ordinance." In the end, however, community leaders decided not to make a test case out of Colvin's arrest, concerned that she might not be able to "withstand the pressures sure to be exerted on any central figure in a protest."[27]

Montgomery's African American community, acting through some sixty-eight "political, religious, social, economic, educational, fraternal, and labor organizations," was poised to battle the segregation laws. But it hesitated. The risks were huge. "'Fighting City Hall,'" wrote Robinson, "was a task nobody had done before." Montgomery's middle-class blacks were embedded in the community. However much segregation limited their opportunities, the South's cities offered African Americans more chances to use their talents than had the countryside. For those in Montgomery who had found a measure of professional and economic success, "their positions were oriented toward Montgomery and sustained by Montgomery." To openly challenge the segregation ordinances meant wrenching oneself out of the city in which one lived, moving into uncharted social terrain, redrawing the boundaries of the city's social geography. "The city was their home," Robinson explained, "the place of their hopes and dreams, their future."[28]

The city provided the grounds for Montgomery's black leaders to dream of, and seize, the freedom to move. When a delegation from the Women's Political Council met with Montgomery's mayor, the mayor told them that if bus patrons "were not satisfied, they could always drive their own cars!"[29] Little did Mayor W. A. Gayle imagine becoming a prophet. On December 1, 1955, Montgomery civil rights activist Rosa Parks, riding home on a city bus with a full bag of groceries, defied local segregation ordinances by refusing to give up her seat to a white man. As we have seen, Parks was not the first African American in Montgomery to challenge either the legal or the social practice of bus segregation, but she was acting on behalf of a community of civil rights activists who had for some years sought the "right" person to test the segregation ordinance. As a middle-aged, professionally skilled, prominent African American woman, she had qualities alongside race—gender, age, and class—that influenced the decision to make hers the test case.

On the night of Parks's arrest, Robinson and others went, about midnight, to their offices at Alabama State. We need to understand the perils of this move, for it involved political and economic as well as social risks. Unlike Montgomery's African American ministers, Jo Ann Robinson was a public employee who stood to lose her job if her leading role in the protest arising from the arrest became too widely known. Not only that, but their midnight errand assuredly violated the general notion that black women should not go about alone at night in southern towns.[30] Nonetheless, at the college, they drafted a letter of protest, calling for a citywide one-day boycott of the bus lines. They mimeographed tens of thousands of notices of the proposed December 5 action, invoking the notion of feminine dignity insulted (Jo Ann Robinson insisted in her memoir on Parks's right to be treated like a lady: she "was a woman, and the person waiting was a man"),[31] and also making African American women present where they had not before been, with the printed declaration, "Another Negro woman has been arrested and thrown in jail. . . . The next time it may be you, or your daughter, or your mother."[32]

Robinson got on the phone to call members of the WPC and enlist their help in getting the leaflets out, all over Montgomery: to "schools, businesses, beauty parlors, beer halls, factories." She and two of her male students set out—in her own car—to places around the city where WPC members and friends were waiting "to take a package of notices as soon as my car stopped and the young men could hand them a bundle of leaflets."[33]

On December 5, 1955, black taxi drivers charged passengers only ten cents a ride, and some two hundred private automobiles joined forces to transport Montgomery's black bus riders. In a mass action "comparable in precision to a military operation," ninety percent of Montgomery's bus riders stayed off the city line. This would prove to be only the first day of thirteen months of stalwart protest, confrontation, negotiation, and, perhaps most unusual of all, independent, alternative volunteer mass transit. Over that thirteen-month period, 325 private automobiles operated out of forty-three dispatch and forty-two pick-up stations, arriving every ten minutes between the hours of 5 and 10 A.M. and 1 and 8 P.M., with hourly pick-ups the rest of the day. Many Montgomery residents, black and white, also gave rides on a more haphazard basis. As contributions arrived from around the nation, the newly formed Montgomery Improvement Association, a coalition of civic and civil rights organizations, and local churches purchased station wagons, hired drivers, and bought gasoline for the protest.[34]

The Montgomery bus boycott blasted a gaping hole in the wall of de jure racism in the American South. Jo Ann Robinson was there every mile of every day, editing the newsletter of the Montgomery Improvement Association, organizing car pools on an unprecedented scale, preparing the defense of those ride pools when segregationist officials tried to prohibit them, herself offering rides to boycotters day after day. When, a year into the boycott, the Montgomery police commissioner joined the White Citizens' Council, Robinson rededicated herself to the struggle in a highly symbolic way: "I put my car in the garage and walked. . . . I suffered with my colleagues and peers."[35]

The car—a Chrysler—suffered too when, one night, the police came by her house and threw acid on it. Robinson experienced the automotive body damage as a kind of combat wound, proof of valor to be displayed with pride. "I kept that car . . . until 1960, after I had resigned from Alabama State. It had become the most beautiful car in the world to me. I turned it in for a new one only when I moved to California, for I did not think the Chrysler would hold up through the deserts I had to cross."[36]

In 1960, the Cold War provided a rationale for Alabama's segregationists to get rid of civil rights activists in the state's institutions of higher learning. The Alabama state legislature launched an investigation of "subversives" and forced a dozen of Alabama State's most outspoken faculty to resign.[37] Robinson taught briefly at Grambling College in Louisiana, but she "realized the boycott had robbed me of something! It had taken its toll on my ability to adapt to new environments, new situations, new people."[38]

In light of this comment, we might be amazed to discover that Robinson's response to this realization was to move clear across the country, to Los Angeles. True, she had friends there, Montgomery friends including Portia Trenholm, wife of the former Alabama State president. But what would make Los Angeles appear to Robinson as familiar terrain?

The answer lies in imagining what Wallace Stegner so memorably called "the geography of hope."[39] For Jo Ann Robinson, that geography was not regional, but national and urban. In *The Montgomery Bus Boycott and the Women Who Started It,* the published version of her memoir of the struggle, Robinson hardly ever used the words "South" or "southern" to situate her story. For her the South was not a framework, but a problem to be solved. In the preface, written as a later reflection on the main narrative, Robinson located Montgomery as "once the capital of the Confederacy of the eleven southern states that waged the Civil War against the rest of the United States," a gesture signaling her belief that the South never had been, and should not in any way be considered, a separate entity from what she would later refer to as "the American land of freedom."[40] The first chapter, titled "Trouble," opens on the cold and cloudy morning of December 5, which was, Robinson explains, "meteorologically speaking . . . no different from other winter days in the South"—an image at odds with the claim that a warm and sunny climate somehow made the Confederacy a natural nation. On that morning, she explains, the WPC had "organized themselves to defeat segregation in the heart of the Confederacy," but in fact the WPC did even more: it challenged the very regional geography that made the institutions of southern racism seem natural.[41]

Throughout *The Montgomery Bus Boycott* Robinson refers, in passing, to southern culture and customs and social institutions as forces impeding progress, but never as forces to be taken for granted or, to be sure, revered. Her community was local—Montgomery, and particularly African American Montgomery—national, and global: "black Americans all over America and all over the world and . . . freedom-loving people everywhere . . . oppressed people the world over." When she became the editor of the newsletter for the Montgomery Improvement Association, she linked Montgomery with a national and even worldwide community of supporters. In Robinson's mind, this wider affinity was forged from common history and aspirations, for on the morning that the African American bus riders began to walk, "the voice of liberty-seeking colonists of 1776, the Minutemen of Lexington, seemed to make itself heard in the hearts of Montgomery Negroes, joyously exclaiming, 'O what a glorious morning this is!'"[42]

By contrast, white southerners who resisted integration had a marked tendency to invoke the South as an explanation for their politics. When Montgomery Improvement Association representatives met with white groups in the mayor's office, they presented a proposal that more black bus drivers be hired. But "the whites agreed that the company could hire whomever it chose, and that since it was not southern custom to hire black bus drivers, the Negroes had no right to propose it."[43] A man who declared himself "heartily in favor of segregation, being a 'born and bred Southerner,'" wrote a letter to the Montgomery *Advertiser* suggesting that Montgomery Negroes would not have disrupted the city's peace had they not been influenced by "Northern agitators of the NAACP"—a sentiment heartily echoed in an editorial in the city's *Alabama Journal,* which figuratively solidified the South against "outside" forces ranging from civil rights organizations to the U.S. government:

> Either fortuitously or with a purpose, Montgomery, the first Capital of the Confederacy, has been made a guinea pig for the great sociological experiment.
>
> The contributors to the experiment have been the Supreme Court of the United States, the NAACP, the ADA [Americans for Democratic Action] and a bunch of wild, well-financed political radicals jealous of the South's peaceful and serene way of life.[44]

As the boycott wore on, resistant white citizens began to wave the Confederate flag, putting stickers on their cars, wearing flag lapel pins, and in the case of a local television newsman, displaying a flag on his desk during broadcasts. Far from being a benign demonstration of attachment to a symbol of harmless nostalgia, the flag-waving, in Robinson's eyes, was a clear reflection of "the 'hate' mood" growing in the city.[45]

But Robinson and others contrasted the seeming unity of their opponents' South with the variety of race ways in "southern cities." Indeed, whites who supported desegregation were wont to point out existing integrated public transportation systems in the cities of a region supposed to be solidly segregated. J. H. Bagley, the bus company's manager, sought to resolve the situation early on by studying the "first come, first served" transit system of Mobile, "Montgomery's sister city," only two hundred miles away. Robinson pointed out that "similar practices were used in Huntsville, Alabama; Macon, Georgia; and other southern cities."[46] Mrs. Frances P. MacLeod asked in a letter to the *Advertiser* why Montgomery could not do as Nashville, Richmond, and "we understand Mobile," and pass a first come, first served law that would ensure that "all citizens have equal opportunities for a ride." And another letter from Mrs. I. B. Rutledge, whom Robinson described as "a leading white civic worker who was well-known in religious, civic, cultural and educational circles," justified desegregation in terms that transcended region:

> We in the South like to think of ourselves as a courageous people. . . .
> Isn't it time that those of us who really believe in Christian and democratic
> principles of consideration of others and of fair play speak out and help
> create a public opinion which will make possible a solution of the present
> situation that will be satisfactory to all?[47]

Even if the U.S. Supreme Court affirmed African Americans' rights to equal treatment in transit through Montgomery and elsewhere, the state legislature's blacklisting in 1960 forced Robinson to take to the road, once again, in search of opportunity. And so she set out across the Great American Desert, long before the interstate highway system had made reliable roads commonplace, on a journey from one city to another. The move to Los Angeles took her farther than she had ventured before, but it was certainly in character for a woman who had already made a living in four states—Georgia, Texas, Alabama, and Louisiana, and who had come to see cities as places of opportunity.

Robinson had again and again seized the moment to move from one place to another, to get away from a bad situation and seek a better one. But just as surely, she did not take mobility for granted. If her experience in the bus boycott had taught her the importance of contesting geographical constraints based on race, she also knew the ways in which gender, as an economic, occupational, and intellectual structure, impeded women's power to move.

Still, by Robinson's time, American women could claim an institutional resource that helped them contest the constraints of womanhood: the national system of public education. She had benefited from that system as a student and would take advantage of the national market for teaching talent. She avowed that her professional achievements gave her the courage to leave, something women didn't generally have. As she recalled, "I had been less afraid than most women, because I knew I could get teaching positions elsewhere." On a summer visit to Los Angeles after her year at Grambling, "for some reason I found myself in the office of the Los Angeles Board of Education, where I was offered a job teaching English in the public school system." She took the job, resigned from Grambling, found a house, sent for her furniture, and lived and taught in Los Angeles, retiring in 1976. After retirement, she did what good Angelenos at least aspire to do, and invested successfully in real estate.[48]

Jo Ann Robinson started out life as a southerner, but a very mobile citizen of that region. She became involved in the cause that, in her words, "gave me courage" as a middle-aged professional, contributing to the bus boycott struggle her eloquence as well as her political savvy and energy. The story of her life, thus, can be read as a dramatic narrative that crests in the 1950s, in the southern United States. During the period of her life deemed most significant by historians, she was at the center of a conflict that, more than virtually any other in American history, demonstrated the race, class, and gender politics of the interconnected domains of public space, personal mobility, and human dignity.

But lives do not build to a climax and then hold still, waiting for their stories to be written as dramas. Jo Ann Robinson brought a determination to move freely to a landscape of arrested motion. Ironically, the role she played in organizing the boycott and in seeing it through to its successful conclusion made it impossible for her to stay in Montgomery. Neither did the significance of her participation become apparent to most students of the struggle until her memoir was published in 1987. By that time she was more than seventy years old, retired, and living quietly on the Pacific edge of the American West, far from the place of her birth.[49] Even after retirement, she remained active in a variety of civic organizations, including the League of Women Voters and Black Women's Alliance, gave one day a week of free service to the Los Angeles city government, worked in a child care center and in senior citizens' assistance, and played contract bridge.[50]

For more than thirty years, Jo Ann Robinson lived at the Pacific edge of the trans-Mississippi West, and it was from the West that her voice rang across the wire to David Garrow, offering to pick him up. But long before she ever set foot in the West, she insisted on her right to the mythic westerner's taken-for-granted power to move freely. Wondering how western women's history might come to terms with such a reflective, moving subject forces us to recognize, once again, that lives like Jo Ann

Robinson's persist beyond the borders of political events, defy containment, insist on emancipation, burst the boundaries of region, demand respect on their own complex terms.[51] Jo Ann Gibson Robinson's story, not strictly southern or western but mobile and national, is the story of the changing landscapes of women's, African American, American history.

CHAPTER 7

THE LONG STRANGE TRIP OF PAMELA DES BARRES

These days ecstasy is indeed out of fashion; it's become conventional to trivialize, when not simply condemning out of hand, the romance of sex and drugs that carried so much of my generation's transcendental baggage. Yet the power of the ecstatic moment—*this is what freedom is like, this is what love could be, this is what happens when the boundaries are gone*—is precisely the power to reimagine the world, to reclaim a human identity that's neither victim nor oppressor, to affirm difference not as separation but as variations on a theme. **Ellen Willis,** *No More Nice Girls*

De Rougement, in his *Passion and Society,* traces the origins of the Tristan myth to the incompatibilities of passion and idealized love, so that, as with the Beatles, the courtly bard is preoccupied with idealized love. Just as the status of women, having these ambivalent psychological qualities, was a problem in the Age of Chivalry, so in our modern culture, women find the ancient dilemma a live issue. **Evan Davies, "Psychological Characteristics of Beatle Mania"**

Am I not a good girl any more? At least when I give my body, I give a chunk of my heart.
Pamela Des Barres, *I'm with the Band*

I WAS SEVEN YEARS OLD WHEN John Kennedy took office, just realizing that there was a world outside the verdant curving streets of my neighborhood. That spring I lay in bed in the room I shared with my teenage sister, listening to her favorite AM station in the dark. That spring I fell in love, for the first time, with a song—a pumping beat, a man with a rough and driving voice that seemed to come from some aching place inside, and lyrics about a girl who'd somehow gotten away. Del Shannon's great hit, "Runaway," was a song about love and loss, yes, but even then, in my comfortable suburban house in my comfortable midwestern life, I knew it was about more.

Music on the radio in the dark moved millions of American girls like me. It was a personal, intimate call from disembodied voices somewhere beyond: "There's something else out here. Something you want." In 1961 it was romance. A few years later it would be things less ethereal, more visceral: loud rock and joy rides and kicks and sex and dope. But it began and continued, for so many of us, with the music that reached out to us, broke through suburban walls, dragged us to new places. Like so many kids of my generation I was, in Maria Muldaur's phrase, "magnetized into the music."[1]

Rock 'n' roll music was a remarkably powerful component of a national culture that was, as historian Beth Bailey has pointed out, undermining local authority, bringing new conflicts and choices to dispersed locales, and providing both the means and the motives to move people.[2] Even as the mass media hyped a constraining and consumerist vision of women's choices, those same messages carried seeds of change. Media critic Susan Douglas explains that even girl groups like the Shirelles "helped cultivate inside us a desire to rebel. . . . When tens of millions of young girls started feeling, at the same time, that they, as a generation, would not be trapped, there was planted the tiniest seed of a social movement."[3]

As we have seen, such movements both require individual action and have the power to thrust people out of their accustomed orbits, off into uncharted territory. Certainly, that was the case with the civil rights movement that rode into Montgomery, Alabama, in the determined hearts of those who boycotted the buses, and spread across the nation with the news of their bravery and their ultimate success. With that success, however, came sacrifice. For Jo Ann Robinson and others, Montgomery had become an impossible place. They would have to move on. Many chose to head west, in the hope of finding greater tolerance, greater scope, greater opportunity. Their movement, in turn, would transform the western landscape: try to imagine Los Angeles without African American migrants from the South.[4]

But African Americans weren't the only southerners making their way west. Ever since the Dust Bowl disaster, a stream of dispossessed farmers and workers from the South and Southwest had poured into California, in search of security at least, fortune at best. Immortalized by John Steinbeck and Woody Guthrie, Buck Owens and Merle Haggard, they too engraved their collective signature on the countryside. Among those was a couple from Pond Creek, Kentucky, O. C. and Margaret Ruth Miller. O. C. was a dreamer who thought he'd find gold one day, and since California's rush had long since busted, he slipped off to Mexico every weekend to dig for treasure. During the week, O. C. brought home a paycheck from a Budweiser bottling plant, while Margaret kept the home fires burning in a bungalow in Reseda, out in the San Fernando Valley. Their daughter Pamela would be born there, a California native and self-proclaimed product of the New West. The Millers and their compatriots, in lighting out for the territory, signaled the fact that American society was beginning to change in ways so far-reaching and multiform that people born after 1960 have a hard time imagining what life was like before. For American women, the end of the twentieth century brought new opportunities and challenges, new responsibilities and problems, new pleasures and dangers in new times and places. The passage from Kentucky to California, and from one generation to another, was a crossing of myriad great divides.[5]

I cannot treat in detail the history of American women since 1960, but I can sketch some of the most important forces affecting women's lives. The growth of the service economy brought an enormous increase in jobs for women, particularly in clerical work, retail sales, and customer service. That same economic expansion spewed forth an array of consumer goods both dazzlingly diverse and within the reach of more and more Americans. Young women who had grown up amid material abundance could contribute to their own keep or to the family's comfort, and even pay for things they wanted, by getting a diverse array of jobs.

Economic changes brought new ways of inhabiting American space. Young women could, in fact, become self-supporting (if relatively underpaid) to the point where they could earn their own room and board. The expansion of higher education, first catalyzed by the GI Bill, drew more and more women into colleges and universities, and in some cases into graduate study and professional training. Across the nation, girls moved into dormitories and sorority houses and apartments, increasingly insisting on making their own house rules. American families too were changing; divorce would become as common a means of ending marriages as the death of a partner. More and more often, women were finding themselves living beyond marriage, on their own. American ways of sex were transfigured by the advent and spread of contraceptive technologies and new ideas about sexual freedom, which women could at last try out in their own dwellings. And not least important, a varied, vigorous, and effective feminist movement claiming women's rights, including the right to live and move independently, swept the country.[6]

In some important regards, Jo Ann Robinson stood as a symbol of these transformations. A wage worker, a college graduate, a divorcée, a political activist, she embodied the new American woman as a brave, independent, effective citizen, thinker, and professional, a woman who had what Virginia Woolf had argued were the two fundamental conditions for women's creativity: an independent income and a room of her own. As we have seen, Robinson also personified female mobility—geographical, economic, and political. Her assertion of her right to a wider world, and the means to navigate that world, helped to power a movement that continues to challenge injustice to this day. Her capacity to move changed the very landscape around her, challenging settled geographies as much as entrenched habits, from the heart of the South to the edge of the Pacific.

But just as Robinson and her colleagues shook the foundations of American racism, other women were moving in ways far less self-consciously political, but ones that nonetheless powered an earthquake in women's everyday lives, amplified and broadcast women's voices, and reconfigured the shapes of cities themselves. As they launched themselves out of their parents' households, not directly into marriage, but instead into college, or the workforce, or the search for creative fulfillment, or a quest for mad adventure, they claimed and charted American space anew, threatening established patterns in sometimes scandalous ways.

Nowhere were their "outrageous acts and everyday rebellions," in Gloria Steinem's marvelous term, more evident than in the countercultural enclaves that claimed California as their physical and spiritual province. Flower children, hippie chicks, sluts, groupies, and rock divas, they shocked the squares and even some of the hip with their bad loud mouths and their body-flaunting garments and their hollering and hitchhiking and myriad comings and goings. Their search for self and for ecstasy terrified and fascinated a global public.

Such women have been trivialized as druggies and sex objects, prisoners of false consciousness, lightweights. They have also served as bad examples in cautionary tales about the perils of self-indulgence and self-destruction. At times, they were all of these things. But without romanticizing their mistakes, or minimizing the risks they took, we must understand that they were also, in Anthony Giddens's phrase, "skilled and knowledgeable actors" whose words and works, however bounded by unrecognized conditions and unintended outcomes, indeed had substantial consequences.[7] It is time we took them seriously.

It is time to open up the sound-filled, eroticized, and dangerous terrain of women's journeys in the West by looking at the strange California trip of O. C. and Margaret Ruth Miller's daughter, Pamela Miller Des Barres. The women of the sixties counterculture, who gave their bodies and minds to the cause of sex, drugs, and rock 'n' roll, have never quite gotten their historical due. But there is plenty of historical material to tell us what we might want to know. We need do no more than turn on our car radios to know that hippie chicks and rock 'n' roll women are still with us, in a visceral and moving way. We know, by now, about the triumph and tragedy of the blues goddess Janis Joplin.[8] More recently, we have had the wry survivor's tale of acid rock avatar Grace Slick.[9] Although these were by no means "typical" women, and the times and places they lived in were neither normative nor representative in any sociological sense, their stories tell us more than we might expect about where women went, what they said and sang and heard and did, and why their movements matter. Both Joplin and Slick, at their peak, enjoyed a power to speak to, and move, a national and even international audience, and their voices can still be heard, blasting along freeways across the land. Both have served as symbols of the sexual and moral excesses of the sixties, Joplin in particular, who has become an iconic figure in narratives that fashion the story of the sixties as a dire warning.

To find the story of a woman traversing and remaking the landscape of the counterculture in more or less skilled and knowledgeable fashion, we need search no further than the comic and troubling odyssey of self-proclaimed groupie Pamela Miller Des Barres. Pamela was locally notorious in her heyday, enjoying fleeting cult fame as a member of the GTOs, the all-girl, all-groupie band produced by the musical experimentalist Frank Zappa. Later, Des Barres achieved national celebrity on her own following the 1987 publication of her sexy tell-all book, *I'm with the Band: Memoirs of a Groupie.*

It was the music that first called Pamela Des Barres, and literally millions of other girls, out of themselves in quest of a bigger, wider, higher reality. Following Pamela around a California made larger by her own legend, watching her record and reflect on her experiences, we can't help hearing the music or tasting the sensations, or seeing a new landscape, at once local and global, taking shape around shouting, sinuous female bodies. Seeing how their desires came into being and took them away, in a terrain notoriously rocked and remade by seismic tremors, we may even feel the earth move. Ultimately, we will see how even in California, the land of dreams and possibility, the weight of tradition, doubt, and expectation, of romance, channeled her bold sorties into old and deep-cut streams, diverted only at great cost.

Pamela Miller Des Barres was by no means the first or only or most influential girl captivated by rock 'n' roll and thrust into a world where music, sex, and drugs shook up identity and reality. She did not travel the farthest, soar the highest, plummet the lowest, or learn the most from her plunge into the counterculture she helped to invent. Yet there was one major difference between Pamela and most of the other girls whose risky adventures created a new scene: Pamela was a writer. From the first moment that sex gleamed in her adolescent eye and throbbed somewhere below her neck, she was turning sensation into words on a page, keeping a diary, writing it all down. And then, looking back at a sexual career so extravagant that the more reticent reader squirms, Pamela Des Barres dredged up her old notebooks and wrote again. "I was always writing," she told a reporter for the *San Diego Union-Tribune* in 1988. "And I always thought I could fall back on it if all else failed."[10]

Why tell the story of Pamela Des Barres? Because no story better illustrates the powers and perils and consequences of women's journeys across shifting landscapes. Like Sacagawea, Pamela was a pathbreaker. Like Susan Magoffin and the myriad sunbonneted women celebrated in "western women's history," she was a ferocious diarist. Like the women's rights advocates of Wyoming Territory, she brought with her the very political baggage she meant to leave behind on her journey to emancipation. Like Grace Hebard, she remapped western space with her body and her mind. Like Fabiola Cabeza de Baca and Jo Ann Robinson, she turned, reflectively, to memoir. Like them all, she wanted to get out and to know more and to be free, even as she took part in historical processes large and small. As the center of a rapidly globalizing mass media, California was a place in which the groupie life could flourish, a fountain that spewed forth new ideas and habits that washed across the continent, and even onto other shores. When women like Pamela did new things and went new places, they became roving ambassadors for a new way of living.

History celebrates not those who first do deeds, but those who leave the earliest permanent records of their actions. Not Viking sailors, but Christopher Columbus. Not unidentified natives trekking the unmapped West, but Lewis and Clark. Pamela Des Barres is the Lewis and Clark of wanton women, who prowled the land anew, from sea to shining sea.

In the spring of 1962, not many people would have predicted the upheavals that would shortly sweep the nation. In Port Huron, Michigan, the student radical Tom Hayden would make a speech on behalf of "people of this generation, bred in at least modest comfort . . . looking uncomfortably to the world we inherit."[11] The sources of that discomfort were distinctly political for Hayden and the other members of Students for a Democratic Society. In the San Fernando Valley suburb of Reseda, California, fourteen-year-old Pamela Miller was feeling another kind of discomfort. It wasn't a matter of material deprivation. Pamela had Pop Tarts and Barbie dolls, a parakeet named Buttons, and not one but two rooms of her own. But she had shivers and twinges, tingles and blushes. "I wanted to be a good girl . . . " she wrote, "but boys and rock 'n' roll had altered my priorities."[12]

There is something about the word "pubescent" that conjures up images of bodily mysteries suddenly exposed. Hair in new places, bumps where there didn't used to be any, involuntary secretions, and urgent desire, furtive and fascinating. Pamela Miller, at fourteen, was a study in the daily drama of female puberty, California-style, and rock 'n' roll played no small part in bringing her new sexual awareness to the surface. Listening to the music on the radio, she began to sense her body in a new way. Looking back at the experience from the vantage point of her late thirties, she revealed more than most of us would, letting her junior high diary do the talking: "Dear Diary . . . DION!! Oh Help!!! I'm so excited, I think I'll just DIE!!! I was runnin' around, chokin' and cryin' and yellin' and screamin'. Wow wow cute cute CUTE!!"[13]

Within weeks of that diary entry she was hanging around the house across the street, where a garage band had begun to practice, necking with the lead guitar player and writing lovesick poetry. One schoolgirl crush after another finally gave way to "a fatal dose of Beatlemania" in 1964, and Pamela Miller was never the same. As Barbara Ehrenreich, Elizabeth Hess, and Gloria Jacobs noted, "Beatlemania was the first mass outburst of the sixties to feature women—in this case girls."[14] Students of the phenomenon have generally argued that Beatlemania made the blatantly sexual appeal of Elvis safer for female fans. The Beatles were, compared with Presley, androgynous, fun-loving, clean-cut. But at the same time, Beatlemaniacs were rowdy, extravagant, even hysterical. "In Beatlemania," wrote Susan Douglas, "the seeds of female yearning and female revolt germinated with the speed of those exploding flowers in time-lapse photography."[15] Every Beatlemaniac who paraded her devotion in a public space put herself and her ecstasy on display in places and ways that threatened the sexual containment of the 1950s.[16]

Pamela Miller's Beatlemania was probably about average for the time: obsessive collecting of Beatles paraphernalia, hour upon hour of listening to Beatles music, writing poems and stories and plays, sometimes in collaboration with fellow Beatlemaniacs, often featuring themselves in sexy situations with the Beatles ("Paul fell across you, pushing you into the soft bed. His tender lips kissed you passionately"). In retrospect Pamela Miller Des Barres admitted, "It's enough to make you throw up," but she carefully preserved the documents in which she had put down the details, embarrassing as they might be, knowing that her loopy Beatlemania had been the catalyst for what was to come.[17]

While many Beatlemaniacs were elementary and junior high school girls with limited capacity to go out unchaperoned, and many more lived in places that the Beatles would never visit, Pamela was sixteen years old and the Beatles were emphatically coming to L.A. In a remarkably adventuresome piece of urban exploration, she and her friends managed to sneak into the Bel Air subdivision where the Beatles were staying, camping out all night until they were hauled off by the police in the morning.[18] It would be several years before being arrested became a commonplace experience for Americans of Pamela's generation.

Pamela rang in 1965 by getting herself a bad-boy boyfriend who took her to a trailer and taught her about oral sex. She was still trying to be good in ways that would please her mother and father—get good grades, remain a virgin—but every time she slipped out of the house and into a sweaty night of clinches, her resolve stretched and weakened. And now she was meeting new friends, palpitating to the more overt sexual come-ons of the Rolling Stones, abandoning her Beatle buddies for the wilder world of real-live rock 'n' roll.

Then came another trailer, this one in the desert, this one belonging to the musician Don Vliet, a.k.a. Captain Beefheart, who made her want to be different. She started hanging out with friends who smoked marijuana and had names like Vixon and Tomato. She got sent home from school for "looking absurd." And amazingly, through the offices of Captain Beefheart, she began to meet the rock musicians who turned her sexual fantasies into sexual encounters, the men who would become her obsession.

American women have long found both peril and delight in the places where musicians gather to ply their trade and the public comes to drink, dance, and flirt.[19] Rock 'n' roll propelled Pamela Miller out of Reseda, down to Hollywood, out onto the Sunset Strip, and into the turmoil of a larger sixties history. More and more young women like Pamela began to promenade on the Strip, wearing sexy clothes reconstructed from thrift shop castoffs and show-off lingerie, setting trends and changing the ways American women displayed their bodies in public. When a road-widening project threatened the demolition of a popular club called Pandora's Box, a thousand demonstrators, Pamela among them, sat in the street, many holding hands. It wasn't all peace and love, though. When some "Gorgeous Hollywood Boys overturned a bus," police moved in with billy clubs. The musician Stephen Stills would write a song about the protest, "For What It's Worth," expressing the same sense of foreboding and tension Tom Hayden had captured at Port Huron. As a single released by the band Buffalo Springfield, Stills's song reached a far wider audience than Hayden's words had, reverberating, indeed, as a kind of generational anthem. For Pamela, the Sunset Strip Riot of 1965 marked the coming together of the long-haired and cool, "people trying to become what others call 'nonconformists' . . . And we meet in Hollywood."[20]

To meet friends on the street in Hollywood was to break out of the straitjacket of fifties one-on-one dating rituals. At the time, middle-class mores mandated that girls wait to be asked out by boys who made all the plans, provided the transportation, picked up the tab. Mothers warned their daughters against making the first move—even picking up the telephone to call a boy—lest they appear too active or aggressive, too easy, too cheap.[21] Pamela Miller, though, was not one to wait around for the phone to ring, and that in itself made her a rebel. She had begun to haunt the backstage doors of Hollywood clubs, hoping for a close encounter with local rock heroes who might become national or even international sensations. She even badgered insiders for the idols' addresses, found them on maps, and got herself out to Laurel Canyon, where the rock royalty lived. Peeping in windows, sleeping on lawns, waiting for her idol of the moment to appear: today she might be called a stalker.

Pamela wanted to be loved, to be hip, to be seen. She was determined to find ways to go wherever the action was, and once there, make some action of her own. She and a girlfriend hitchhiked "out past many, many spanking-new shopping malls," architectural emblems of the mobility of women like her own mother, to attend the eulogy for political comedian and counterculture icon Lenny Bruce. There she ogled and was ogled by older men who assumed that high school girls in slinky clothes were fair game. She joined with the other girls who, moving in twos and threes and groups, paraded along the Strip and danced in the clubs. "We dared to do things together that we wouldn't have done alone," Pamela recalled. But assuredly they also did things, when they were alone with men, that they wouldn't have done without encouragement. For Pamela, that meant frequent, fleeting sexual encounters of the oral kind, with musicians. She did feel guilty, on occasion. "Perhaps if I'd been born in Idaho none of these things would be burdening my head," she wrote in her diary, "but I'm in L.A. and here I'll stay."[22]

There were, of course, to be trips out of Los Angeles. In January 1967 Pamela and a friend caught a ride to San Francisco, to see for themselves the hippie scene taking root in the Haight-Ashbury district, near Golden Gate Park. Pamela cruised the Haight and went to the Human Be-In, the event that brought the nascent Bay Area counterculture into the glare of national media attention and set the stage for the remarkable and terrifying Summer of Love. Many writers have described the ugliness of the scene that greeted her. Nicholas von Hoffman wrote of a fog-bound landscape of seediness and desperation, race tensions and homophobia, madness and pathetic alienation. He likened the place to a Hieronymus Bosch painting, peopled by pathetic children whose parents had thrown them away and evil-eyed hustlers closing in fast on the innocents, surrounded by garbage and addiction and lying and sudden violence. Most people in the Haight, von Hoffman suggested, might sense the menace but were usually too stoned to respond. "The fog and drugs filter out precision, leave a mood, an apocalyptic premonition."[23]

Pamela Des Barres was not much more impressed with the Haight than von Hoffman, though she was untroubled by apocalyptic premonitions. She recalled wryly that she had been eager to "breathe the unwashed hippie air, see all the dirty bare feet . . . maybe meet some pretty hippie boy and discover the true meaning of life." But from the first, she was disgusted by the accommodations (bare mattresses and filthy bathrooms), the food ("sticky brown rice and smelly old vegetables"), and the general air of dowdiness and dreariness. She'd loved the festivity of the Be-In ("I was floating around in the Garden of Eden . . . draped in flowers, bestowed upon me by my brothers and sisters. I was a laughing, loving, living, breathing Princess of Peace") but was glad enough to head the four hundred miles back down the road to Reseda and sleep in her own bed.[24]

Sleep in her own bed? Haight-Ashbury had become a crossroads for unprecedentedly mobile young men and women from all over the United States. For the girls in particular, migrating to San Francisco in search of love and peace (and sex and drugs and music) was a long step out of security and into a profoundly suspect terrain. But unlike those sometimes witlessly bold adventurers, Pamela was not ready, precisely, to abandon the shelter of family. For all the nights she spent crushed into jam-packed Sunset Strip clubs, writhing to the music, and ending up crashing wherever the early hours of the morning found her, for all the "love orgy" parties, all the bad behavior on band buses and in the backs of limousines, Pamela was hanging on to home. She was desperately protective of her "virginity," and was still putatively living with her parents.

But she was making more sorties into the unknown. Even if she had not yet gotten to the point of paying rent anywhere, she was spending more and more nights at houses in Laurel Canyon, an area that was becoming a gathering spot for bold, aspiring girls like herself. She was beginning to dabble in drugs and finding, to her surprise, that attracting sexual attention was not always a good thing. "It seemed like I was always in the danger zone," she recalled, "without knowing how I got there."[25]

Drugs were a danger. Pamela had a friend who worked at a hospital, who brought her quart bottles of Trimar, a powerful tranquilizer used as a "saddleblock" on women in labor. Poured on a hanky and sniffed, it produced a dizzying, brain-frying high. And men were a danger, too, like Jim Morrison of the Doors, who kissed her and slapped her and impressed her with what she believed was "perfect insanity." For Pamela and other young women on the scene, traveling in a group of girlfriends afforded some protection, but spending time even with girlfriends could be perilous. They were often without a car, and hitchhiking was, as mothers are wont to point out, not a safe way of getting around. "We had zero trouble getting rides," Pamela explained, "but quite often a pervert would be sitting behind the wheel." Being high while hitchhiking increased the hazards. On one drunken adventure, she and a friend ended up in jail (six months' probation and a two-week curfew put barely a dent in their revels). On others, they ended up at orgies hosted by a popular party-giver and sexual predator named Vito, who was eventually deported for sexual exploitation of underage girls.[26]

There was, of course, the problem of making a living. Like most middle-class girls her age, Pamela had no particular employable skills. She did, however, put work into making her hair and her skin and her body resemble an ideal feminine type of the time, the blonde, beach-loving California Girl. She tried to cash in on her looks by auditioning for modeling and acting jobs, pronouncing herself "desperate to be famous." For years she took acting lessons, and managed to get parts in forgettable movies with titles like *Massage Parlor* and in commercials. The high point of her acting career was a stint on the afternoon soap opera *Search for Tomorrow*. She admitted in retrospect that she had little acting talent, but clearly she hoped that she could find some way to enter Los Angeles's highest-profile industry, show business, on her own. As for the music trade, although a very few women were beginning to take the stage as performers—Mamas Michelle Phillips and Cass Elliot, Janis Joplin, Grace Slick, Tracy Nelson of Mother Earth, Linda Ronstadt, and of course folk pathbreakers Mary Travers and Joan Baez—Pamela couldn't sing. For the most part, then, she patched together an income in rather conventionally female ways: working the candy counter in a discount store, sewing clothes that she sold to friends.

Pamela was thus in many regards typical of girls of her generation, struggling to find a way to make a decent living until they could find a man to foot the bills. She was in other ways ahead of the curve. She could manage to appear conventional, when necessary, but she preferred outrageous. As long as there were other girls doing what she did, the outrageous could become trend-setting. By the late 1960s, women like Pamela were identified as "groupies"—devotees of rock 'n' roll who lived for the rock "scene" and, not incidentally, for sexual intimacy with their heroes as well. There were young women doing similar things in any number of urban locales, especially in New York and Chicago and San Francisco, although Southern California's groupies had unparalleled access to mass media. However misguided their intentions, however self-defeating their strategies, these young women were claiming, and remaking, the American cultural landscape. As *Rolling Stone* magazine writers John Burks and Jerry Hopkins explained, in Los Angeles groupies who moved from scene to scene were creating a new local geography:

> The actual lay of the land tells . . . about the character of the Los Angeles groupie. The "scenes" in this city are spread wide. The Rose Palace in Pasadena is 17 miles away from the Whisky a Go Go in West Hollywood; Capitol Records (office and studios) is 16 miles from the new Electric Theater on the Santa Monica beach (site of the old Cheetah); the Landmark Motor Hotel is nearly 50 miles from the Golden Bear in Huntington Beach. With all this mileage between groupie haunts, it means the groupies must, generally, have access to ready transportation . . . or join southern California's throng of hitchhikers. Most do the latter.
>
> Throughout the Los Angeles Basin (from the somewhat arid suburban San Fernando Valley to the salty beach communities of Laguna and Huntington) these packs of happy carnivores roam from one dressing room to another, from one motel to another, looking for where it's at.[27]

Pamela zigged and zagged through this landscape with a vengeance, from the Valley to the crags of Laurel and Topanga canyons, from the Strip to the Hollywood Hills. Her menial jobs and hand-sewn, flashy-trashy cowboy shirts helped to finance her nightly forays into the clubs of the moment—the Troubadour, the Palomino, the Whisky a Go Go, Thee Experience—although, often enough, she found some man willing to "treat."[28] Her parents provided a place to live, a childhood haven to crawl back to. However, at the very moment that Pamela was making her most daring raids into uncharted territory, her parents lost their house. Her father's long-cherished dream of getting rich mining gold in the hills of Mexico came up a bust, and they couldn't pay the mortgage. She helped her parents find "a ghetto in North Hollywood," a place she obviously hated. To make matters much worse, somewhere along the way she'd contracted hepatitis, and since her family couldn't pay for medical care, she spent two frighteningly lonesome weeks in a charity ward at County General Hospital.[29]

Pamela, like so many young Americans of her time, was learning a hard lesson: the restless search to get out, to move, sometimes made it hard to find the way home. There were, for groupies, myriad scenes in which to be seen. Yet amid all the frenzy, they had to work to make ends meet, and to find places they could call their own. "It was easy to dig up a pad around town in a day or two for seventy-five a month," wrote Pamela, but she and her friends wanted quarters in Laurel Canyon where they could frolic. Frank Zappa, the experimental musician and free speech lightning rod, provided such a place, a rambling log cabin he occupied with his wife, Gail, and their daughter, Moon Unit.[30] One of Pamela's friends, a transplanted New Yorker called "Miss Christine," was living in the basement of Zappa's house, and he welcomed Pamela and the other girls. Soon they were hanging out, capering in motley costumes made of flimsy scraps and secondhand finds, even, on one occasion, oversized baby bibs and diapers. Zappa began taping interviews with the groupies and collecting diaries and letters; *Rolling Stone* magazine declared that "Zappa may wind up the ultimate historian of the groupies, whom he sees as freedom fighters at the avant-garde of the sexual revolution that is sweeping Western civilization."[31]

Although Zappa had no illusions about the girls' ability to sing or play instruments, he viewed their public displays as performance art with "real rock and roll potential, fabulous original ideas, and maybe even some hidden talent that might be tapped." Zappa decided that Pamela and her friends would make a perfect accompaniment to his rock band, Mothers of Invention. He invited them to dance onstage as the GTOs, an acronym for "Girls Together Only." "We adored the idea and expanded on it," Pamela wrote, "deciding that the O could stand for anything we wanted it to: Outrageously, Overtly, Outlandishly, Openly, Organically. The potential was obviously endless."[32]

The GTOs represented the convergence in Los Angeles of women who had found their way to a scene they were even then making. Some had been thrown out by distant parents, some had tired of San Francisco. All were dedicated to pushing the envelope of public decorum, with their dress, their wild dancing, their loud voices and laughter, their aggressive pursuit of rock musicians, their sexual exhibitions. They kissed and hugged each other, lifted their blouses and touched each other's breasts, declared their love. Their mobile, brazenly displayed, and openly sexualized bodies were the canvases on which they painted their collective, insurgent, eroticized art. Zappa reported that "the incidence of lesbianism between groupies is high," and allowed that "it's good that they can be bisexual. It shows they're adapting to their needs. If it feels good, do it!"[33]

But the GTOs, bowing to the conventions of what Adrienne Rich identified as "compulsory heterosexuality," made a point of denying that their physicality with one another amounted to lesbianism. *Rolling Stone* stated baldly, "The GTOs (the group) are not lesbians, they are merely girls who happen to like other girls' company." One member told the reporters, "We complement each other. There are closer relationships between girls than boys." Another said, "We love boys to death. But you shouldn't be pushed into things. Some people think we're dykes and they're disappointed when they find out we aren't."[34]

Sex in the environs of Hollywood was a journey with many branching paths, retraced steps, crossroads, cul-de-sacs. As people experimented with their bodies, they sampled gay and lesbian and bisexual as well as heterosexual encounters. Pamela reveled in cross-dressing, in exhibitionism, in appearing in public with girls who "had *no* inhibitions and helped me to squelch any that I was hanging onto," in kissing and touching her friends' bodies. But sexual polymorphousness scared her. "I am so confused with my life," she wrote in the book that she was now calling not "diary," but "journal." "Where am I? In between a girl and a boy, in between sane and insane."[35]

In an atmosphere of endless potential, of unprecedented choices, and in constant, gyrating motion, there lurked endless possibility for bad decisions and even fatal risks. As American girls had been brought up to do, Pamela never really questioned her dedication to heterosexuality. But that choice, conservative in some particulars, was by no means a secure bet. When she relinquished her much prized virginity, the experience was, to say the least, disappointing, although she continued to pine for the man she would describe, much later, as an "exquisite moron." Even in the throes of her infatuation, crossing the final heterosexual frontier led her to a bitter and remarkably clear-headed evaluation of what she and her girlfriends were doing, of what she saw around her:

> So much heroin, so much diseases, scum, filth, crabs, clap, needles, fucking, boys not caring, methedrine, people existing only for their penises and needles. . . . God must be trembling and nervous waiting, watching us, wondering if we're going to stumble into something inescapable. . . . Why have we found it so urgent lately to parade our bodies in front of ogling spectators?[36]

Hesitating as she looked around at such rugged terrain, Pamela Miller soon plunged ahead, and embarked on an improbable search for Mr. Right. If rock 'n' roll musicians seem almost ludicrously unpromising candidates for that job, they were, after all, the men that a girl who gave her life to the music was likely to encounter. As Jenni Dean, a New York City musician/groupie, told *Rolling Stone*, she filled her life with musicians "because my life is music. . . . Musicians are my contemporaries, for one thing. . . . They're creative, artistic young people—and that's my trip. If I were in college and a premed student, I'd probably be after the hottest young intern in the school."[37]

Unlike interns, rock musicians also made their living singing about love and sex, in terms that ranged from the gently romantic to the brutally exploitative. In the sexist world the rock 'n' roll people fashioned for themselves, simply getting an important man's permanent attention was supposed to be worth whatever pain a girl had to endure. American teenage girls like Pamela had been taught to seek their own value in attractiveness to men, and to see catching a prime husband as proof of their own spiritual and material worth. For Pamela and other groupies, finding a "Prince Charming" to sweep them off their feet, carry them away, marry them, was the nearest thing to a heroic quest. Male heroes gone to battle could wield wit and skill and strength as their chief assets. It hardly mattered, from a mythic point of view, whether the weapon of choice was sword, six-gun, or guitar. In Pamela's world, the men who made big money making music held power. *Very* few women, no matter how talented, broke into the business of rock 'n' roll, and almost none made it to the top. Pamela and the other female Argonauts of the Sunset Strip lacked both the opportunity to play music professionally and the money success could bring. For them, the armaments at hand were sex and service.

In one sense, Pamela hunted for a rocking Prince Charming like a general going to war. She sought and engaged a variety of intimate adversaries in lesser skirmishes, but saved up her firepower for bigger game, for superstars in major bands. She branched out, after a time, following a hip boutique owner to London, falling for an ambitious young actor, but each of these relationships, narrated in retrospect, took on martial cadences. As one sexual moment piled up on the next, one moment of heat and coupling and climax gave way to another, and each heady beginning pressed on to its crises and consequences, her most extended missions exhibited all the doggedness and tedium of long marches.

Military commanders name their battles for landmarks, for rivers or towns, churches or courthouses. Pamela met the beloved enemy not in forest and field, but in a dizzying, shifting array of hotel rooms and limousines, nightclubs and arenas, bungalows and apartments, passed through, left behind. She mapped her landscape not by sight or by place, but by something much more memorable, pervasive, significant: by sound. Rock 'n' roll songs were the compass by which she steered her desirable and desiring body on its crazy course through the California night and the more diffuse terrain Peter Townshend called "teenage wasteland," toward the goal of happily-ever-after marriage. Looking back to write, she divided her memoir into nine chapters, each marking a major romantic campaign, with snippets of song or album titles related to the particular object of conquest. The chapter devoted to her affair with Jimmy Page, who invented heavy metal guitar with the fabled Led Zeppelin, she called "Every Inch of My Love," a phrase from Zeppelin's first hit, "Whole Lotta Love." She related her escapades with the Rolling Stones' Mick Jagger, likewise, in a chapter titled "It's a Gas Gas Gas," a quote from the Stones' "Jumping Jack Flash."

Her journey was, to say the least, picaresque. And as we saw, in the case of Susan Magoffin, picaresque travels in suspect terrain can wander into trouble. Like Susan, Pamela believed in romantic love and put her faith in happy marriage. Unlike Susan, Pamela plied her risky course without the lodestone of husband or family fortune, or even respectability. Where Susan took pains to remain a true woman, an embodiment of purity, Pamela was at least as determined to throw off the yoke of sexual restraint. She claimed her body and its urges as not a burden, but a reservoir of pleasure. And yet, as a girl, she had to justify the search for sensation as a noble crusade for true love. The men she met relished her brazenness, but most, ultimately, expected subservience. Love and sex, fortune and fame, quest and war, brassy assertiveness and womanly submission, were volatile ingredients in an unstable social brew.

No wonder things got a little mixed up. At the very moment she was closest to becoming a performer in her own right, recording the album with the GTOs, she worried that she might be missing her chance at finding her guy: "I knew my Prince Charming was trotting around out there somewhere on a white charger, wondering where the fuck I was."[38] One relationship after another ended in heartbreak, and Pamela spun into weepy victimhood, and then off into another sexual encounter overburdened with expectations. Some vestige of moral misgiving made her want to believe that she only went to bed with men she fell in love with, so she convinced herself that she was in love with each of her partners. Along the way, she strayed into trysts that were, she knew, merely for the moment—a mad encounter with Jim Morrison, backdoor tangles with the ultimately unattainable Jagger, cross-dressing hijinks with Keith Moon, the tortured drummer for the Who. As she staged these sexual guerrilla raids, she put herself on more equal footing with her partners. Nothing in her upbringing had prepared her for so much freedom, and much as she wallowed and rollicked, seizing sexual power was, well, scary.

The perpetual risk of venereal and other infectious diseases made it scarier still. Rock 'n' roll musicians, transient, drug-taking, and sexually hyperactive, were remarkably efficient disease vectors, as were groupies.

When her steady boyfriend of the moment accused her of giving him "an intimate infection," Pamela confessed to having had sex with a rock star passing through, although she refrained from mentioning that she had gone to a doctor for "just in case" shots.[39] Not surprisingly, it was hard for her to establish the trust that lasting intimacy required.

The rock world became even more frightening as more and more people used more and harder drugs. Heavy drinking was commonplace, as were marijuana, hashish, and various forms of hallucinogens. As feminist writer and rock critic Ellen Willis and others have pointed out, seeing the world from a radically stoned perspective did, in fact, open up some new ways of thinking, provoking a questioning of the status quo that was not without value.[40] But the mind-altering gumbo also created problems aplenty for the users. To make matters worse, cocaine and heroin were becoming increasingly common. What had first appeared as recreation, or as an attempt to shed inhibitions, or as seeking after cosmic enlightenment, or as a temporary vacation from dull or difficult reality, all too often mutated into addiction. Pamela did her share of getting high, but terrified of needles, she stopped short of shooting up. Sooner or later, she found herself mourning many friends, including several of the GTOs, who died of drug overdoses.

Like those around her, Pamela used drugs to try to blot out emotional pain. She had plenty of reason to hurt—her parents' financial straits, her own economic difficulties, and not least, her ever-dramatic man problems. When the London boutique owner, a man who said he didn't "feel like a man when he couldn't pick up chicks," finally kicked her out, she crashed with a girlfriend across town, "rolling hash joints, smoking opium, and whimpering into my vodka."[41]

She poured her self-pity onto the pages of her diary: "My soul is devastated, it's like the emptiness of a city when a bomb has blown it to smithereens. The closest thing to Hell I've ever felt. . . . At times I thought my search was finally over. . . . Unless an affair is for eternity, it will always end in heartbreak." The older, wiser, memoirist Pamela reflected on her younger diarist self with wry frankness: "I was so stoned I couldn't see."[42]

And after all, she did want to see. As much as the late 1960s and early 1970s were years of intoxication and hedonism, that time was also an era of spiritual questing. On the individual level, social change was multiple and confusing, sometimes headlong, sometimes hesitant. People who obliterated their senses with dope one day might spend the next forty-eight hours fasting or meditating, or cleaning house, or baking bread, or going to work at the phone company. Even as she chased her rock quarries from one hotel or concert venue to another, sometimes across continents or even oceans, Pamela also pursued enlightenment. Without irony, she pressed toward nothingness and self-awareness, serenity and breakthrough. Brought up in a good Christian home, descended from a fire-eating Kentucky preacher grandfather, she knew Jesus early, and maintained the connection. Beyond doubt, rock 'n' roll took her to places others attain through organized religion, but Pamela, as Californians had from the state's early days, sought many forms of worship.[43] Along her meandering course, she looked for spiritual truth in hallucinogens, vegetarianism, the I Ching, a Japanese church called Jo Rei, yoga, the teachings of Krishnamurti, and even Ehretism, a purifying, "mucusless" diet consisting entirely of raw fruits and vegetables, reinforced by regular enemas. Withal, boyfriends acted as her most powerful and proximate gurus. Because, above all, Pamela wanted to please men.

In the aspiring actor Don Johnson (later to achieve stardom in the hit television series *Miami Vice*), Pamela found the emotional, sexual, and spiritual connections she was seeking, in a stunningly conventional relationship based on his dominance, her submission. Johnson was a hard man to please, but she was more than willing to let him make all the rules, and enforce them. "Donnie told me he loved me, I told him I loved him too, and after the big announcement had been made, he started the creative process of molding me to meet his specifications. . . . I wanted to be what he wanted me to be: perfect," she recalled. She and Johnson moved in together, struggled financially, fought and made up. But the terms were clear: Don was the artist, the dispenser of wisdom and orders. Pamela was the housewife, the acolyte, the provider of comfort. "Donnie's creative opinion reigned supreme . . . and that's the way I wanted it. . . . My creativity was spent adoring him."[44]

Economically dependent, and accustomed as she was to believing that men ought to be in charge, Pamela was willing, even eager, to curtail her scene-seeking and put up with her boyfriend's almost constant criticism. "He had me in a swirling state of turmoil at all times, trying to mend my magnified flaws," she wrote, and she thought he was "absolutely right" to heap disapproval on her. Pamela kept house, cooked and cleaned, worked on her hang-ups, and tried to earn a little cash. They had great sex and long talks about their struggles toward personal growth. But as so often happened to couples of the time and place, they ran out of money and she found out that he'd been cheating on her. The connection was broken. She fled to Wyoming "to meditate and eat a lot of home-grown vegetables . . . [and] escape my obsessive, ulcerous ache for monogamy."[45]

Pamela Des Barres's Wyoming bore little resemblance to the country marked off by the Union Pacific Railroad or by Grace Raymond Hebard. The ranch Pamela visited was instead an outpost of a counterculture that knew no regional bounds. Escaping the heartbreak of Los Angeles, she found a little serenity with hippie farmers who ate barley stews and alfalfa sprouts and read *Siddhartha*. The geographical distance from California, paradoxically, made it possible for her to do precisely the things that thousands of people much closer to her home were doing. At the same time, out in Wyoming, she was on her own. Wary of pompous pronouncements, Pamela did not portray her trip as a turning point in her spiritual journey, but clearly, getting away helped her move toward a laudable goal. It was not long before she began to gather the resources to "scrape up a kind of sideways self-acceptance." When she returned she looked, for the first time, for a place to live all by herself.[46]

Back in L.A., she pursued her acting career and began, once again, the frantic search for somebody to love. Things were not the same. The vibrant social world she'd helped to invent had, by 1974, begun to decay. Drugs killed one friend after another. She continued to haunt the clubs, to spend nights with stars falling deeper and deeper into dope, but she had begun to feel like "a floundering, faded Jezebel." Faced with younger and younger "rock and roll girls" who told her that, at twenty-five, she was "over the hill," she determined to give up the life. Feeling that she wasn't getting any younger, "looking for Mr. Right became a full-time occupation," she remembered. Still, this was Pamela Miller, one-time GTO. Her search, however desperate, was not exactly self-effacing. She pursued Prince Charming, in part, by appearing onstage at the Whisky, sporting a black push-up bra, garter belt, and black-seamed stockings.[47]

Perhaps not surprisingly, Pamela's husband-hunting strategy netted the kind of man most likely to look for a wife who wore her underwear on the outside. Michael Des Barres was a titled member of the British nobility. He was also a glitter-rock singer with a cadaverous face, terrible personal hygiene, and a peerless appetite for sex and drugs. Her mother was appalled—"You're not serious about this one, are you?" she implored, and with good reason. Michael Des Barres was a singer with a second-rate band, an emaciated, walking cauldron of drug problems, venereal disease, and family dysfunction who lived, as Pamela herself so often did, from night to night, smoking and drinking and dropping and snorting, orgasm by orgasm. Michael's battle with alcohol and cocaine would, in time, turn into full-fledged war. He was, in short, not most people's idea of a trophy. But he was also, evidently, an intelligent, funny man, a talented actor, and a person who, in Pamela's term, "was the first man who let me be me; in fact, he let me *become* me."[48] After so many relationships in which men held all the power, Pamela had finally met someone who was willing to take her on her own terms. When she married him, she'd have to do the same.

And now we may ask: All that risk, all that work, all that dashing from here to there, all that ingenuity and optimism and resourcefulness, just to take, in the end, the walk down the aisle? All that angst and effort in the name of freedom, just to get married? Was there nothing new under the sun? For this, the tree of sexual liberty had been so liberally drenched in the blood of patriots?

Yes—and no. Pamela and Michael married, had a son, struggled together to make a living in show business. Michael abandoned music for acting in television, and sometimes in the movies. Pamela's own acting career never took hold, and she slid more and more into the life of a hip Hollywood housewife—cooking gourmet meals, working out with Jane Fonda, continuing her spiritual search at the church of the Science of the Mind, in sunrise meditations, in psychotherapy, and with a Las Vegas psychic who led Pamela through her past lives. Michael owned up to the hell of his addictions and became a stalwart in Alcoholics Anonymous; Pamela finally admitted to being "co-dependent." They found parenthood far more engrossing and difficult than they had anticipated, as parents will.

And after thirteen years, their marriage fell apart. They divorced and, eventually, fell in love with other people. In many regards, it was an ordinary story of the last decades of the American century. The facts of the matter would seem to suggest that the counterculture had left intact the frame of women's lives—marriage, motherhood—and had not produced much more than problems: weakening of family ties, spiritual dissatisfaction, a raft of addictions and depressions nearly too demoralizing to contemplate.[49]

But American women had traveled many miles between the time Pamela's mother accompanied her husband to Los Angeles, and the time the daughter first ventured onto the Sunset Strip, and the moment Pamela began to take stock of her life. The diaries and journals, the letters, souvenirs, poems, and scrapbooks, lay fallow for years as Pamela struggled to preserve her marriage, raise her troubled son, keep her looks.

Meanwhile, the world changed around her. The women's movement had already begun to transform lives by the millions. Pamela refrained from joining feminist organizations and disparaged "hard-bitten gals determined to wear the slacks and hold the reins." Still she held, after her fashion, that "I've always considered myself a freewheeling feminist, a lover of men and a champion of chicks."[50]

Whatever her reservations, the movement provided the catalyst that changed her life. "I started a writing course at Everywoman's Village, a lib-type ladies' school in the Valley that specialized in yanking out artistic female expression." She wrote a little essay about seeing the Rolling Stones in 1965, and the instructor "encouraged me to continue with my story, adding that she enjoyed my 'voice.' I didn't even know I had a voice."[51] When, at last, she sat down to try to make sense of it all on paper, she was moving into uncharted territory. She had never made money writing, never tried to do so. To reveal, at the hysterical height of the just-say-no Reagan era, the details of her sex, drugs, and rock 'n' roll life was an act of bravery bordering on insanity. Amazingly, perhaps, her mother and Michael encouraged her in the project. Ultimately she produced, and sold, *I'm with the Band,* a funny, frank, perceptive memoir, written in a voice that recalled Kay Thompson's Eloise and Anita Loos's Lorelei Lee, wry ingenues on the make, wreaking havoc.

I'm with the Band marked Pamela Des Barres's transformation from failed actress and financial dependent to professional writer. Before long she was doing magazine articles, working on a novel, even developing a rock 'n' roll cookbook. No longer dependent on someone else's wages, she had found, at last, her vocation. And now, the world offered women the latitude to pursue their professional aspirations, on their own.

Pamela hit the road—or rather, the air—promoting her book from coast to coast, rediscovering the drive, chutzpah, and focus she'd once lavished on the likes of Jimmy Page and Don Johnson, qualities she seemed to have lost track of since her groupie days. Life, in some regards, went on as before. She still had a household, the demands of motherhood, and a complicated emotional life; now she also had obligations in the workaday world. Some women called it "the double day." Not many called it "having it all."

But Pamela was no grim, dress-for-success careerist. She insisted, after all, that her journeys, and those of her often hapless friends, had opened new territory. If her metaphysical preoccupations appear, to non-Californians, fairly wacky, her persistence in pursuing them bespoke sincerity. The ways of soul-seeking are never transparent to persons on different paths. And of the unholy countercultural trinity of sex, drugs, and rock 'n' roll, she unflinchingly faced the costs of the second and insisted on the merits of the first and the last.

Sex: Pamela Des Barres rejected the idea that women had to repress the desires of their bodies and insisted on her right, as a woman, to the power and pleasure of her sexuality. If the men she slept with sometimes treated her as a sex toy, she turned the tables by regarding them as conquests. Hobbled by the need to preserve some shred of feminine respectability, she justified her search for ecstasy by insisting that what she really wanted was romance, and surrender. In the end, she insisted on at least the right to look for both ecstasy and intimacy. She demanded the most fundamental prerequisite of the right to move freely: the power of the body.

At least as importantly, Pamela, together with the millions of women who carried on sexual relationships outside of marriage, learned, sometimes at high cost, that sex did not define the boundaries of human connection. The GTOs had insisted that "girls" could be together any number of ways—openly, outrageously, organically, and assuredly, orgasmically. And they could be with men in a variety of ways too: as friends, lovers, mentors, disciples, adversaries—any combination of things. Doubtless such complex connections generated plenty of disappointment, despair, and damage along the way, but there were blessings too.

Pamela valued the idea that she could turn sexual relationships into lifelong friendships. She was proud of the notion that she and Michael became close friends with her former boyfriend, Don Johnson, and with the woman who had come between Pamela and Don, the actress Melanie Griffith. She was just as proud that for all the pain of the marriage's breakup, she and Michael insisted on nurturing friendship and respect for one another. She doubtless shaded the truth when she gushed that "I always retained a stunning friendship with most of my *amores*," but she undeniably believed in that most lasting positive component of the sexual revolution: the friendship revolution, the possibility that men and women could be, to each other, not simply mysteries or lovers, but also friends. That hope, indeed, "made me feel like life was worth living. All the hours of lunacy and love had actually amounted to something."[52] California girls like Pamela Miller had been pioneers and pathbreakers in this revolution, and all over the nation, human relations had become, for better and worse, more complicated and more fluid.

And what of rock 'n' roll? "The right music can still find a place inside me that has never been opened, lifting the top off an unborn feeling, creating a new space to be filled up with more living," she wrote.[53]

Art transforms reality; for a generation of American women and men, rock 'n' roll was transformative art at its most pervasive. Today rock music haunts our mundane byways, echoes through supermarkets and shopping malls, signifies "hold the phone." Sounds that began their journeys in dark, smoky rooms in American towns and cities have become disembodied, infinitely reproducible, weightless, omnipresent. For many who once followed the counterculture's errant and exciting paths, the songs are all that remain of the dream of breaking on through to something larger, something more meaningful, than the circuit of getting and spending.

The songs, commodified from the first, do have some persistent power. The voices ring out of car radios across the land, sexy and funny, desperate and full of desire—Mick Jagger looking for a honky-tonk woman; Janis Joplin smashing her own heart; Bob Dylan reciting his nightmare vision of Highway 61; Grace Slick howling for somebody to love. Millions of women like Pamela Des Barres make a living, make a life, drive home from their demanding jobs, bags of groceries in the back of the car, dry cleaning to pick up, maybe a child waiting at the day care center. They chauffeur the carpools, deliver the kids and the goods and the next necessity, clog the roads, contour the landscape with their working, moving, thinking, and wanting. As workers and homemakers, they reconfigure the countryside with their movements, mile after mile of pavement uncoiling before them, to a rock 'n' roll beat.

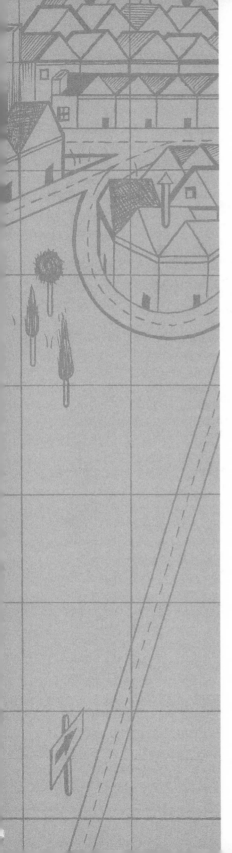

CHAPTER 8

THEY PAVED PARADISE

I N THE BEGINNING, THERE WERE NO WORDS. The land and the creatures needed no names, no directions, no verbal cues. When humans came to live, perhaps thirty thousand years ago, the words came with them. But only in the last half millennium did Europeans arrive to pronounce that what had once been known by other names would be designated, thereafter, a remote part of a New World, first a North, then, at length, a West. The West was a protean, transient entity, first myth, then wish, then a series of episodes and encounters; a spiderwork of trails into and through terrain not yet western; a system of steel rails and gridded tracts that transformed intention and expectation and transaction into landscape, culture, continuity.

In the second half of the nineteenth century, the West was born as a region, a jostling collection of locales, states, subregions. Even then, its diverse inhabitants insisted on their distinctive domains and identities. And before very long, the money, the power, and the people that had created it in the first place began to penetrate, and fragment, and transform that regional order. By the year 2000, many places in what had once been unmistakably "western" locales were in substance indistinguishable from similar areas scattered not only around the country, but around the world—suburb and shopping mall, city strip and airport, office building and factory floor marked a new geography of mobile capital that transcended borders. The grid had morphed into flow and flux, and it circled the globe.

As we have seen, women preceded, created, contested, eluded, and survived the American West. They participated in, and challenged, every process involved in the making and unmaking of the West. From the indigenous women who encountered European adventurers, to the housewives and workers who span contemporary western cities, their movements have been crucial to making the landscape what it is.

Consider Highlands Ranch, a "planned community" at the heart of Douglas County, Colorado, the fastest-growing county in the United States at the end of the second millennium.[1]

Not so long ago, this was high golden prairie. The first homesteaders filed a claim in 1867, and by the turn of the twentieth century myriad small claims had been consolidated into the John W. Springer Cross Country Horse and Cattle Ranch, a spread covering more than 20,000 acres. The ranch would change hands several times, becoming host to the Arapahoe Hunt Club, a company of prosperous men who took their pleasure in riding to the hounds, shooting coyotes from horseback. By 1976, the property known since 1937 as Highlands Ranch, encompassing some 22,000 acres of rolling plains, was bought by Denver oilman Marvin Davis, who three years later sold out to the Mission Viejo Company, a California land development concern.[2]

As recently as 1988, antelope grazed in the breaking heart of Highlands Ranch. In the dead of winter, they picked their way down to the creek, leaving tracks in the endless snow-blanketed swales. Come spring, prairie dogs and pocket gophers peeked up from their burrow villages. As summer baked on, wild sunflowers sprang riotous from the cracking red-brown ground.

Naturally, to live there, you had to have a car. In those days, you had to leave the county to go to the grocery store. It wasn't all that far—just across County Line Road, into Arapahoe County and the shopping centers anchored by Safeway and King Sooper, where you could buy groceries and get a haircut. It was farther to a day care center, farther still to a doctor. When I try to fathom what it might have been like for a young mother who didn't drive, or for a teenager not yet old enough for a license, I feel an iron fist closing in my chest.

For a brief time, the antelope and the bulldozers lived side by side. But change was well under way. At the behest of Mission Viejo, and later of a dozen construction companies ("homebuilders"), of Denver realtors scrambling for sales and banks ready to extend loans, and of families on the move looking for a pleasant, "affordable" place to live, the big machines scraped flat more and more of the Colorado prairie. Huge rotating blades tore through the sunflowers and the wild grasses. Cement mixers came, pouring the roads: Ventura Boulevard, Bermuda Run Circle. Lumber trucks dropped off thousands of board feet of pine and oak, great heaping piles of bricks. Crews of carpenters and plumbers and electricians made the air ring with their screaming machines. Families toured split-level, two-story, and ranch-style "model homes" in a variety of mid-to-high price ranges. They picked out the shape of the house and the location of the land that they and the bank would buy, much as they would have selected a shirt in a mail-order catalogue.

The prairie grew up in cul-de-sacs and For Sale signs. As the snow melted, the curving concrete streets ran red with mud. Moving vans pulled up in front of houses, disgorging shrouded furniture, brown boxes full of paper-wrapped dishes, rakes and lawnmowers bespeaking the expectation that the sucking mud would in time be coaxed into producing plants again. Dazed, uncertain, the newly arrived citizens of Highlands Ranch took possession of their domain as howling spring winds blew swirling dust under door sills and window sashes. The housewives hung sheets over the vaulting windows, and yet again vacuumed their mauve and oatmeal carpets, scrubbed their Formica counters, and swept their vinyl floors. They found solace in the sound of sod trucks rumbling up the streets. Every heavy load of rolled dirt and short grass promised deliverance from grainy red stuff that seeped into every corner and cranny. Springtime in the Rockies.

Optimistic suburbanites poured into Highlands Ranch to practice reverse sodbusting. Again, per agreement between the developers and the homeowners, came crews of workers to unroll the strips of sod in front yards, to walk heavy rollers over the grass and finish the effect by placing, on alternate sides of each front walk, a single, struggling, spindly tree. What families did with their barren back yards was, within the limits of certain restrictive covenants, their own business. To prospective buyers cruising the instant neighborhoods from the curbside vantage point, wishfully imagining that this might, after all, be the place where they could settle down, hold jobs, raise kids, Highlands Ranch raised the street front of a hometown.

The West is pocked with ghost towns that testify to the difficulties of sticking in a tough country, of turning prairie and plain and mountain fastness into abiding home. In many places, the antelope have proven more tenacious than the people. Not so at Highlands Ranch. The first master plan was approved in 1979, and the first residents came to live there in 1981. The population had grown to 70,923 by 2001. Eventually, some 90,000 people are expected to live there, in 36,700 houses. The Highlands Ranch project kicked into high gear a development boom that transformed the Colorado Front Range, from Fort Collins to Colorado Springs. What was once rangeland is fast being swallowed up by suburbs and edge cities, spreading out along I-25 southward and northward from Denver, creeping up into the mountains to the west and slouching out over the plains to the east, replete with glass-and-steel office buildings, supermarkets, shops, strips, megamalls, acres of parking lots, more and more miles of rolling freeway.[3]

I was a housewife in Highlands Ranch. My husband, two-year-old son, and I moved there in the winter of 1988, when the population was listed at 7,000. We unloaded the contents of a moving van into a barely finished split-level on a winding dead-end street lined with houses in various stages of completion. It was the first house we'd ever owned. We had a sweeping view of the Front Range through cathedral ceiling–high windows, a sloping muddy lot, a concrete slab and bare dirt basement that made us wonder about radon gas.

As a housewife, I lived according to certain rhythms, followed particular circuits, which differed in substance and style from those of the majority of adults living in Highlands Ranch—the people who worked full time, bringing home the wages that paid the house note, the car payments, the monthly credit card bills, the grocery tab. I was often at home when fully employed men and women and school-age children were gone. My husband was off to his job with Chevron Oil, sitting at a desk somewhere in the Denver Tech Center, in a mirrored high-rise that gleamed like a state trooper's sunglasses. Even my little boy vacated the premises during the day, heading off to child care, while I remained home in front of a computer screen, trying to coax a dissertation to become a book. It was mighty lonesome, and also mighty quiet. Virginia Woolf would have said I had the requisites for creativity: financial security, a place to write, time enough. And there was that mountain view.

As the winter wore on, other families moved in. My doorbell began to ring during the day. The people who came to my door were the other daytime inhabitants of the neighborhood, corporate wives like me, mostly, unemployed or underemployed. They liked to drop in for coffee. They went to aerobic classes at the recreation center, traded baby-sitting, hosted Tupperware parties. They joined churches and civic groups, softball teams. I slipped, half willing, into their routine.

Some of the women planned to "stay home" at least until their children went off to school, perhaps indefinitely. They didn't mean they wouldn't leave the house; they meant they weren't going to look for jobs. The salaries they could earn as secretaries or dental technicians would barely cover the cost of child care, and given the caprices of husbands' corporate transfers, they might have to quit when they'd hardly gotten started. Better, in the meantime, to have time with the kids, time to devote to home and community.

Still, their deal seemed a bad bargain to me. I wondered why they were so determined to embrace a segregated way of life, drifting in and out of their houses in the spectral hours between 8 A.M. and 5 P.M., going to the supermarket and the drug store, to and from schools. We all had a furtive knowledge of our own transience, knew that we were only a transfer or a divorce away from the arrival of the next moving van, the plunge again into the unknown.

But we also clung to the hope that we'd found security and permanence. We pretended Highlands Ranch was the place where our children would grow up, where we'd make lifelong friendships. We planted lawns and more sapling trees.

We weren't just crazy. We were heroes of an outmoded but still powerful dream. Women who "stay home" do not do so literally: the phrase is symbolic, expressing deep longing for a settled, comforting way of life embodied in the figure of a mother always waiting, at home, to feed, nurture, and sustain, to create a haven in a heartless world.[4] In the "master planned hometown" of Highlands Ranch, as in suburban developments across America, making a home means creating a landscape of privacy, ruthlessly separated from the corridors and clusters of commerce and industry. The development plan for Highlands Ranch calls for a mere nine percent of land to be devoted to business or commercial use. The rest is designated for housing, parks, schools, and recreational facilities, including an 8,200-acre parcel designated as the Wildcat Mountain Reserve.[5]

The passion for privacy extends even to the ways the work that goes on in households is visible to, or part of, the neighborhood streetscape. When we lived there, covenants for our neighborhood mandated that all garage doors be closed, that cars be parked in driveways and not on the curb. Clotheslines were prohibited. Keeping house in Highlands Ranch might require everything from doing laundry to driving a car, but to all appearances, such work was to remain invisible. The ideal of domestic tranquillity was not merely desirable: it was actionable.

Paradoxically, the dream of permanence, of domestic containment, requires perpetual movement. In the nearly twenty years of its existence, Highlands Ranch has seen thousands of residents come and go, a fortunate thing indeed for those who stake their life savings on or make their livelihoods from the market in housing. Those who stay to build community, the "stickers," have so fierce a devotion to the ideal of the self-enclosed bedroom community that they rise up and organize at any threat that their enclave might be breached. They regard the roads that connect one neighborhood to another with a measure of suspicion. From the early days, neighborhood associations have opposed developers' efforts to extend major streets that turn cul-de-sacs into through-routes or bring retail developments too close to neighborhoods, or erect government facilities that attract patrons who are not, in the narrowest sense, neighbors. In 1988, the Highlands Ranch post office was in the back of a video store. When, two years later, the Mission Viejo Company presented a plan for a permanent structure large enough to manage anticipated mail traffic, residents picketed both the site and the company's offices.[6]

Even the public sector is private. Highlands Ranch has yet to incorporate as a municipality, to become, legitimately, a town. For police protection, street maintenance, public street snow removal, traffic signal maintenance, and some park management, the development depends on Douglas County. Other government functions—fire protection, street landscaping, water and wastewater services, for example—are managed by special districts. The Mission Viejo Company (a subsidiary of Philip Morris) ran the burgeoning development like a colony, from 1981 until it sold out to J. F. Shea Company, builder of Hoover Dam and contractor on the Golden Gate Bridge, in 1997.[7] Shea continues to operate much in the manner of its predecessor, though both companies have had to deal with homeowners' attempts to exert control over growth and to foster community spirit. In an effort to enforce architectural covenants, keep commercial development to a minimum, and address homeowners' concerns, Mission Viejo formed the Highlands Ranch Community Association in 1980.

The HRCA avows a vision of community that celebrates the myth of the West as a grand, unspoiled, exceptional, and wild place. Developers' brochures foreground panoramic mountain views, women and children in cowboy hats, people riding horseback through tall-grass prairie, joggers and bicyclists rolling along trails through sweeping green meadows, and Indian paintbrush, red spikes thrusting skyward.[8] The master plan included greenbelt areas behind rows of homes, as well as larger parks. In 1998 the HRCA and Mission Viejo agreed to set aside 7,000 acres of the Wildcat Mountain Reserve as a refuge for elk, mountain lions, golden eagles, red-tailed hawks, and other wildlife (including the grazing antelope and coyotes once so despised by the members of the Arapahoe Hunt Club), as well as the eight hundred head of cattle already grazing the area. The other 1,200 acres of the reserve were to be open to recreational development.[9]

Maintaining the myth that the master-planned hometown is also, in some sense, archetypal western wilderness has, perhaps inevitably, presented problems.[10] Some homeowners, far from revering the greenbelts, have seen fit to "improve" the areas by putting in horseshoe pits and dog runs, or else use them as personal dumping grounds. Collectively, too, Highlands Ranch managers and residents soon began to cast speculative eyes on land set aside for the wild. By 1996 the HRCA and Mission Viejo were considering commercial development plans for the recreational area in the Wildcat Reserve, including proposals for campgrounds, cemeteries, an in-line skating rink, and even a water park.[11]

In theory, open space was a wonderful thing, but in practice, for householders seeking safe domestic harbor, there were drawbacks to living cheek-by-claw with nature. Where prairie, canyon, and mountain butted up against the neighborhoods, cats and dogs fell prey to coyotes, hawks, eagles, even here and there a mountain lion or bear. As late as 1997, Marti Woo, a Highlands Ranch woman out mowing her lawn, thought she heard her neighbors' automatic sprinklers go on unexpectedly, and turned to find herself face-to-fang with a rattlesnake, coiled and ready to strike. Douglas County deputies were summoned, and they solved the problem in the usual fashion (decapitation by shovel), presenting the woman with the snake's body and rattles, to be preserved in the manner of the Old West (Mrs. Woo "thought they might make a hatband out of it").[12]

Highlands Ranchers have always faced a dilemma. If they hold tight to the idea of a bedroom community nestled in the wild and splendid West, Highlands Ranch will be unable to develop the commercial tax base that would finance fully autonomous self-government. If they promote commercial development, their vision of community has to change.[13] In the meantime, preserving the landscape of privacy and majesty means that nearly everyone in Highlands Ranch has to leave home, by car, on a daily basis. Wage-earners and students commute, and "stay-at-home" moms embark on the daily rounds that make houses built on speculation into those venerated objects of promotional literature: homes. Women whose families are their vocation are the coveted clients of a vast array of retail businesses, not to mention the volunteer labor force that staffs institutions from youth sports organizations to hospitals and public schools and, in Highlands Ranch, government. If in the past forty years housewives have moved into a cultural twilight zone, they remain essential to the welfare of both public and private life in the United States, navigating landscapes that have been transformed to meet women consumers' needs and desires. As politicians have learned at their peril, the figure of the soccer mom in the minivan is not a joke. She is an engine of social, economic, political, and indeed geographical change.[14]

And of course, most soccer moms have more than one job. As we move

into the twenty-first century, most adult American women work for pay
as well as laboring at home. Most American children, even the ones under six months old, have a mother whose domestic and public responsibilities require her presence in any number of places in the course of a
working day. American women, charged with the obligation to do more
things and be more places in the same amount of time, become willing,
even demanding, partners in the postmodern reinvention of time and
space.[15]

In the stretched-out landscapes of contemporary metropolitan America, women drivers provide the alternative to mass transit of people and
goods. Imagine the Highlands Ranch worker-housewife, making her
daily rounds. On the way to work, she delivers the children to school
and day care. Lunch hour may find her again in the car, shopping or
taking a child to a doctor or dentist appointment. On the way home,
she attempts to link errands—grocery store, mall—and passenger pick-
ups and drop-offs—music lessons, sports practices—in a "trip chain."
Add a cellular phone to the toolkit, and she manages to work even more
stops into a given trip chain. To make separate sorties to accomplish
each task would be simply impossible; it is more implausible still to imagine her trying to get everything done by taking mass transit. And meanwhile, the woman driver manages changing traffic patterns caused by
construction, congestion (more and more people like her, out there on
the road), contingency.

The landscape responds, as thoroughfares like the prosaically named
County Line Road, marking the border between Douglas and Arapahoe
counties, become development corridors. Formerly quiet rural byways,
laid out along the Jeffersonian grid, sprout the franchise businesses that
look, from one angle, like the excrescence of a convenience- and amenity-
mad culture, and from another angle, like efficient provisioning stations
for women stretched too thin across time and space. As one commercial
real estate broker explained the growth spree on County Line Road,
"There are lots of people in Highlands Ranch. They have kids, cars, and
they need stuff."[16]

Highlands Ranch homeowners have fought developers' attempts to
bring strip malls within their borders. But Highlands Ranch women venture over into strip mall territory every day, taking advantage of the prox-
imity of supermarket and bank, dry cleaner and health club, Starbuck's
and Boston Market and McDonald's. Hard by Highlands Ranch, on 115
acres of unincorporated Douglas County land, the gigantic, lavish Park
Meadows Mall, which opened in 1996, trumpets itself as "Colorado's

Only Retail Resort." Park Meadows encompasses 1.6 million square feet of space featuring 130 retailers and offering more than 8,000 parking spaces. In an attempt to capitalize on the mystique of Colorado's mountain setting, Park Meadows is designed to look like a Rocky Mountain ski lodge, with soaring timbered ceilings, landscaping featuring boulders and a waterfall, and a limestone and granite fireplace big enough for a car to drive through.[17] Park Meadows shows what $164 million can do, put to the use of reconciling affluent, mobile women consumers' desires and fantasies with the demands on their time and travel.

Transportation planners predicted that the construction of the mall would generate an average of 70,200 vehicle trips a day, a traffic burden that would, of course, require expansion of existing roadways and construction of new ones, including a freeway interchange on the new C-470 highway extension through Highlands Ranch. Some planners worried about the effect of all that car exhaust on air quality. Denver, after all, is the city in which air pollution has achieved sufficient notoriety to deserve its own name: The Brown Cloud. Thus many were skeptical of a Federal Highway Administration study indicating that construction of the new interchange would not lead to violations of the Clean Air Act. "It's going to be a zoo out there when the mall opens," said Colorado Department of Transportation engineer Larry McKenzie, manager of one Park Meadows construction project.[18] Arapahoe County residents, just across the road, complained that they were getting more traffic and no tax revenues from the new mall. "Arapahoe County will eat it," remarked Dave Phifer, mayor of Greenwood Village, an Arapahoe County municipality. Arapahoe County Commission chairwoman Polly Page suggested that the sales tax dollars generated by the mall ought to lead to discussions about revenue sharing between the counties.[19]

Terrible traffic notwithstanding, Park Meadows has become a magnet for upscale shoppers throughout the Rocky Mountain West. One New Mexico woman I know—a nuclear scientist, as it happens—has timed, to the minute, the drive from her house in Corrales to the parking area adjacent to Nordstrom's in Park Meadows. Yet Park Meadows surely would not have been built in the absence of residential development in Douglas County, in the absence of "lots of people with kids and cars who need stuff." Highlands Ranch was there first. Mommy didn't come to the mall; the mall came to Mommy.

But Mommy, after all, must be ready to move. If the illusion of permanence drives the daily, weekly, monthly peregrinations of suburban women, the reality is that families, more than ever, move on. In a world where business is conducted on a global scale, families move from one house to another, one city to another, even one country to another. My own family lived in Highlands Ranch a total of ten months before Chevron gave my husband the word that he would be transferred to Houston. Ten months after that, Chevron let us know, once again, that relocations were contemplated, with most transferees to be sent to Midland, Texas, or Hobbs, New Mexico. Others went to California or St. Louis, or Lagos, Nigeria, or Djakarta, Indonesia.

Making a home across an immense and shifting corporate landscape requires a positive genius for mobility, a willingness to enter endlessly into the process of domestication and to leave to the next round of occupants nearly new drapes, trees just sprouting their first leaves, gardens not yet harvested. Sacagawea would have been better at the task than Susan Magoffin. Fabiola Cabeza de Baca might have offered cooking classes at the recreation center; Grace Hebard would have lobbied to get herself elected to the HRCA Board of Directors. Jo Ann Robinson might have looked for justice, and for friendship. Pamela Des Barres would have sought out the nightlife. For most of us, how much easier, by far, to come and go in a landscape of convenience and franchised familiarity, comfortable enough, if ultimately anonymous. Preserving the privacy of home, we prepare to move on.

The last time I passed through Highlands Ranch, I managed to find my way to that house of ours, after making numerous wrong turns into neighborhoods that hadn't been there when we lived in the area, subdivisions so like the one we'd left that I was hard put to distinguish one from another. I peered between the slats of the backyard fence. Where we'd created opulent flower borders, cozy beds for asparagus and strawberries, and two great, lushly fertilized rectangles that had brought forth abundant tomatoes and beans and corn and chiles and squash, somebody in the years since had seen fit to replace our efforts with . . . sod. Our labor-intensive little Eden had given way to monoculture; only a few dispirited lilac bushes stood in the corners of the yard to testify to the fact that, once, passionate gardeners had lived there.

Nowadays, I'm told, Highlands Ranch covenants prohibit the planting of vegetable gardens, exceptions to be granted only with prior written approval from the neighborhood architectural committee. So much for Thomas Jefferson's dream of an expanding nation thriving on the labor of virtuous yeomen.[20] But why be surprised at the sod, in any event? If we had known, when we landscaped our yard, that we'd be heading out for Houston before we tasted the first stalk of asparagus from that optimistic bed, would we have bothered with all the expense and sweat, the manure shoveling and weed pulling, the time and the water and the work? How much more sensible to keep a simple expanse of green, a place to kick a soccer ball around, throw a baseball, play with a baby. As the homeowners of Highlands Ranch have hoped, their property values have risen steadily and handsomely. For the kind of people who have the money to live there these days—two-job families, mostly, hard-pressed for time—those gardens are too much.

The segregated bedroom enclave, home to a parcel of wilderness and bounded by strip malls and office parks, "retail resorts" and chain restaurants, preserves a cherished illusion of women creating a home on the range, even as those women ricochet from office to school to store to soccer field to keep the dream going, day by day. Even as they had best be ready to move on, at the call of corporate caprice. Shea Homes, recognizing the revenue possibilities of commercial development as well as the fact that some people aspire to work where they live, contemplates bringing in a big employer as tenant in a proposed "business park." Highlands Ranch, still fighting incorporation, nonetheless imagines itself in 2005 as not an edge city but an anticity, a community of 36,700 homes and well-fenced open spaces with a closely bounded "town center" intended not to replace offices or factories or Park Meadows Mall or County Line Road but, instead, to simulate a small-town main street in a community of 90,000 souls. "We're doing a full-fledged analysis of town centers in Colorado and nationwide, both big and small, to see what makes them work and what does not work," Shea Homes president Bert Selva told the *Rocky Mountain News*. "If its main street is more than two blocks long, it loses its charm."[21]

I imagine that nostalgic two-block "center," that business park, those open spaces, and those thousands of homes connected by twenty thousand roads: a dozen great boulevards and parkways leading through the development and out into the edge city, threaded with clusters of common places; dozens more arteries linking neighborhoods with necessities, thousands upon thousands of meandering, ferociously defended dead-ends. A safe, clean, pleasant place in some eyes, an apocalyptic nightmare of control and sterility in others, successor to the wide, Wild West.

Every one of those twenty thousand roads is alive with women in motion. If they bear scant resemblance to the free-spirited, emancipated western girls of lore and legend, they have something in common with tenacious and adaptable women like Sacagawea and Susan Magoffin, with women who braved the uncertainties of Reconstruction Wyoming, with Grace Hebard, Fabiola Cabeza de Baca, Jo Ann Robinson, Pamela Des Barres. The signs of their presence extend to the very air they breathe, air that has, lamentably, acquired color and texture and taste all too palpable in their wake. The fate of the earth is in their hands, and under their wheels. For better or worse, as the West becomes, again, more myth than place, this landscape is a geography of women's movements.

Love it or hate it, here—and there—it is.

Stand on a hill gazing out at the endless sprawl of Highlands Ranch, and you will conclude that the myth of renewal may be just about all we have left of the West. But maybe there is some point to believing in the possibility of a newer world, something fairer and finer. There may be no real alternative. The West was never, in any meaningful sense, untrammeled wilderness, any more than the Highlands Ranch Wildcat Mountain Reserve is virgin land. Virginity should not be the standard for respectful treatment, any more than purity guarantees wisdom. The stories of women's movements do not offer reassuring tales of innocence, but they do show us how people make places, knowledgeably, if not always wisely, and how places change, according to similarly changeable human values. We have the capacity to reflect on what we value, to account more fully for who we have been and what we have done, and to think about what we will do. With one eye on the rearview mirror, perhaps we will chart a path to a better place, farther along.

NOTES

INTRODUCTION

1. Bernard Christian Steiner, *A History of the Plantation of Menunkatuck and of the Original Town of Guilford, Connecticut, Comprising the Present Towns of Guilford and Madison, Written Largely from the Manuscripts of the Honorable Ralph Dunning Smyth* (Baltimore: Published by the Author, 1897), pp. 26–31; John W. De Forest, *History of the Indians of Connecticut from the Earliest Known Period to 1850* (1851; repr. Archon Books, 1964), pp. 162–168. The 1639 agreement of purchase, along with a map drawn by Henry Whitfield representing "the land wholly and only colonys to the Squaw Sachem" Shaumpishuh, is in the collections of the Massachusetts Historical Society; see Henry Whitfield, "Account of his lands in Guilford, Connecticut," #71.G.2b, and Henry Whitfield, "Agreement on behalf of the English planters of Menunchetuck, with the sachem squaw and the Indian inhabitants of that place for purchase of the land" (copy). I am indebted to Jack Swift for this information, and to Nicholas Graham, reference librarian at the Massachusetts Historical Society. On Native women's power and authority, see Laura F. Klein and Lillian Ackerman, eds., *Women and Power in Native North America* (Norman: University of Oklahoma Press, 1995); and Nancy Shoemaker, ed., *Negotiators of Change: Historical Perspectives on Native American Women* (New York: Routledge, 1995).

2. William Cronon, *Changes in the Land: Indians, Colonists, and the Ecology of New England* (New York: Hill and Wang, 1983), brilliantly describes the cycles of mobility of New England Indian life in the period before and during European contact and demonstrates the ways in which Indian women played crucial roles in maintaining mobile subsistence.

3. James Clifford, "Identity in Mashpee," in *The Predicament of Culture: Twentieth Century Ethnography, Literature, and Art* (Cambridge, Mass.: Harvard University Press, 1988), pp. 277–346.

4. I have offered precisely this argument in Virginia Scharff, "Mobility, Women, and the West," in *Over the Edge: Remapping the American West,* ed.

Valerie J. Matsumoto and Blake Allmendinger (Berkeley: University of California Press, 1999), pp. 160–171; and Virginia Scharff, "Lighting Out for the Territory: Women, Mobility, and Western Place," in *Power and Place in the North American West,* ed. Richard White and John M. Findlay (Seattle: University of Washington Press, 1999), pp. 287–303. On women and landscape in the West, see Annette Kolodny, *The Land before Her: Fantasy and Experience of the American Frontiers, 1630–1860* (Chapel Hill: University of North Carolina Press, 1984); Vera Norwood and Janice Monk, eds., *The Desert Is No Lady: Southwestern Landscapes in Women's Writing and Art* (Tucson: University of Arizona Press, 1997); Jane Tompkins, *West of Everything: The Inner Life of Westerns* (New York: Oxford University Press, 1992); Kerwin Lee Klein, *Frontiers of the Historical Imagination: Narrating the European Conquest of Native America, 1890–1990* (Berkeley: University of California Press, 1997); Brigitte Georgi-Findlay, *The Frontiers of Women's Writing: Women's Narratives and the Rhetoric of Western Expansion* (Tucson: University of Arizona Press, 1996); and Krista Comer, *Landscapes of the New West: Gender and Geography in Contemporary American Women's Writing* (Chapel Hill: University of North Carolina Press, 1999).

5. Karen Anderson, "Western Women: The Twentieth Century Experience," in *The Twentieth Century West: Historical Interpretations,* ed. Gerald D. Nash and Richard W. Etulain (Albuquerque: University of New Mexico Press, 1989), pp. 99–122, offered a visionary and sweeping critique of the limitations of the western history paradigm for the study of women's history.

6. Richard White, *The Middle Ground: Indians, Empires, and Republics in the Great Lakes Region, 1650–1813* (Cambridge: Cambridge University Press, 1991); Patricia Nelson Limerick, *Legacy of Conquest: The Unbroken Past of the American West* (New York: W. W. Norton, 1987); Patricia Nelson Limerick, "Turnerians All: The Dream of a Helpful History in an Intelligible World," in Limerick, *Something in the Soil: Legacies and Reckonings in the New West* (New York: W. W. Norton, 2000), pp. 141–165.

CHAPTER 1. SEEKING SACAGAWEA

The epigraph sources are, in order: "Testimony Taken on the Shoshone Indian Reservation, Wyoming, July 21, 1929, by Grace Raymond Hebard, through an Interpreter, James E. Compton, of Fort Washakie, with James McAdam," Sacajawea Notes and Manuscript—Testimony folder, Box 20, Grace Raymond Hebard Collection, Acc. 8, American Heritage Center, University of Wyoming, Laramie (hereafter cited as Hebard Papers); "Statement of Mrs. Weidemann, Elbowwoods, N.D. The daughter of hereditary Chief of Poor Woolf of the Hidatsa Indians (She speaks Gros Ventres, Sioux, and English)," February 3, 1925, Sacajawea Manuscript—Eastman Vindication folder, Box 17, Hebard Papers; "Testimony Taken on Shoshone Indian Reservation, July 22, 1929, by Grace Raymond Hebard through an Interpreter, James E. Compton, of Fort Washakie," Sacajawea Notes and Manuscript—Testimony folder, Box 20, Hebard Papers; and William Clark, cash accounts book for 1825–1828, Graff Collection, Newberry Library, Chicago, Illinois, cited in James Ronda, *Lewis and Clark among the Indians* (Lincoln: University of Nebraska Press, 1988), p. 258; and Harold

P. Howard, *Sacajawea* (Norman: University of Oklahoma Press, 1971), p. 189 (this document was discovered in 1955).

1. Rayna Green, "The Pocahontas Perplex: The Image of Indian Women in American Culture," *Massachusetts Review* 16, no. 4 (autumn 1975): 698–714; Patricia Albers, "Introduction: New Perspectives on Plains Indian Women," in *The Hidden Half: Studies of Plains Indian Women,* ed. Patricia Albers and Beatrice Medicine (Washington, D.C.: University Press of America, 1983), pp. 1–28; Alice B. Kehoe, "The Shackles of Tradition," ibid., pp. 53–75; Clara Sue Kidwell, "Indian Women as Cultural Mediators," *Ethnohistory* 39, no. 2 (spring 1992): 97; Nancy Shoemaker, "Introduction," in *Negotiators of Change: Historical Perspectives on Native American Women,* ed. Nancy Shoemaker (New York: Routledge, 1995), p. 2.

There is a growing and increasingly sophisticated literature on indigenous women. See Sylvia Van Kirk, *Many Tender Ties: Women in Fur-Trade Society, 1670–1870* (Norman: University of Oklahoma Press, 1983); Jacqueline Peterson, "Women Dreaming," in *Western Women: Their Land, Their Lives,* ed. Lillian Schlissel, Janice Monk, and Vicki L. Ruiz (Albuquerque: University of New Mexico Press, 1988); Devon Mihesuah, *Cultivating the Rosebuds: The Education of Women at the Cherokee Female Seminary, 1851–1909* (Urbana: University of Illinois Press, 1994); Tsianina Lomawaima, *They Called It Prairie Light: The Story of the Chilocco Indian School* (Lawrence: University Press of Kansas, 1994). For a useful bibliography, see Elizabeth Jameson and Susan Armitage, eds., *Writing the Range: Race, Class, and Culture in the Women's West* (Norman: University of Oklahoma Press, 1997), pp. 616–621.

2. For the most complete tracing of the importance of Sacagawea as an American myth, see Donna J. Kessler, "Sacagawea: A Uniquely American Legend" (Ph.D. diss., Emory University, 1993).

3. On these points, see Albers, "Introduction"; and Kehoe, "Shackles of Tradition."

4. For biographies of Sacagawea, see Grace Raymond Hebard, *Sacajawea* (Glendale, Calif.: Arthur H. Clark Company, 1933); Howard, *Sacajawea;* and Ella E. Clark and Margot Edmonds, *Sacagawea of the Lewis and Clark Expedition* (Berkeley: University of California Press, 1979). For a comprehensive study of representations of Sacagawea, see Kessler, "Sacagawea." Sacagawea was the subject of a best-selling epic novel by Anna Lee Waldo, *Sacajawea* (New York: Avon, 1979). For an extended treatment of the Sacagawea story from the point of view of a Shoshone woman and descendant, see Esher Burnett Horne and Sally McBeth, *Essie's Story: The Life and Legacy of a Shoshone Teacher* (Lincoln: University of Nebraska Press, 1998).

5. Thus I use "West" here to refer to the process so insightfully described by Patricia Nelson Limerick in *Legacy of Conquest: The Unbroken Past of the American West* (New York: W. W. Norton, 1987). I use "American" to refer to activities and ideas associated with the expanding modern nation, the United States of America.

6. "Interview of December 12, 1926, with Mr. Charles William Bocker," Sacajawea Notes and Manuscript—Testimony folder, Box 20, Hebard Papers.

7. Statement of Mrs. Weidemann (also spelled Waidemann): "These two Sho-shoni women were very young, one being 16 years old and the other about 18. One was called the 'Bird Woman' or Sacajawea, the other was 'Otter Woman.'"

8. Hebard, *Sacajawea*, pp. 90–93, 111.

9. William Clark, journal entry of Sunday, November 11, 1804, in *The Journals of the Lewis and Clark Expedition*, ed. Gary Moulton (Lincoln: University of Nebraska Press, 1983–1999), 3:232–233. Four other expedition members, Lewis, Sergeants John Ordway and Patrick Gass, and Private Joseph Whitehouse, kept journals as well. Commentators since Grace Raymond Hebard have noted the propensity of white male observers to refer to Indian women not by name but generically. See Hebard, *Sacajawea*, p. 290; Kessler, "Sacagawea," p. 75; Albers, "Introduction," p. 3; and Green, "Pocahontas Perplex."

10. On the controversy over Sacajawea's name, see Helen Crawford, "Sakaka-wea," *North Dakota Historical Quarterly* 1 (April 1927): 5–15; Hebard, *Sacajawea*, pp. 98n, 283–295; Howard, *Sacajawea*, p. 16n; Irving Anderson, "Saca-jawea, Sacagawea, Sakakawea?" *South Dakota History* 8 (1978): 303–311; and Kessler, "Sacagawea," pp. 274–282.

11. Clark was said to have referred to Sacagawea as "Janey" on two occa-sions, once at Fort Clatsop, and later in an August 20, 1806, letter to Charbon-neau following the expedition. There has been a further controversy over whether to read Clark's handwritten rendering of her name as "Janey" or "Jawey." Grace Hebard wrote letters to dozens of people attempting to settle the matter, but decided in the end to accept Thwaites's rendering of the nick-name as "Janey." For a specimen of that correspondence, see William E. Con-nelley to Grace Raymond Hebard, March 15, 1928, Sacajawea Manuscript—William Connelley file, Box 17, Hebard Papers.

12. On practice involving women captives, see Katherine Weist, "Beasts of Burden and Menial Slaves: Nineteenth Century Observations of Plains Indian Women," in Albers and Medicine, eds., *Hidden Half*, p. 41; on gender in Hi-datsa culture, see Janet Spector, "Male/Female Task Differentiation among the Hidatsa: Toward the Development of an Archaeological Approach to the Study of Gender," ibid., pp. 77–100.

13. Charles Alexander Eastman to the Commissioner of Indian Affairs, March 2, 1925, typescript in Sacajawea Manuscript—Eastman (Dr.)—His Conclusions folder, Box 17, Hebard Papers; Hebard, *Sacajawea*, pp. 285–293; "Affidavit of Andrew Basil or Oha-wa-nud, age 74 years, Shoshone alottee No. 206" and "Affidavit of Enga Peahrora, Shoshone allottee No. 305," both January 15, 1925, Sacajawea Manuscript—Eastman (Dr.) and Others folder, Box 17, Hebard Pa-pers; "Testimony Taken on July 21, 1929, Sunday Morning, by Grace Raymond Hebard through an Interpreter, James E. Compton of Fort Washakie, Wyoming, *Quantanquay*," and "Testimony Taken on Shoshone Indian Reservation, July 22, 1929, by Grace Raymond Hebard through an Interpreter, James E. Comp-ton, of Fort Washakie, *Hebe-chee-chee*," Sacajawea Notes and Manuscript—Testimony folder, Box 20, Hebard Papers. I emphasize that these spellings are variable and approximate.

14. Affidavit of Enga Peahrora; "Sacajawea, by Andrew Basil," Sacajawea Notes and Manuscript—Testimony folder, Box 20, Hebard Papers.

15. Ronda, *Lewis and Clark,* pp. 256–260, offers a synthesis of testimony from members of the expedition on Sacagawea's early years.

16. Ibid., pp. 150–151.

17. Ibid., pp. 70–75.

18. Lewis's entry for February 11, 1805, in Moulton, ed., *Journals,* 3:291. On women and childbirth on overland trails, see John Mack Faragher, *Women and Men on the Overland Trail* (New Haven: Yale University Press, 1979); Julie Roy Jeffrey, *Frontier Women* (New York: Hill and Wang, 1979); Sandra Myres, *Westering Women and the Frontier Experience, 1800–1915* (Albuquerque: University of New Mexico Press, 1982); and chapter 2 of this book.

19. Lewis, August 17, 1805, in Moulton, ed., *Journals,* 5:109. An edition of Lewis's journal by Nicholas Biddle, cited in Bernard De Voto, *The Journals of Lewis and Clark* (Boston: Houghton Mifflin, 1953), p. 203, renders the same episode even more emotionally:

> We soon drew near to the camp, and just as we approached it a woman made her way through the croud towards Sacajawea, and recognising each other, they embraced with the most tender affection. The meeting of these two young women had in it something peculiarly touching, not only in the ardent manner in which their feelings were expressed, but from the real interest of their situation. They had been companions in childhood, in the war with the Minnetarees they had both been taken prisoners in the same battle, they had shared and softened the rigors of their captivity, till one of them had escaped from the Minnetarees, with scarce a hope of ever seeing her friend relieved from the hands of her enemies.

20. See, for example, Thomas Jefferson, *Notes on the State of Virginia* (New York: Harper Torchbooks, 1964), pp. 57–59: "The women are submitted to unjust drudgery. This, I believe, is the case with every barbarous people. With such, force is law. The stronger sex imposes on the weaker. It is civilization alone which replaces women in the enjoyment of their natural equality." For a critique of such language, see Weist, "Beasts of Burden and Menial Slaves."

21. Clark, journal entry of September 26, 1804, in Moulton, ed., *Journals,* 3:117.

22. Clark, journal entry of October 12, 1804, ibid., p. 161.

23. Lewis, journal entry of August 19, 1805, ibid., 5:161.

24. Lewis, journal entry of August 21, 1805, ibid., p. 140.

25. Lewis, journal entry of August 26, 1805, ibid., p. 171.

26. Ronda, *Lewis and Clark,* pp. 159–160.

27. Ronda, ibid., p. 159, provides a splendid bit of detective work in tracing Watkuweis.

28. Sherry Ortner, in "Is Female to Male as Nature Is to Culture?" in *Woman, Culture, and Society,* ed. Michelle Zimbalist Rosaldo and Louise Lamphere (Stanford: Stanford University Press, 1974), analyzes the widespread tendency to identify women with nature and men with culture.

29. Clark, journal entry of May 16, 1805, in Moulton, ed., *Journals,* 4:157.

30. Clark, journal entry of January 6, 1805, ibid., 6:168.

31. Clark, journal entry of December 25, 1805, ibid., p. 157.

32. Clark, journal entry of August 17, 1806, ibid., 8:306.

33. Hebard, *Sacajawea,* pp. 83–84, quotes the letter in full, and explains in

a footnote that "Captain Clark's letter to Charbonneau of Aug. 20, 1806, was discovered in the possession of Mrs. Julia Clark Voorhees and Miss Ellen Voorhees. It was published in the *Century Magazine,* October, 1904. It was also published in the Thwaites edition of the Lewis and Clark journals, vol. III, 247."

34. Ibid., 88–90.

35. Ibid., pp. 90, 93, citing Henry M. Brackenridge, "Journal of Voyage up the River Missouri," in Reuben Gold Thwaites, ed., *Early Western Travels, 1748-1846,* ed. Reuben Gold Thwaites (Cleveland: Arthur H. Clark, 1904–1907), vol. 6.

36. Hebard, *Sacajawea,* p. 111, citing John C. Luttig, *Journal of Fur-Trading Expedition on the Upper Missouri, 1812–13* (reprinted later in an edition by Stella M. Drumm, New York: Argosy-Antiquarian, 1964).

37. Clark, cash accounts book.

38. Hebard, like a number of other white women in the woman suffrage movement, saw Sacagawea as a symbol of women's leadership. See Jan C. Dawson, "Sacagawea: Pilot or Pioneer Mother?" *Pacific Northwest Quarterly* 83, no. 1 (January 1992): 22–28; Gail Landsman, "The 'Other' as Political Symbol: Images of Indians in the Woman Suffrage Movement," *Ethnohistory* 39, no. 3 (summer 1992): 247–284; and Kessler, "Sacajawea," pp. 94–141.

39. See correspondence in Sacajawea Manuscript—Kendrick, John B. (Senator) file, Box 19, Hebard Papers; Sacajawea Manuscript—Eastman (Dr.)—Testimony file, Box 17, Hebard Papers.

40. Eastman to Commissioner of Indian Affairs, March 2, 1925. See also Hebard, *Sacajawea,* p. 93.

41. Hebard, *Sacajawea,* p. 93.

42. Ibid.

43. For the most recent example of Indian narratives of the Sacagawea story, see Horne and McBeth, *Essie's Story.*

44. "Statement of Bull Eye's," to Charles Eastman through interpreters Charles Hoffman and Eagle, typescript, Sacajawea Manuscript—Eastman Vindication folder, box 17, Hebard Papers.

45. "Statement of Chief Wolf Chief, Judge of the Indian Court and Chief of Gros Ventre," Sacajawea manuscript—Eastman Vindication folder, box 17, Hebard Papers. Both Eastman and Hebard were careful to note when they had conducted interviews with the aid of translators. In this case, Eastman noted "two interpreters present," but did not indicate that the interview had been translated.

46. Ibid.

47. Janet Spector, in "Male/Female Task Differentiation among the Hidatsas: Toward the Development of an Archaeological Approach to the Study of Gender," in Albers and Medicine, eds., *Hidden Half,* p. 94, notes that "the distinctiveness of male and female activity patterns among the Hidatsa (and other sexually segregated groups) suggest that generalizations about the 'culture' of the group must be made with great caution."

48. Statement of Mrs. Weidemann.

49. Ibid.

50. Ibid.

51. Ibid.

52. Statement of Bull Eye's.

53. Statement of Mrs. Weidemann.

54. The best description of such terrain is Richard White, *The Middle Ground: Indians, Empires, and Republics in the Great Lakes Region, 1650–1815* (Cambridge: Cambridge University Press, 1991).

55. Statement of Mrs. Weidemann; Statement of Bull Eye's.

56. Statement of Mrs. Weidemann.

57. "Statement of We-sue-poie, Lawton, Oklahoma, a Comanche woman 75 years old, concerning the Tradition of Porivo, or supposed to be Sacajawea, 'or Bird Woman,'" Sacajawea Manuscript—Eastman (Dr.) and Others file, Box 17, Hebard Papers.

58. Testimony of James McAdam.

59. Ibid.

60. "Sacajawea, by Barbara Meyers, Testimony taken September 7, 1926," Sacajawea Notes and Manuscript—Testimony folder, Box 20, Hebard Papers.

61. "Affidavit of Susan Perry or Te-ah-win-nie, Shoshone allottee No. 238, born 1836, interviewed by Charles Eastman, January 15, 1925," Sacajawea Manuscript—Eastman (Dr.) and Others folder, Box 17, Hebard Papers; Affidavit of Enga Peahrora.

62. Affidavit of Andrew Basil.

63. Testimony of James McAdam.

64. Affidavit of Andrew Basil.

65. For a thoughtful examination of the relation between human mobility, Indian reservations, and the built environment, see John M. Findlay, "An Elusive Institution: The Birth of Indian Reservations in Gold Rush California," in *State and Reservation: New Perspectives on Federal Indian Policy,* ed. George Pierre Castile and Robert L. Bee (Tucson: University of Arizona Press, 1992), pp. 13–37.

66. "Testimony Taken on Shoshone Indian Reservation, July 22, 1929 . . . *Hebe-chee-chee.*"

67. Testimony of James McAdam.

CHAPTER 2. THE HEARTH OF DARKNESS: SUSAN MAGOFFIN

The epigraph sources are, in order: Stella M. Drumm, ed., *Down the Santa Fe Trail and into Mexico, 1846–1847* (New Haven: Yale University Press, 1926), p. xi (typescript of original Drumm edition is in the Santa Fe Papers Collection, Missouri Historical Society, St. Louis); Stella M. Drumm, ed., *Down the Santa Fe Trail and into Mexico: The Diary of Susan Shelby Magoffin, 1846–1847* (Lincoln: University of Nebraska Press, 1982), p. 178; and Joseph Conrad, *The Heart of Darkness and the Secret Sharer* (New York: Signet, 1997), p. 150.

1. Howard R. Lamar, "Foreword," to Drumm, ed., *Down the Santa Fe Trail,* p. ix.

2. Sandra Myres, *Westering Women and the Frontier Experience, 1800–1915* (Albuquerque: University of New Mexico Press, 1982), p. xvii.

3. Lamar, "Foreword," p. xiv.

4. DeVoto wanted, he said, not only to "realize the pre–Civil War, Far Western frontier as personal experience," but also "to study the Far West at the moment when it became nationally important." If there was some tension between the small and the tall tales, wrote DeVoto, "My hope is that, in combining the two jobs, I have not bungled both" (Bernard DeVoto, *The Year of Decision: 1846* [Boston: Houghton Mifflin, 1960], p. xxv). See also David Lavender, *Bent's Fort* (Garden City, N.Y.: Doubleday, 1954); and Max Moorhead, *New Mexico's Royal Road: Trade and Travel on the Chihuahua Trail* (Norman: University of Oklahoma Press, 1958).

5. There is nothing new about this observation. See, for example, Myres, *Westering Women;* John Mack Faragher, *Women and Men on the Overland Trail* (New Haven: Yale University Press, 1979); Julie Roy Jeffrey, *Frontier Women* (New York: Hill and Wang, 1979); and Glenda Riley, *The Female Frontier: A Comparative View of Women on the Prairie and the Plains* (Lawrence: University Press of Kansas, 1988). At the same time, the categories of race and gender were mutually constitutive, as Neil Foley has so elegantly shown in *The White Scourge: Mexicans, Blacks, and Poor Whites in Texas Cotton Culture* (Berkeley: University of California Press, 1997), as Grace E. Hale has demonstrated in *Making Whiteness: The Culture of Segregation in the South, 1890–1940* (New York: Pantheon Books, 1998), and as Peggy Pascoe has demonstrated in "Miscegenation Law, Court Cases, and Ideologies of 'Race' in Twentieth-Century America," *Journal of American History* 83, no. 1 (June 1996): 44–69.

6. In *Catherine Beecher: A Study in American Domesticity* (New Haven: Yale University Press, 1973), Kathryn Kish Sklar deftly analyzes the class dimensions and expansionist program of nineteenth-century American female domesticity. The literature on middle-class women and empire is rich and fast-growing. See, for example, Antoinette Burton, *Burdens of History: British Feminists, Indian Women, and Imperial Culture, 1865–1915* (Chapel Hill: University of North Carolina Press, 1994); Ann Laura Stoler, "Making Empire Respectable: The Politics of Race and Sexual Morality in Twentieth-Century Colonial Cultures," *American Ethnologist* 16, no. 4 (1989): 634–660; Margaret Strobel, *European Women and the Second British Empire* (Bloomington: Indiana University Press, 1991); Chandra Mohanty, Ann Russo, and Lourdes Torres, eds., *Third World Women and the Politics of Feminism* (Bloomington: Indiana University Press, 1991); and Nancy Duncan, ed., *Bodyspace: Destabilizing Geographies of Gender and Sexuality* (London: Routledge, 1996). The notion of *habitus*, that complex of things, thoughts, and actions that reproduces everyday life, has been most fully elaborated by Pierre Bourdieu in *Outline of a Theory of Practice* (Cambridge: Cambridge University Press, 1977), and usefully expanded by Michel De Certeau in *The Practice of Everyday Life* (Berkeley: University of California Press, 1984).

7. Lamar, "Foreword."

8. Mary Louise Pratt, in *Imperial Eyes: Travel Writing and Transculturation* (London: Routledge, 1992), p. 5, explains that "travel and exploration writing produced 'the rest of the world' for European readerships at particular points in Europe's expansionist trajectory."

9. John McPhee, *In Suspect Terrain* (New York: Farrar, Straus, and Giroux, 1983); Peter Coney, Steven R. May, and Myrl E. Beck, Jr., *Paleomagnetism and*

Suspect Terranes of the North American Cordillera [microform] (Reston, Virginia: U.S. Department of the Interior, Geological Survey, 1983).

10. Magoffin, *Down the Santa Fe Trail,* p. 1. All quotations from this work, unless otherwise noted, are from the University of Nebraska Press Bison Books edition, edited by Stella M. Drumm. Quotations from the text of Magoffin's diary are cited as "Magoffin"; Drumm's footnote comments are cited as "Drumm." Those who wish to consult the original diary may see "Magoffin, Susan Shelby, Journal, 1846–1847," WA MSS S-867, Western Americana Manuscript Collection, Beinecke Rare Book and Manuscript Library, Yale University, New Haven, Connecticut. I do not note discrepancies involving minor differences of spelling or punctuation, but do point out omitted words or phrases.

11. Missouri History Scrapbook, column by M. W. Childs, *St. Louis Post Dispatch Sunday Magazine* (n.d., probably 1931), Missouri Historical Society.

12. Typescript of introduction to Drumm, 1926, Santa Fe Papers Collection, Missouri Historical Society.

13. "Mrs. Magoffin is mistaken in this date," Drumm, p. 54n.18; "Mrs. Magoffin's comment on General Taylor's personal appearance suggests the reason for his soubriquet," Drumm, p. 252n.110.

14. Wedding announcement, *St. Louis Post Dispatch,* September 22, 1943; "Stella Atkinson Dies of Auto Injuries," *St. Louis Post Dispatch,* October 17, 1946, Missouri Historical Society Scrapbook, vol. 4, Missouri Historical Society.

15. Marguerite Ely, "She Is a Member of the Gros Ventre Tribe: St. Louis Girl Historian, Who Is Librarian of the Missouri Historical Society, Was Adopted by the Redskins during the Columbia River Historical Expedition Ceremony at Fort Union, Colo., Being Given the Name of Ah-Ki-Kia-Ka-Som by Chief Head Dress," *St. Louis Globe-Democrat Magazine,* September 30, 1928, Stella M. Drumm vertical file, Missouri Historical Society. Like many historical researchers, Stella Drumm wanted to prove the importance of the local. In her case, that meant putting St. Louis at the center of the American past, projecting the city's influence not simply across the West but into the present and future. St. Louis was, then as now, a city with a chronic case of urban envy. For three-quarters of a century, St. Louis had been the American Gateway to the West. By the late nineteenth century, however, Chicago had vastly outpaced St. Louis as the hub of midwestern business, industry, and transportation (see William Cronon, *Nature's Metropolis: Chicago and the Great West* [New York: W. W. Norton, 1991], pp. 295–309). Studying the history of frontier commerce and conflict provided Drumm the chance to reprise her hometown's glory days and commemorate its historical role in the international trade that flowed through the town in the eighteenth and nineteenth centuries; this she did in several historical publications, including the Magoffin diary and John Luttig and Stella M. Drumm, eds., *Journal of a Fur Trading Expedition on the Upper Missouri, 1812–1813* (New York: Argosy-Antiquarian, 1964). Another of her passions was to venerate the city's prominent families.

16. The Missouri Historical Society, like all archives, attracted genealogical researchers who used collections emphasizing "Missouri and southern genealogy." Drumm assisted researchers and edited the society's *Collections,* a publication that foregrounded Missouri family histories. The Reverend G. R. Dod-

son, who reviewed *Down the Santa Fe Trail* for a St. Louis newspaper, felt sure that "what will most interest many people" in the volume was "the great number of references to well-known Missouri and Kentucky families." For those not inclined to actually read the book, Dodson listed the family names. See Ely, "Interesting Diary of the Woman Who Rode the Santa Fe Trail," *St. Louis Globe-Democrat*, November 17, 1926, Drumm vertical file, Missouri Historical Society.

17. According to Hobsbawm and Terence Ranger (*The Invention of Tradition* [Cambridge: Cambridge University Press, 1997], p. 2), genealogy constitutes one among many possible "responses to novel situations which take the form of references to old situations, or which establish their own past by quasi-obligatory repetitions." Hobsbawm notes the middle-class American fascination with genealogy in the 1890s in "Mass-Producing Traditions: Europe, 1870–1914," ibid., pp. 292–293.

18. Lamar, "Foreword," pp. xix–xxi.

19. Drumm never trifled to mention the woman who appeared most frequently in the pages of the diary, Jane, Susan's slave maid; and the only Mexican woman Drumm commemorated in a footnote (pp. 119–120n.44) was the notorious Gertrudis Barceló, Doña Tules, a Santa Fe gambling house operator who is portrayed as the embodiment of local color, not in the least veiled by or implicated in domesticity. For more on Barceló, see Deena J. Gonzalez, "La Tules of Image and Reality: Euro-American Attitudes and Legend Formation on a Spanish-Mexican Frontier," in *Building with Our Hands: New Directions in Chicana Scholarship*, ed. Adela de la Torre and Peatriz M. Pesquera (Berkeley: University of California Press, 1993), pp. 75–90. The few other women named in Drumm's footnotes were absent wives or sisters or daughters of westering men.

20. Magoffin manuscript, p. 1; Drumm's edition omits the word "rather" from this sentence (Magoffin, p. 1).

21. Conrad, *Heart of Darkness,* p. 71.

22. Magoffin, p. 6. On the preparation of shrubs, see Samuel P. Arnold, *Eating Up the Santa Fe Trail* (Niwot: University Press of Colorado, 1990), pp. 31–32.

23. Magoffin, p. 10; Drumm notes that "Captain Benjamin Moore's company of United States Dragoons . . . was sent to overtake [a] caravan, carrying arms and ammunition to the Mexicans."

24. Magoffin, p. 11.

25. Magoffin, pp. 16, 18. (All italicized matter in quotations is emphasized in the original.)

26. Magoffin, pp. 20–21.

27. Magoffin, pp. 21, 23.

28. Magoffin, pp. 26–30.

29. Magoffin, p. 31.

30. Magoffin, pp. 32–34.

31. Magoffin, pp. 40–41.

32. Magoffin, pp. 40–42.

33. Magoffin, p. 44.

34. Magoffin, pp. 44, 47–50.
35. Magoffin, p. 53.
36. Drumm, p. 53n.
37. Magoffin, pp. 55–58.
38. Lavender, *Bent's Fort,* esp. pp. 254–267. For a fascinating look at Bent's Fort as a machine for modernization, see Douglas Comer, *Ritual Ground: Bent's Old Fort, World Formation, and the Annexation of the Southwest* (Berkeley: University of California Press, 1996).
39. Magoffin, pp. 60–61.
40. Magoffin, p. 62. Drumm identified Solidad Abreu in a typical genealogical footnote about the husband, Dr. Leitensdorfer, a Missourian and Santa Fe trader.
41. Magoffin, pp. 61–63.
42. Magoffin, pp. 63–66.
43. Magoffin, pp. 67–69.
44. Magoffin, p. 68.
45. Magoffin, p. 69.
46. Magoffin, pp. 70–71.
47. Magoffin, pp. 72–74.
48. Magoffin, pp. 78–82.
49. Magoffin, pp. 83–85.
50. Magoffin, pp. 89–90.
51. Magoffin, p. 91.
52. Magoffin, pp. 92–93.
53. Magoffin, pp. 94–95.
54. Magoffin, p. 95.
55. Magoffin, pp. 96–98.
56. Magoffin, pp. 100–102.
57. According to restaurateur and culinary historian Sam Arnold (*Eating Up the Santa Fe Trail,* p. 8), the oysters Susan enjoyed would have been canned, although fresh oysters were available along the trail in cooler months. They were packed in barrels, shells opening upward, so that they could be fed. At every stage stop along the trail, chipped ice would be packed in. Cornmeal was sprinkled on top, trickling down to feed the oysters as the ice melted. "Oysters," said Arnold, "arrived fatter and better fed than when they left the Chesapeake Bay."
58. Magoffin, pp. 103–108.
59. Magoffin, pp. 106–107.
60. Magoffin, pp. 110–115.
61. Magoffin, pp. 108–109, 117–124.
62. Magoffin, pp. 126–131.
63. Magoffin, pp. 130–135.
64. Magoffin, pp. 137–148.
65. Magoffin, pp. 147–149.
66. Magoffin, pp. 150–152.
67. Magoffin, pp. 151–160.
68. Magoffin, pp. 160–161.

69. Magoffin, pp. 160–163.
70. Magoffin, p. 164.
71. Magoffin, pp. 165–168.
72. Magoffin, pp. 169–171.
73. Magoffin, p. 171.
74. Magoffin, pp. 173–176.
75. Magoffin, pp. 176–177.
76. Magoffin, pp. 177–179.
77. Magoffin, p. 178.
78. Magoffin, p. 180.
79. Magoffin, pp. 179–183.
80. Magoffin, pp. 183–184.
81. Magoffin, pp 190–193.
82. Magoffin, pp. 193–194.
83. On women and evangelicalism, see Kathryn Kish Sklar, *Catherine Beecher: A Study in American Domesticity* (New Haven: Yale University Press, 1973).
84. Magoffin, pp. 194–195.
85. Magoffin, pp. 195–200.
86. Magoffin, p. 200.
87. Magoffin, pp. 201–203.
88. Magoffin, pp. 204–205.
89. Magoffin, pp. 205–207.
90. Magoffin, pp. 207–209.
91. Magoffin, pp. 209–212.
92. Magoffin, p. 212.
93. Magoffin, pp. 213–215.
94. Magoffin, pp. 215–216.
95. Magoffin, pp. 217–223.
96. Magoffin, pp 223–230.
97. Magoffin, p. 231.
98. Magoffin, pp. 231–234.
99. Magoffin, pp. 236, 234.
100. Magoffin, p. 245.
101. Magoffin, pp. 248–249.
102. Magoffin, pp. 237–238, 249–251. Carroll Smith-Rosenberg's landmark article "The Female World of Love and Ritual: Relations between Women in Nineteenth-Century America," *Signs: Journal of Women in Culture and Society* 1, no. 1 (1975): 1–29, opened up the possibility of understanding the intimate relations of middle- and upper-class white women in the nineteenth-century United States.
103. Magoffin, pp. 253–257.
104. Conrad, *Heart of Darkness*, p. 140.
105. Magoffin, p. 259.
106. Magoffin, p. 260.
107. Magoffin, p. 260.
108. Lamar, "Foreword," p. xxxii.

CHAPTER 3. EMPIRE, LIBERTY, AND LEGEND:
WOMAN SUFFRAGE IN WYOMING

1. Peter S. Onuf, "Thomas Jefferson, Missouri, and the 'Empire for Liberty,'"
in *Thomas Jefferson and the Changing West,* ed. James P. Ronda (Albuquerque:
University of New Mexico Press, 1997), p. 140.

2. Here I follow Anthony Giddens's theory of structuration for understanding the various means by which modern nations consolidate social and political
power. See Anthony Giddens, *A Contemporary Critique of Historical Materialism* (Berkeley: University of California Press, 1985). For a useful gloss on Giddens, see William H. Sewell Jr., "A Theory of Structure: Duality, Agency, and
Transformation," *American Journal of Sociology* 98, no. 1 (July 1992): 1–29.

3. John R. Stilgoe, *Common Landscape of America, 1580 to 1845* (New
Haven: Yale University Press, 1982), pp. 106–107. See also Peter S. Onuf, *Statehood and Union: A History of the Northwest Ordinance* (Bloomington: University of Indiana Press, 1987).

4. Richard White, *"It's Your Misfortune and None of My Own": A New History of the American West* (Norman: University of Oklahoma Press, 1991), pp.
155–178.

5. T. A. Larson, *History of Wyoming* (Lincoln: University of Nebraska Press,
1978), p. 67.

6. My explanation owes much to the "relational" history of the West best
exemplified in the work of Richard White, as well as to Patricia Limerick's insistence on conquest as a main theme of western history. I believe, at the same
time, that the intellectually robust western history these scholars practice has
much to learn from feminist scholars, including Ellen Dubois, Ann Stoler, Chandra Talpade Mohanty, and Antoinette Burton, who have explored the racial and
imperial politics of feminism. None of these historians has offered an explanation of western precedence in woman suffrage, but together, their work provides
conceptual tools I employ today. See Richard White, *It's Your Misfortune;* Patricia Nelson Limerick, *Legacy of Conquest: The Unbroken Past of the American West* (New York: W. W. Norton, 1987); Ellen Carol Dubois, *Feminism and
Suffrage: The Emergence of an Independent Women's Movement in America,
1848–1869* (Ithaca: Cornell University Press, 1978); Ann Laura Stoler, "Making Empire Respectable: The Politics of Race and Sexual Morality in Twentieth-
Century Colonial Cultures," *American Ethnologist* 16, no. 4 (1989): 634–660;
Ann Laura Stoler, "Carnal Knowledge and Imperial Power: Gender, Race, and
Morality in Colonial Asia," in *Gender at the Crossroads of Knowledge: Femi-
nist Anthropology in the Postmodern Era,* ed. Micaela di Leonardo (Berkeley:
University of California Press, 1991); Chandra Talpade Mohanty et al., eds.,
Third World Women and the Politics of Feminism (Bloomington: Indiana Uni-
versity Press, 1991); and Antoinette Burton, *Burdens of History: British Femi-
nists, Indian Women, and Imperial Culture, 1865–1915* (Chapel Hill: University
of North Carolina Press, 1995). See also Edward Said, *Culture and Imperialism*
(New York: Knopf, 1993). Scholars of race, too, help us see Wyoming anew; see
Peggy Pascoe, *Relations of Rescue: The Search for Female Moral Authority in
the American West, 1874–1939* (New York: Oxford University Press, 1990);

Alexander Saxton, *The Rise and Fall of the White Republic: Class Politics and Mass Culture in Nineteenth-Century America* (New York: Verso, 1990); and David Roediger, *The Wages of Whiteness: Race and the Making of the American Working Class* (New York: Verso, 1999).

On the subject of woman suffrage in Wyoming, see the diverse views of Grace Raymond Hebard, "How Woman Suffrage Came to Wyoming" (1920), Box 6, Grace Raymond Hebard Collection, Acc. 8, American Heritage Center, University of Wyoming, Laramie (hereafter cited as Hebard Papers); T. A. Larson, "Petticoats at the Polls: Woman Suffrage in Territorial Wyoming," *Pacific Northwest Quarterly* 44 (April 1953): 74–78; T. A. Larson, "Dolls, Vassals, and Drudges: Pioneer Women in the West," *Western Historical Quarterly* 3 (January 1972); T. A. Larson, *History of Wyoming*, 2d ed., rev. (Lincoln: University of Nebraska Press, 1978); Miriam Gantz Chapman, "The Story of Woman Suffrage in Wyoming, 1869–1890" (M.A. thesis, University of Wyoming, 1952); Virginia Scharff, "The Case for Domestic Feminism: Woman Suffrage in Wyoming," *Annals of Wyoming* 56, no. 2 (fall 1984): 29–37; and Michael A. Massie, "Reform Is Where You Find It: The Roots of Woman Suffrage in Wyoming," *Annals of Wyoming* 62, no. 1 (spring 1990): 2–21.

7. Larson, *History of Wyoming*, p. 36.

8. The classic formulation of the concept of imperial middle ground is Richard White, *The Middle Ground: Indians, Empires, and Republics in the Great Lakes* (Cambridge: Cambridge University Press, 1991); my analysis also owes an enormous debt to Elliott West, *The Contested Plains: Indians, Goldseekers, and the Rush to Colorado* (Lawrence: University Press of Kansas, 1998).

9. *Cheyenne Leader,* September 9, 1870. On sex ratios among non-Indians, see Larson, *History of Wyoming,* p. 80.

10. On the setting of the Sweetwater settlements, see Virginia J. Scharff, "South Pass since 1812: Woman Suffrage and the Expansion of the Western Adventure" (M.A. thesis, University of Wyoming, 1981).

11. For a summary of Indian-white relations in the territory during this time, see Larson, *History of Wyoming,* chap. 2. Every issue of the *Sweetwater Mines,* the *Frontier Index,* the *Cheyenne Leader,* and the *Wyoming Tribune* from 1868 through 1871 carried stories about Indian-white conflict, generally blaming Indians for incidents of violence and criticizing the government for dealing with "savages" and "devils" in the first place. The *Sweetwater Mines,* March 28, 1868, for example, criticized the peace commissioners for sentimentality toward "noble" natives, averring that as a newspaper "published in an Indian country," the *Mines* could attest that the Indian was "'cruel and revengeful,' because he possesses, in many respects, the instincts of the wild beast rather than because he has been outlawed by 'civilized man.'" Edward Said offered the classic theorization of the predilection to dehumanize colonial subjects, exemplified in such statements, in *Orientalism* (New York: Vintage Books, 1974).

12. On men's social singleness, see Sarah Deutsch, *No Separate Refuge: Culture, Class, and Gender on an Anglo-Hispanic Frontier in the American Southwest, 1880–1940* (New York: Oxford University Press, 1987). For comparison, see Belinda Bozzoli on South African gender systems and empire, in *Women of*

Phokeng: Consciousness, Life Strategy and Migrancy in South Africa, 1900–1983 (Portsmouth, Eng.: Heinemann, 1991).

13. *Sweetwater Mines,* May 27, 1868.

14. On "true womanhood," see Barbara Welter's pathbreaking article, "The Cult of True Womanhood, 1820–1860," *American Quarterly* 18 (summer, 1966); see also Kathryn Kish Sklar, *Catherine Beecher: A Study in American Domesticity* (New Haven: Yale University Press, 1973); Christine Stansell, *City of Women* (Urbana: University of Illinois Press, 1987); Darlene Clark Hine, *Black Women in American History: From Colonial Times through the Nineteenth Century* (Brooklyn, N.Y.: Carlson, 1990); and Evelyn Brooks Higginbotham, *Righteous Discontent: The Women's Movement in the Black Baptist Church, 1880–1920* (Cambridge, Mass.: Harvard University Press, 1994). See also Stoler, "Carnal Knowledge and Imperial Power"; and Burton, *Burdens of History,* on white feminism, femininity, and empire.

15. Welter, "Cult of True Womanhood"; Nancy Cott, *The Bonds of Womanhood: "Woman's Sphere" in New England, 1780–1835,* 2d ed. (New Haven: Yale University Press, 1997); Sklar, *Catherine Beecher.*

16. U.S. Department of the Interior, *Compendium of the Ninth Census (June 1, 1870),* pp. 372, 592. See also Wyoming Territory Manuscript Census 1870, American Heritage Center, University of Wyoming, Laramie.

17. Lola M. Homsher, ed., *South Pass, 1868* (Lincoln: University of Nebraska Press, 1978), p. 204.

18. See, for example, *Sweetwater Mines,* June 3, 1868.

19. *Sweetwater Mines,* December 30, 1868; January 9, 1869.

20. Linda Kerber, in "Separate Spheres, Female Worlds, Woman's Place: The Rhetoric of Women's History," *Journal of American History* 75 (June 1988): 9–39, demonstrated the problems with believing that the Victorians practiced what they preached.

21. The *Sweetwater Mines* reported on December 2, 1868, that one "Anna Wright arrested by officer Carson on charge of being drunk and fighting, fined $10 and cost."

22. Anne M. Butler, *Daughters of Joy, Sisters of Misery: Prostitutes in the American West, 1865–1890* (Urbana: University of Illinois Press, 1991); Marion Goldman, *Gold Diggers and Silver Miners: Prostitution and Social Life on the Comstock Lode* (Ann Arbor: University of Michigan Press, 1981); Paula Petrik, "Capitalists with Rooms: Prostitution in Helena, Montana, 1865–1900," *Montana: The Magazine of Western History* 31 (spring 1981): 28–41; Benson Tong, *Unsubmissive Women: Chinese Prostitutes in Nineteenth-Century San Francisco* (Norman: University of Oklahoma Press, 1994).

23. *Frontier Index,* June 5, 1868. The historian Richard Etulain is tracing the path of Calamity Jane, and has found evidence of her presence in Wyoming railroad and mining towns in the late 1860s.

24. *Sweetwater Mines,* March 28, 1868.

25. *Frontier Index,* August 18, 1868; microfilm in Coe Library, University of Wyoming, Laramie.

26. *Frontier Index,* March 6, 1868.

27. *Frontier Index,* June 2, 1868.

28. Homsher, ed., *South Pass,* p. 80; Marjorie C. Trevor, "History of Carter-Sweetwater County, Wyoming to 1875" (M.A. thesis, University of Wyoming, 1954), pp. 111–112.

29. Chisholm is quoted in Homsher, ed., *South Pass,* pp. 81, 104.

30. *Sweetwater Mines,* June 3, 1868.

31. *Frontier Index,* March 24, 1868.

32. James Sherlock, *South Pass and Its Tales* (New York: Vantage Press, 1978), p. 44.

33. Trevor, "History of Carter-Sweetwater County," p. 95. Smith demurred from explaining to Hebard that since no church was ever built in South Pass City, the devout were forced to meet in the Magnolia Saloon; see *South Pass News,* August 31, 1870.

34. Sherlock, *South Pass and Its Tales,* pp. 68–69.

35. *Sweetwater Mines,* March 25, 1868.

36. Ibid., April 4, 1868.

37. Ibid., May 30, 1868.

38. Carrie Chapman Catt and Nettie Rogers Shuler, *Woman Suffrage and Politics* (New York: Charles Scribner, 1923), p. 76.

39. Larson, *History of Wyoming,* pp. 70–74.

40. *Frontier Index,* August 18, 1868.

41. Ibid., April 21, 1868.

42. John A. Campbell to Ely S. Parker, June 10, 1869, Records of the Office of Indian Affairs, University of Wyoming Library, Laramie. On Indian-white relations in Wyoming Territory, see Larson, *History of Wyoming,* pp. 12–35, and Scharff, "South Pass since 1812," pp. 22–56.

43. Among such bills were measures appointing officials for Wyoming Territory's (then) four counties. Campbell vetoed the bills on the grounds that the appointive power belonged to the executive branch. See Larson, *History of Wyoming,* pp. 75–76.

44. *House Journal of the Legislative Assembly of the Territory of Wyoming, First Session, 1869* (Cheyenne: Tribune Office, 1870), pp. 210, 262; *Council Journal of the Legislative Assembly of the Territory of Wyoming, First Session* (Cheyenne: Tribune Office, 1870), pp. 79, 167. See also Roger D. Hardaway, "Prohibiting Interracial Marriage: Miscegenation Law in Wyoming," *Annals of Wyoming* 52, no. 1 (spring 1980): 55–60. On miscegenation law more generally, see Peggy Pascoe, "Miscegenation Law, Court Cases, and Ideologies of 'Race' in Twentieth-Century America," *Journal of American History* 83, no. 1 (June 1996): 44–69.

45. *Cheyenne Leader,* August 27, 1870.

46. *Wyoming Tribune,* December 18, 1869.

47. Campbell to Ely S. Parker, February 21, 1870, Records of the Office of Indian Affairs; *Wyoming Tribune,* January 29, 1871.

48. Larson, *History of Wyoming,* p. 81; Larson, "Dolls, Vassals, and Drudges"; and T. A. Larson, "Petticoats at the Polls," *Pacific Northwest Quarterly* 44 (April 1953): 74–79. See also G. Thomas Edwards, *Sowing Good Seeds: The Northwest Suffrage Campaigns of Susan B. Anthony* (Portland, Ore.: Oregon Histor-

ical Society Press, 1990); and, regarding Susan B. Anthony in the Pacific Northwest, Dubois, *Feminism and Suffrage.*

49. See, for example, *Frontier Index,* March 6, 24, June 5, November 13, 1868; *Cheyenne Argus,* November 12, 1869; *Sweetwater Mines,* December 2, 5, 23, 1868; *Cheyenne Leader,* November 22, 24, December 2, 10, 1869; *Wyoming Tribune,* December 4, 1869. See also Larson, *History of Wyoming,* pp. 78–83.

50. Elizabeth Cady Stanton, Susan B. Anthony, and Matilda Joslyn Gage, *History of Woman Suffrage,* vol. 3 (Rochester, N.Y.: Charles Mann, 1887), p. 730.

51. Ben Sheeks to Grace Raymond Hebard, n.d. [1920?], Hebard Papers.

52. *Council Journal,* 1st session, pp. 54, 66, 110, 121, 122–123, 141, 155, 158, 188.

53. *Cheyenne Leader,* November 10, 1869.

54. *Frontier Index,* March 6, 1868. The Stanton-Anthony racial argument is carefully detailed in Dubois, *Feminism and Suffrage,* chaps. 3 and 4.

55. Larson, *History of Wyoming,* pp. 78–83; Scharff, "Case for Domestic Feminism," p. 34; Massie, "Reform Is Where You Find It," pp. 8–10.

56. *Wyoming Tribune,* December 18, 1869.

57. Larson, *History of Wyoming,* pp. 78–83.

58. For one of the first summaries of women's activism, see John W. Kingman, "Woman Suffrage in Wyoming: Six Years' Practical Workings" (unpublished pamphlet, 1876), Folder 1, Woman Suffrage Collection, American Heritage Center, University of Wyoming, Laramie (hereafter cited as Woman Suffrage files). For general discussions, see Hebard, "How Woman Suffrage Came to Wyoming"; Larson, *History of Wyoming,* pp. 84–90; Scharff, "Case for Domestic Feminism," p. 36; Massie, "Reform Is Where You Find It," p. 13.

59. Edward T. James and Janet W. James, eds., *Notable American Women, 1607–1950: A Biographical Dictionary* (Cambridge, Mass.: Harvard University Press, 1971), 2:319.

60. *Laramie Republican Booomerang,* July 25, 1937.

61. Robert Morris to the *Revolution,* December 27, 1869; copy in Hebard Papers.

62. *South Pass News,* March 19, 1870.

63. Edward M. Lee, "The Woman Movement in Wyoming," *Galaxy* 13 (June 1872): 756.

64. Undated newspaper clipping, Hebard Papers.

65. Kingman, "Woman Suffrage in Wyoming"; "Woman Suffrage in Wyoming" (pamphlet published by the American Woman Suffrage Association, Boston, 1889), Woman Suffrage files, Folder 9.

66. "Woman Suffrage in Wyoming," Woman Suffrage files, Folder 9.

67. Ibid.

68. Kingman, "Woman Suffrage in Wyoming." The *Wyoming Tribune* exulted on September 17, 1870, that women's first trip to the polls was a great success: "Whenever a woman, no matter what her race, color, or condition might be, was seen approaching with a ballot in her hand, the multitude of male sovereigns opened a wide and convenient aisle, so that the newly enfraschised might meet with no obstruction while indulging in the right of suffrage."

69. "Nine Years' Experience: Woman Suffrage in Wyoming" (unpublished pamphlet, 1878), Woman Suffrage files, Folder 9.

70. The most extensive discussion of the repeal effort is in Massie, "Reform Is Where You Find It," pp. 16–17.

71. *Cheyenne Leader,* November 10, 1871.

72. The quarrel originated when Lee bypassed Baker for the contract printing the legislature's journals and awarded it instead to Bristol. Shortly thereafter, on November 23, 1869, the *Cheyenne Leader* accused Baker of "afflict[ing] the people of Wyoming by his foul presence" and of bearing "the conduct of a drunkard and licentious libertine. . . . He is shunned by all respectable ladies, as they would shun a foul and loathsome viper ., . . . an unprincipled pimp." For a discussion of the quarrel between Baker and Lee, see Larson, *History of Wyoming,* pp. 120–123.

73. *Cheyenne Leader,* December 11, 1871.

74. There was a third party in Wyoming, the People Party, composed of disaffected Democrats and Republicans who thought they otherwise wouldn't have a chance against the powerful Democrats. One Council member, John Fosher of Atlantic City, and one House member, H. G. Nickerson of Miner's Delight, represented the People Party, and voted with the Republicans. See Massie, "Reform Is Where You Find It," p. 17.

75. *House Journal of the Legislative Assembly of the Territory of Wyoming, Second Session* (Cheyenne: Tribune Office, 1872), pp. 112–118.

76. Ibid., p. 115.

77. Woman Suffrage files.

CHAPTER 4. MARKING WYOMING:
GRACE RAYMOND HEBARD

The epigraph sources are, respectively: Grace Raymond Hebard, "The First White Women in Wyoming," *Washington Historical Quarterly* (1917); and Janelle M. Wenzel, "Dr. Grace Raymond Hebard as Western Historian" (M.A. thesis, University of Wyoming, 1960), p. 10.

1. Wenzel, "Dr. Grace Raymond Hebard," p. 7.

2. List of "Organizations," Box 36, Personal File, Grace Raymond Hebard Papers, American Heritage Center, University of Wyoming, Laramie (hereafter cited as Hebard Papers).

3. On the first college women, marriage, and professionalism, see Patricia Albjerg Graham, "Expansion and Exclusion: A History of Women in American Higher Education," *Signs: Journal of Women in Culture and Society* (fall 1978): 759–773; and Rosalind Rosenberg *Beyond Separate Spheres: Intellectual Roots of Modern Feminism* (New Haven: Yale University Press, 1982). On Hebard in particular, see "In Memoriam: Grace Raymond Hebard, 1861–1936," Box 35, Hebard Papers; undated clipping, *Wyoming News,* Box 35, Hebard Papers; and Wenzel, "Dr. Grace Raymond Hebard." On the university and the state, see Deborah Hardy, *Wyoming University: The First 100 Years, 1886–1986* (Laramie: University of Wyoming, 1986); T. A. Larson, *History of Wyoming,* 2d ed. rev. (Lin-

coln: University of Nebraska Press, 1978); and Virginia Scharff, "The Independent and Feminine Life: Grace Raymond Hebard, 1861–1936," in *Lone Voyagers: Academic Women in Coeducational Institutions, 1870–1937*, ed. Geraldine Joncich Clifford (New York: Feminist Press, 1989), pp. 125–137.

4. On the pioneering generation of college women, see Jessie Bernard, *Academic Women* (University Park: Pennsylvania State University Press, 1964); Mabel Newcomer, *A Century of Higher Education for Women* (New York: Harper and Brothers, 1959); Rosenberg, *Beyond Separate Spheres;* Barbara Miller Solomon, *In the Company of Educated Women: A History of Women and Higher Education in America* (New Haven: Yale University Press, 1985); Clifford, ed., *Lone Voyagers;* and John Mack Faragher and Florence Howe, eds., *Women and Higher Education in American History* (New York: W. W. Norton, 1989). On women's role in the academy, see Katherine Jensen, "Women's Work and Academic Culture," *Higher Education* 11 (1982): 67–83.

5. On Mead, see Donald Worster, *Rivers of Empire: Water, Aridity, and the Growth of the American West* (New York: Pantheon Books, 1985), pp. 154–160, 180–188.

6. Hebard used the term to describe herself in a letter to Carrie Chapman Catt of November 9, 1926, regarding the defeat of Governor Nellie Tayloe Ross, Box 3, Hebard Papers. I use the term "feminist" here in the historical sense explicated in Nancy Cott, *The Grounding of Modern Feminism* (New Haven: Yale University Press, 1987).

7. Scrapbook, Box 34, Hebard Papers; Grace Raymond Hebard (hereafter GRH) to William C. Deming, April 30, 1930, Hebard Papers.

8. On the horrible winter of 1886–1887, see Larson, *History of Wyoming,* pp. 190–192. On the founding of the university, see Hardy, *Wyoming University,* pp. 1–7.

9. Larson, *History of Wyoming,* p. 262.

10. Eva E. Downey to GRH, n.d., Box 31, Hebard Papers.

11. "In Memoriam," p. 24; Roger L. Williams, *Aven Nelson of Wyoming* (Boulder: Colorado Associated University Press, 1984), pp. 28–29.

12. For the most critical view of Hebard's career as University of Wyoming administrator and professor, see Williams, *Aven Nelson,* pp. 28, 151–154. On Hebard's own willingness to exercise power, see Wenzel, "Dr. Grace Raymond Hebard," p. 10.

13. On the "Svengali-like hold," see Susan Macki and Eric D. Kohler, "Fencing Out the Foreigner: Influences on the 18th Wyoming Legislature and Its Exclusion of Foreign Physicians," *Wyoming History Journal* 69, no. 2 (spring 1997): 24.

14. "In Memoriam," p. 29.

15. Wenzel, "Dr. Grace Raymond Hebard," p. 10.

16. *Semi-Weekly Boomerang,* April 13, 1908; Wenzel, "Dr. Grace Raymond Hebard," pp. 11–12.

17. GRH, "Dedication of the New Library," March 14, 1924, p. 2, Hebard Papers.

18. Ibid., p. 4.

19. There is an extensive literature on the history and political significance

of librarianship and on women's important part in that history. See Dee Garrison, *Apostles of Culture: The Public Librarian and American Society, 1876–1920* (New York: Free Press, 1976); Kathleen Weibel, Kathleen M. Heim, and Dianne J. Ellsworth, *The Role of Women in Librarianship: The Entry, Advancement, and Struggle for Equalization in One Profession* (Phoenix: Oryx Press, 1979); Michael F. Winter, *The Professionalization of Librarianship* (Champaign: University of Illinois Press, 1983); Joanne E. Passet, *Cultural Crusaders: Women Librarians in the American West, 1900–1917* (Albuquerque: University of New Mexico Press, 1994); David Shauit, *The Politics of Public Librarianship* (New York: Greenwood Press, 1986); Abigail Van Slyke, *Free to All: Carnegie Libraries and American Culture, 1890–1920* (Chicago: University of Chicago Press, 1995); Andrew G. Kirk, "That 'Fearful Brightness': The Conservation Library, and the American Environmental Movement, 1950–1980" (Ph.D. diss., University of New Mexico, 1998).

20. GRH to Dr. C. A. Duniway, April 18, 1914, Box 1, Hebard Papers.

21. GRH to Dr. C. A. Duniway, April 14, 1917; GRH to Aven Nelson, April 4, 1918; both in Box 1, Hebard Papers. On Hebard as mentor to women librarians, see Agnes Wright Spring, *Near the Greats: Prominent People Known to Agnes Wright Spring* (Frederick, Colo.: Platte 'n Press, 1981), pp. 72–76.

22. "In Memoriam," p. 3.

23. Ibid., p. 3; Wenzel, "Dr. Grace Raymond Hebard," pp. 14–15; Williams, *Aven Nelson*, pp. 153–154.

24. Williams, *Aven Nelson*, p. 29.

25. Hardy, *Wyoming University*, pp. 18, 32. On national trends, see *Recent Social Trends in the United States: Report of the President's Research Committee on Social Trends* (New York: McGraw-Hill, 1933), p. 338.

26. Hebard, "Report to the President, 1913," Box 1, Hebard Papers; author's interview with Caroline Mortimer, Green River, Wyoming, July 23, 1984; Frank Van Nuys, "'My One Hobby': Grace Raymond Hebard and Americanization in Wyoming," *Wyoming History Journal* 67, no. 2 (autumn 1995): 2–15.

27. Leslie B. Cook to GRH, March 1, 1916, Box 35, Hebard Papers.

28. Spring, *Near the Greats*, p. 76.

29. Student to GRH, n.d., Box 35, Hebard Papers.

30. On the question of women's work in maintaining familial and social networks across distances, see Micaela di Leonardo, "The Female World of Cards and Holidays," in *The Women's West*, ed. Susan H. Armitage and Elizabeth Jameson (Norman: University of Oklahoma Press, 1987).

31. Virginia Scharff and Katherine Jensen, "The Professors' Club and the Complexities of Women's Culture," paper presented to a conference on "Women's Culture in the Great Plains," sponsored by the Institute for Great Plains Studies, Lincoln, Nebraska, March 19, 1987.

32. Lillian Faderman, *Surpassing the Love of Men: Romantic Friendships between Women from the Renaissance to the Present* (New York: William Morrow, 1981); Blanche Wiesen Cook, "Female Support Networks and Political Activism: Lillian Wald, Crystal Eastman, and Emma Goldman," *Chrysalis* 8 (1979): 17–27; Rosenberg, *Beyond Separate Spheres;* Scharff, "Independent and Feminine Life."

33. GRH to Dumas Malone, September 11, 1933, Box 5, Hebard Papers; Agnes Mathilde Wergeland file, Box 33, Hebard Papers.

34. Excerpt from "Thy Hand," unpublished poem by Agnes Mathilde Wergeland, Box 36, Hebard Papers.

35. "Dr. Agnes Wergeland Was Early History Professor," *Wyoming Alumnus*, May–June 1974, pp. 6–7, Agnes Mathilde Wergeland vertical file, American Heritage Center, University of Wyoming, Laramie.

36. Van Nuys, "'My One Hobby.'"

37. GRH, "Immigration and Needed Ballot Reform," *Illinois Wesleyan Magazine*, October 1896, Box 33, Hebard Papers.

38. Van Nuys, "'My One Hobby,'" pp. 2–15.

39. GRH, "Why We Exclude the 97," *Woman Citizen*, January 18, 1921, Box 37, Hebard Papers.

40. "In Memoriam"; Paul Frison, "Dr. Hebard, Wyoming's Foremost Historian, Is True Daughter of Pioneer Parents," *Wyoming News* (undated clipping); GRH to Dr. C. A. Duniway, Annual Report for Department of Economics and Sociology, April 14, 1917, Box 1; GRH to D.A.R., October 4, 1916, Box 1; GRH to Senator John B. Kendrick, April 19, 1924, Box 2: all in Hebard Papers.

41. Van Nuys, "'My One Hobby,'" pp. 3, 8, 11.

42. "Dr. Hebard Given Credit for Child Labor Legislation," *Wyoming State Tribune*, May 21, 1923, Hebard Papers.

43. On Hebard's suffrage work, see Scharff, "Independent and Feminine Life," pp. 131–132.

44. I am indebted to Melanie Gustafson for the idea that Hebard marketed suffrage as a Wyoming export.

45. "Woman Suffrage," Box 6, Folder 6, Hebard Papers.

46. "Speeches Delivered at Suffrage Tablet Unveiling Saturday," *Cheyenne Leader*, July 24, 1917, Box 6, Hebard Papers.

47. "Dr. Hebard Appeals for Suffrage Cause," *Wyoming State Tribune,* May 11, 1920, Hebard Papers.

48. "Advance Guard of Suffrage Emergency Corps Arrives," *New York Tribune*, May 2, 1920; *Laramie Daily Boomerang*, May 15, 1920: both in Box 6, Hebard Papers.

49. GRH, "How Woman Suffrage Came to Wyoming," Box 6, Hebard Papers.

50. Wenzel, "Dr. Grace Raymond Hebard," p. 41.

51. Ibid., p. 68.

52. GRH, "First White Women in Wyoming," Hebard Papers

53. Scharff, "Independent and Feminine Life." Larson, *History of Wyoming*, pp. 91–92, has demonstrated the problems with Hebard's account of the coming of woman suffrage in Wyoming.

54. GRH to June Etta Downey, October 13, 1930, Box 35, Hebard Papers.

55. GRH, "Journal of Trip in Wyoming Following and Marking Trails," 1915, Box 4, Hebard Papers.

56. Ibid.

57. GRH, "How Woman Suffrage Came to Wyoming," Box 6, Hebard Papers.

58. On this controversy, see Larson, *History of Wyoming*, pp. 78–94; T. A. Larson, "Woman Suffrage in Wyoming," *Pacific Northwest Quarterly* 56 (1965): 57–66; and Virginia Scharff, "The Case for Domestic Feminism: Woman Suffrage in Wyoming," *Annals of Wyoming* 56, no. 2 (fall 1984): 29–37.

59. GRH, *Sacajawea* (Glendale, Calif.: Arthur C. Clark Company, 1933), pp. 17–18.

60. "In Memoriam," p. 10; GRH, *Sacajawea*, p. 26.

61. Correspondence in John B. Kendrick file, Box 19, Hebard Papers.

62. Lewis F. Crawford to Nelson A. Mason, March 28, 1925, Box 17, Hebard Papers. Stella M. Drumm mentions the controversy in her "Heroic Women of the Fur Trade," 1926–1927, typescript, Missouri Historical Society Library, St. Louis.

63. GRH to Louise Phelps Kellogg, February 4, 1928, Box 18, Hebard Papers. Hebard's correspondence regarding the Sacagawea monument controversy is scattered through numerous files in Boxes 17, 18, and 19, Hebard Papers.

64. GRH to Kellogg, February 4, 1928.

65. Drumm, "Heroic Women of the Fur Trade."

66. Wenzel, "Dr. Grace Raymond Hebard," p. 51.

67. GRH, "Journal of Trip in Wyoming Following and Marking Trails."

CHAPTER 5. "SO MANY MILES TO A PERSON": FABIOLA CABEZA DE BACA

The epigraphs are from Fabiola Cabeza de Baca, *We Fed Them Cactus* (Albuquerque: University of New Mexico Press, [1954] 1994), pp. 138–139 and 129, respectively.

1. The classic study of land, empire, and the history of New Mexicans is George I. Sánchez, *Forgotten People: A Study of New Mexicans* (Albuquerque: University of New Mexico Press, 1940). See also María Montoya, *Translating Property: The Maxwell Land Grant and the Conflict over Land in the American West, 1840 to 1920* (Berkeley: University of California Press, 2002).

2. See Vera Norwood and Janice Monk, eds., *The Desert Is No Lady: Southwestern Landscapes in Women's Writing and Art* (New Haven: Yale University Press, 1987); Paula Gunn Allen, "Magic and Realism in the Southwest," in *Many Wests: Place, Culture, and Regional Identity*, ed. David M. Wrobel and Michael C. Steiner (Lawrence: University Press of Kansas, 1997); Chris Wilson, *The Myth of Santa Fe: Creating a Modern Regional Tradition* (Albuquerque: University of New Mexico Press, 1997); and Hal K. Rothman, *Devil's Bargains: Tourism in the Twentieth-Century American West* (Lawrence: University Press of Kansas, 1998), pp. 81–112.

3. Sánchez, *Forgotten People*, pp. 3–4.

4. The most comprehensive study of Mexican American women to date is Vicki L. Ruiz, *From Out of the Shadows: Mexican Women in Twentieth-Century America* (New York: Oxford University Press, 1998). On the significance of *mestizaje* in the Southwest, see Gloria Anzaldúa, *Borderlands/La Frontera: The New Mestiza* (San Francisco: Aunt Lute Books, 1999); and Gloria Anzaldúa,

ed., *Making Face, Making Soul/Haciendo Caras: Creative and Critical Perspectives by Feminists of Color* (San Francisco: Aunt Lute Books, 1990). On Hispanic women confronting modernity in New Mexico and Colorado, see Sarah Deutsch, *No Separate Refuge: Culture, Class and Gender on an Anglo-Hispanic Frontier in the American Southwest, 1880–1940* (New York: Oxford University Press, 1987). More recently, Deena J. González has made the case for women's resistance to colonization in *Refusing the Favor: The Spanish-Mexican Women of Santa Fe, 1820–1880* (New York: Oxford University Press, 1999). Terms of preference for ethnic identification vary over time, and differ from place to place. New Mexicans who trace their local roots to the Spanish and Mexican periods most often affirm the designation Hispanic, rather than Mexican, Spanish, Chicano, or Latino.

5. Such speech in itself comprises a form of resistance. See Gayatri Chakravorti Spivak and Ranajit Guha, eds., *Selected Subaltern Studies* (New York: Oxford University Press, 1988).

6. Deutsch, *No Separate Refuge*, p. 206.

7. Chicana and Anglo feminist scholars and critics of Chicana/o literature have explored the careers of Nina Otero-Warren, Cleofas Jaramillo, Concha Ortiz y Pino, Carmen Espinoza, and the woman whose work and life I will discuss, Fabiola Cabeza de Baca. See Gloria Velasquez Treviño, "The Cultural Ambivalence of Early Chicana Prose Writers" (Ph.D. diss., Stanford University, 1985); Joan M. Jensen, "Crossing Ethnic Barriers in the Southwest: Women's Agricultural Extension Education, 1914–1940," in Jensen, *Promise to the Land: Essays on Rural Women* (Albuquerque: University of New Mexico Press, 1991), pp. 220–230; Erlinda Gonzalez-Berry, ed., *Paso por Aqui: Critical Essays on the New Mexican Literary Tradition, 1542–1988* (Albuquerque: University of New Mexico Press, 1989); Genaro M. Padilla, "Imprisoned Narrative? Or Lies, Secrets, and Silence in New Mexico Women's Autobiography," in *Criticism in the Borderlands*, ed. Hector Calderon and Jose David Saldivar (Durham, N.C.: Duke University Press, 1991); Ramon Saldivar, *Chicano Narrative: The Dialectics of Difference* (Madison: University of Wisconsin Press, 1990); Tey Diana Rebolledo, "Tradition and Mythology: Signatures of Landscape in Chicana Literature," in Norwood and Monk, eds., *The Desert Is No Lady;* Tey Diana Rebolledo, Introduction to Cabeza de Baca, *We Fed Them Cactus;* and Merrihelen Ponce, "The Life and Work of Fabiola Cabeza de Baca, New Mexican Hispanic Woman Writer: A Contextual Biography" (Ph.D. diss., University of New Mexico, 1995).

8. In this chapter I use the terms "Hispanic" and "Spanish" to describe cultural identities and alignments in early-twentieth-century New Mexico for a very simple reason: they were the words Fabiola Cabeza de Baca herself used. Again, these are contested political categories that have since given way to other terms of identification, including Chicana/o, Mexican American, and Latina/o, similarly political.

9. See Montoya, *Translating Property.*

10. Carey McWilliams, *North from Mexico: The Spanish-Speaking People of the United States* (Philadelphia: J. B. Lippincott, 1949). John M. Nieto-Phillips has brilliantly explored the roots, transformations, politics, and possibilities of Spanish identity in "'No Other Blood': History, Language, and Spanish Amer-

ican Ethnic Identity in New Mexico, 1880s–1920s" (Ph.D. diss., University of California, Los Angeles, 1997).

11. For an extraordinary view of the preservation of Indo-Hispano ritual, see Miguel Gandert, *Nuevo México Profundo: Rituals of an Indo-Hispano Homeland* (Santa Fe: Museum of New Mexico Press, 2000), with essays by Ramón A. Gutiérrez, Enrique Lamadrid, Lucy Lippard, and Chris Wilson.

12. Nieto-Phillips, "'No Other Blood,'" pp. 255–256.

13. Fabiola Cabeza de Baca Gilbert, *The Good Life: New Mexico Traditions and Food* (Santa Fe: Museum of New Mexico Press, 1986).

14. Fabiola Cabeza de Baca, "This Is New Mexico," Box 1, Folder 9, Fabiola Cabeza de Baca Gilbert Papers, Center for Southwest Research, University of New Mexico General Library, Albuquerque (hereafter cited as Cabeza de Baca Papers). In my view, Cabeza de Baca's appreciation for the dynamism and complexity of New Mexico history anticipated the best of current scholarship, including William de Buys, *Enchantment and Exploitation: The Life and Hard Times of a New Mexico Mountain Range* (Albuquerque: University of New Mexico Press, 1985).

15. On Nina Otero-Warren, see Charlotte Whaley, *Nina Otero-Warren of Santa Fe* (Albuquerque: University of New Mexico Press, 1994); on New Mexico Hispanas in politics more generally, see Joan M. Jensen, "'Disfranchisement Is a Disgrace': Women and Politics in New Mexico, 1900–1940," in *New Mexico Women: Intercultural Perspectives,* ed. Joan M. Jensen and Darlis Miller (Albuquerque: University of New Mexico Press, 1986), pp. 301–332; and Elizabeth Salas, "Soledad Chávez Chacón, Adelina Otero-Warren, and Concha Ortiz y Pino: Three Hispana Politicians in New Mexico Politics, 1920–1940," in *We Have Come to Stay: American Women and Political Parties, 1880–1960,* ed. Melanie Gustafson, Kristie Miller, and Elisabeth Israels Perry (Albuquerque: University of New Mexico Press, 1999), pp. 161–174.

16. Cabeza de Baca, "This Is New Mexico." Jane Slaughter, in *Women and the Italian Resistance, 1943–1945* (Denver: Arden Press, 1997), points out that the opposition between private and public obscures connections between women's acts of resistance and agency and larger political developments, even as it invokes and reifies "gender scripts and symbols." As former partisan Giovanna Zangrandi told Slaughter (p. 1), the Italian resistance during World War II was "a war 'nested in kitchens.'"

17. Cabeza de Baca, "The People and the Community," Box 1, Folder 11, Cabeza de Baca Papers.

18. Ponce, "Life and Work," pp. 18–69; Manuscript inventory, Cabeza de Baca Papers.

19. Cabeza de Baca, "La Liendre," n.d., Box 1, Folder 16, Cabeza de Baca Papers.

20. Ibid.

21. Ibid.

22. Ibid.

23. Cabeza de Baca, *We Fed Them Cactus,* p. 135.

24. Ibid., pp. 129, 138–139; "The Work," n.d., Box 1, Folder 11, Cabeza de Baca Papers.

25. Cabeza de Baca, *We Fed Them Cactus,* p. 139.

26. Ibid.

27. On "knowing nature through work," see Judy Smith, "Something Old, Something New, Something Borrowed, Something Due: Women and Appropriate Technology" (pamphlet) (Butte, Mont., and Washington, D.C.: National Center for Appropriate Technology, 1978); Richard White, "Are You an Environmentalist, or Do You Work for a Living? Work and Nature," in William Cronon, ed., *Uncommon Ground: Toward Reinventing Nature* (New York: W. W. Norton, 1995), pp. 171–185; Virginia Scharff, "Man and Nature! Sex Secrets of Environmental History," in *Human Nature: Biology, Culture, and Environmental History,* ed. John P. Herron and Andrew G. Kirk (Albuquerque: University of New Mexico Press, 1999), pp. 31–48.

28. Miscellaneous Spanish colonial documents and fragments of documents, Box 1, Folders 3, 5, 18, Cabeza de Baca Papers.

29. Cabeza de Baca, "This Is New Mexico." For a compelling discussion of the importance of print to Hispanic political and cultural resistance in the Southwest, see Gabriel Melendez, *So All Is Not Lost: The Poetics of Print in Nuevomexicano Communities, 1834–1958* (Albuquerque: University of New Mexico Press, 1997).

30. Ponce, "Life and Work," p. 33, citing oral history of Fabiola Cabeza de Baca Gilbert by Paula Thaidigsman, Santa Fe, New Mexico, April 29, 1975, Special Collections, University of New Mexico General Library, Albuquerque; also ibid., p. 88.

31. See Kathryn Kish Sklar, *Catherine Beecher: A Study in American Domesticity* (New Haven: Yale University Press, 1973); Kathleen Underwood, "The Pace of Their Own Lives: Teaching Training and the Life Course of Western Women," *Pacific Historical Review* 55 (November 1986): 513–530; Polly Welts Kaufman, *Women Teachers on the Frontier* (New Haven: Yale University Press, 1984); Mary Hurlbut Cordier, *Schoolwomen of the Prairies and Plains: Personal Narratives from Iowa, Kansas, and Nebraska, 1860s–1920s* (Lincoln: University of Nebraska Press, 1997); and Kathleen Weiler, *Country Schoolwomen : Teaching in Rural California, 1850–1950* (Stanford: Stanford University Press, 1998).

32. Cabeza de Baca, *We Fed Them Cactus,* p. 154.

33. Over the past twenty years, scholars and community activists in nearly every western state have collected hundreds of oral histories of women who spent at least some time teaching in rural schools. Undertakings like the Wyoming Heritage and Contemporary Values Project were funded by state humanities councils and presented chiefly in the form of public programs. Most found funding only for transcriptions of oral history interview tapes, which are archived in various locations in each state (in Wyoming, for example, the transcripts can be found at the Wyoming State Archives in Cheyenne). Some other interview material has been published; see, for example, Mary Logan Rothschild and Pamela Hronek, *Doing What the Day Brought: An Oral History of Arizona Women* (Tucson: University of Arizona Press, 1992).

34. Cabeza de Baca, *We Fed Them Cactus,* p. 156.

35. Ibid., p. 157.

36. Ibid., p. 158.

37. Ibid., p. 167.
38. Fabiola Cabeza de Baca, "The Homes," n.d., Box 1, Folder 11, Cabeza de Baca Papers.
39. Cabeza de Baca, *We Fed Them Cactus,* p. 159.
40. Ponce, "Life and Work," pp. 77–79.
41. Cabeza de Baca, *We Fed Them Cactus,* p. 154.
42. On Cabeza de Baca's marriage to Gilbert, see Ponce, "Life and Work," pp. 100–101; personal communication, Cynthia Orozco.
43. Cabeza de Baca, *Good Life,* p. v.
44. Cabeza de Baca, "The Homes."
45. Ibid.
46. See Joan M. Jensen, "Canning Comes to New Mexico: Women and the Agricultural Extension Service, 1914–1919," in Jensen and Miller, eds., *New Mexico Women,* pp. 201–226.
47. Fabiola Cabeza de Baca, "Pioneering in Home Economics," n.d., Box 1, Folder 15, Cabeza de Baca Papers.
48. Cabeza de Baca, "The Homes."
49. Ibid.
50. Cabeza de Baca, "Pioneering in Home Economics."
51. Cabeza de Baca, "The Homes."
52. Jensen, "Crossing Ethnic Barriers," pp. 227–230.
53. Untitled typescript of speech, Box 1, Folder 17, Cabeza de Baca Papers.
54. Cabeza de Baca, "Hunger," n.d., Box 1, Folder 15, Cabeza de Baca Papers.
55. Cabeza de Baca, "The Homes." The significance of mutual aid traditions in the history of Mexican American women cannot be overstated. See Ruiz, *From Out of the Shadows.*
56. Unpublished materials in Box 1, Folder 11, "Narratives—Northern New Mexico, land, people, homes," Cabeza de Baca Papers; "Narratives, Folklore,— Chile, Home Remedies, Medicine Women, Sheep Industry, Colchas, Hunger, Food, Home Economics," Box 1, Folder 15, Cabeza de Baca Papers; Fabiola Cabeza de Baca, *Historic Cookery of New Mexico* (Santa Fe: Ancient City Press, 1997), *Good Life,* and *We Fed Them Cactus;* and Susan Pieper, "Fabiola's Good Life," *New Mexico Resources* 13 (spring 1995): 3–11, in Fabiola Cabeza de Baca vertical file, MSS. 603, Center for Southwest Research, University of New Mexico, Albuquerque.
57. Cabeza de Baca, *Good Life,* p. v.
58. Paula Thaidigsman, notes from oral history interview with Fabiola Cabeza de Baca, August 1975, Box 1, Folder 14, Women in New Mexico Collection, MSS. 303, Center for Southwest Research, University of New Mexico, Albuquerque; manuscript inventory, Cabeza de Baca Papers; news clippings, Box 1, Folder 20, Cabeza de Baca Papers.
59. Cabeza de Baca, "The Wake," Box 1, Folder 17, Cabeza de Baca Papers; see also material in Box 1, Folder 19.
60. Cabeza de Baca, "The Wake."
61. Cabeza de Baca, "Folklore," n.d., Box 1, Folder 16, Cabeza de Baca Papers.

62. Cabeza de Baca, "An Indian Feast Day," n.d., Box 1, Folder 17, Cabeza de Baca Papers. Miguel Gandert's photographs of Indo-Hispano ritual in *Nuevo México Profundo* reflect precisely this mingling of tradition and innovation in cultural borderlands.

63. Miscellaneous documents and fragments dealing with Spanish colonial women's legal and property rights, Box 1, Folders 1, 3, 4, 5,6, 7, 24, Cabeza de Baca Papers. Like Fabiola Cabeza de Baca, Chicana historians have found legal documents a rich source of information on the lives and rights of women in Spanish and Mexican New Mexico. See González, *Refusing the Favor;* Montoya, "Dispossessed People"; and Yolanda Chávez Leyva, "'A Poor Widow Burdened with Children': Widows and Land in Colonial New Mexico," in *Writing the Range: Race, Class and Culture in the Women's West,* ed. Elizabeth Jameson and Susan Armitage (Norman: University of Oklahoma Press, 1997), pp. 85–96.

64. Frank McCullock to Fabiola Cabeza de Baca, July 17, 1967, Box 1, Folder 1, Cabeza de Baca Papers.

65. John Landon to Fabiola Cabeza de Baca, May 6, 1972, Box 1, Folder 1, Cabeza de Baca Papers.

66. John Landon to Fabiola Cabeza de Baca, February 14, 1973, Box 1, Folder 1, Cabeza de Baca Papers.

67. Untitled, undated ms., Box 1, Folder 11, Cabeza de Baca Papers.

68. Ibid.

69. Cabeza de Baca, "People and Community."

70. Ibid.

71. My thinking on geographic matters has been influenced by Anthony Giddens, *A Contemporary Critique of Historical Materialism* (Berkeley: University of California Press, 1987); David Harvey, *The Condition of Postmodernity: An Enquiry into the Origins of Cultural Change* (Cambridge: Blackwell, 1992); Akhil Gupta and James Ferguson, "Beyond 'Culture': Space, Identity, and the Politics of Difference," *Cultural Anthropology* 7 (February 1992): 6–23; and Edward Soja, *Postmodern Geographies: The Reassertion of Space in Critical Social Theory* (London: Verso, 1993). On regionalization within the West in particular, see Wrobel and Steiner, eds., *Many Wests.*

CHAPTER 6. RESISTING ARREST: JO ANN ROBINSON

The epigraph sources are Jo Ann Gibson Robinson, *The Montgomery Bus Boycott and the Women Who Started It* (Knoxville: University of Tennessee Press, 1987), pp. 105 ("Either fortuitously . . . ") and 40 ("The city was their home . . . "); and Quintard Taylor, *In Search of the Racial Frontier: African Americans in the American West, 1528–1990* (New York: W. W. Norton, 1998), p. 311.

1. David J. Garrow, Foreword to Robinson, *Montgomery Bus Boycott,* pp. viii–xv.

2. See Douglas Flamming, "A Westerner in Search of 'Negro-ness': Region and Race in the Writing of Arna Bontemps," in *Over the Edge: Remapping the American West,* ed. Valerie J. Matsumoto and Blake Allmendinger (Berkeley: University of California Press, 1999), pp. 85–104.

3. Here I am making a rather obvious point about the ways in which the West as a frame of reference asserts itself through the mythic presence of white people and the relative absence of pretty much everyone else. This point has been made by many historians writing in the last twenty years, particularly women's historians, who have labored mightily against racist geography that erases people of color. See, for example, Elizabeth Jameson, "Toward a Multicultural History of Women in the Western United States," *Signs: Journal of Women in Culture and Society* 13, no. 4 (summer 1988): 761–791. The most eloquent and informative example of resistance to the intrinsic whiteness of western women's history is Elizabeth Jameson and Susan Armitage's monumental edited volume, *Writing the Range: Race, Class, and Culture in the Women's West* (Norman: University of Oklahoma Press, 1997).

4. Taylor, *In Search of the Racial Frontier.*

5. Ibid.; Quintard Taylor, *The Forging of a Black Community: Seattle's Central District, from 1870 through the Civil Rights Era* (Seattle: University of Washington Press, 1994); Gretchen Lemke-Santangelo, *Abiding Courage: African American Women and the East Bay Community* (Chapel Hill: University of North Carolina Press, 1996); Shirley Ann Wilson Moore, *To Place Our Deeds: The African American Community in Richmond, California, 1910–1963* (Berkeley: University of California Press, 1999).

6. Gerald Nash, *The American West in the Twentieth Century: A Short History of an Urban Oasis* (Albuquerque: University of New Mexico Press, 1977).

7. On Cold War politics and culture in the United States, see Elaine Tyler May, *Homeward Bound: American Families in the Cold War Era* (New York: Basic Books, 1988); Robert Dallek, *The American Style of Foreign Policy: Cultural Politics and Foreign Affairs* (New York: Oxford University Press, 1983); and Paul Boyer, *By the Bomb's Early Light: American Thought and Culture at the Dawn of the Atomic Age* (New York: Pantheon Books, 1984). A recent collection of essays edited by Kevin Fernlund, *The Cold War American West, 1945–1989* (Albuquerque: University of New Mexico Press, 1998), explores the political, cultural, and geographic impacts of the Cold War on the region, and the ways in which Cold War ideology made use of symbols from western mythology.

8. On civil rights and other struggles, see especially A. Yvette Huginnie, "Containment and Emancipation: Race, Class, and Gender in the Cold War West," in Fernlund, ed., *Cold War American West*, pp. 51–70.

9. Nash, *American West in the Twentieth Century*, p. 191.

10. Ferenc Morton Szasz, *The Day the Sun Rose Twice: The Story of the Trinity Site Nuclear Explosion, July 16, 1945* (Albuquerque: University of New Mexico Press, 1984); Tad Bartimus and Scott McCartney, *Trinity's Children: Living Along America's Nuclear Highway* (Albuquerque: University of New Mexico Press, 1991); Peter Bacon Hales, *Atomic Spaces: Living on the Manhattan Project* (Urbana: University of Illinois Press, 1997); María E. Montoya, "Landscapes of the Cold War West," in Fernlund, ed., *Cold War American West*, pp. 9–28.

11. Robinson, *Montgomery Bus Boycott*, pp. xii, 9–10.

12. J. Mills Thornton, III, "Challenge and Response in the Montgomery Bus Boycott of 1955–56," in *The Walking City: The Montgomery Bus Boycott,*

1955–1956, ed. David J. Garrow (Brooklyn, N.Y.: Carlson, 1989), p. 330; Stephen M. Millner, "A Boycott Consciousness Takes Form," ibid., pp. 439, 448; Stephen M. Millner, "The Leap to Activation," ibid., p. 450.

13. Mary Fair Burks, "Trailblazers: Women in the Montgomery Bus Boycott," in *Black Women in United States History,* vol. 16, ed. Darlene Clark Hine, Elsa Barkley Brown, Tiffany R. L. Patterson, and Lillian S. Williams (Brooklyn, N.Y.: Carlson, 1990), p. 76.

14. Ibid.

15. Ibid., p. 78.

16. Ibid., pp. 78–79.

17. Ibid., p. 80.

18. Ibid., p. 81.

19. Ibid., p. 74.

20. Robinson, *Montgomery Bus Boycott,* p. 15.

21. Ibid., pp. 79, 90. For a detailed account of the rise of segregation practices, see Howard N. Rabinowitz, *Race Relations in the Urban South, 1865–1890* (New York: Oxford University Press, 1978).

22. Robinson, *Montgomery Bus Boycott,* p. 79.

23. Ibid., pp. xiii, 15–16.

24. Taylor, *In Search of the Racial Frontier,* p. 93; Helen Holdredge, *Mammy Pleasant* (New York: G. P. Putnam, 1953), p. 62. Paula Giddings details a history of black women's opposition to discrimination in transportation in *When and Where I Enter: The Impact of Black Women on Race and Sex in America* (New York: William Morrow, 1984), pp. 261–270; see also Barbara Y. Welke, "When All the Women Were White, and All the Blacks Were Men: Gender, Class, Race, and the Road to *Plessy, 1855–1914,*" *Law and History Review* 13, no. 2 (fall 1995): 261–316; and Robin D. G. Kelley, "'We Are Not What We Seem': Rethinking Black Working-Class Opposition in the Jim Crow South," *Journal of American History* 80, no. 1 (June 1993): 75–112.

25. Robinson, *Montgomery Bus Boycott,* p. 31.

26. Ibid., pp. 37–39.

27. Steven M. Millner, "Interview: U. J. Fields, November 25, 1977," in Garrow, ed., *Walking City,* p. 534. For more on the Colvin incident, see Ralph D. Abernathy, "The Natural History of a Social Movement: The Montgomery Improvement Association," ibid., p. 110; Thomas J. Gilliam, "The Montgomery Bus Boycott of 1955–1956," ibid., p. 206; and Thornton, "Challenge and Response," p. 336.

28. Robinson, *Montgomery Bus Boycott,* p. 40.

29. Ibid., pp. 22, 31–32.

30. Ibid., p. 43; Giddings, *When and Where I Enter,* pp. 262–264.

31. Taylor Branch, *Parting the Waters: America in the King Years, 1954–63* (New York: Simon and Schuster, 1988), p. 131.

32. Robinson, *Montgomery Bus Boycott,* pp. 45–46.

33. Ibid.

34. Ibid., pp. 92–94.

35. Ibid., pp. 39–74, 115,

36. Ibid., p. 140.

37. Branch, *Parting the Waters*, p. 312.

38. Robinson, *Montgomery Bus Boycott*, pp. 169–171.

39. Richard W. Etulain, *Conversations with Wallace Stegner on Western History and Literature* (Salt Lake City: University of Utah Press, 1990).

40. Robinson, *Montgomery Bus Boycott*, pp. 7, 11.

41. Ibid., pp. 19, 24.

42. Ibid., pp. 58, 62, 75, 88, 100.

43. Ibid., p. 88.

44. Ibid., pp. 104–105.

45. Ibid., p. 126.

46. Ibid., p. 79.

47. Ibid., p. 102.

48. Ibid., p. 171. Kelley, "'We Are Not What We Seem,'" p. 95, notes that "central to black working-class politics was mobility, for it afforded workers relative freedom to escape oppressive living and working conditions and power to negotiate better working conditions."

49. Robinson, *Montgomery Bus Boycott*, pp. xii, xv.

50. Ibid., pp. 171–172.

51. Robin Kelley ("'We Are Not What We Seem,'" p. 77n.9) uses the term "infrapolitics" to approach the political meaning of black working-class opposition in the South, and acknowledges a scholarly tradition examining the meaning of everyday life ranging from the work of anthropologist James C. Scott to that of theorist Michel de Certeau to that of labor historian E. P. Thompson. Kelley, however, fails to acknowledge a long, global, and sophisticated tradition of feminist theoretical analysis of sexual and personal politics, including the work of, among many others, Mary Wollstonecraft, Alexandra Kollontai, Simone de Beauvoir, Kate Millett, and Joan Wallach Scott.

CHAPTER 7. THE LONG STRANGE TRIP OF PAMELA DES BARRES

The sources of the chapter epigraphs are, in order: Ellen Willis, *No More Nice Girls: Countercultural Essays* (Hanover, N.H.: Wesleyan University Press, 1992), p. xxii; Evan Davies, "Psychological Characteristics of Beatle Mania," *Journal of the History of Ideas* 30, no. 2 (April–June 1969): 276; and Pamela Des Barres, *I'm with the Band: Confessions of a Groupie* (New York: Jove Books, 1988), p. 121.

1. Alice Echols, *Scars of Sweet Paradise: The Life and Times of Janis Joplin* (New York: Metropolitan Books, 1999), p. 45.

2. Beth Bailey, *Sex in the Heartland* (Cambridge, Mass.: Harvard University Press, 1999). Studies of rock 'n' roll abound; they include Greil Marcus, *Mystery Train: Images of America in Rock 'n' Roll Music,* 3d rev. ed. (New York: Plume, [1975] 1990); David P. Szatmary, *Rockin' in Time: A Social History of Rock-and-Roll* (Englewood Cliffs, N.J.: Prentice-Hall, 1991); and Simon Frith, *Sound Effects: Youth, Leisure, and the Politics of Rock 'n' Roll* (New York: Pantheon Books, 1981).

3. Susan J. Douglas, *Where the Girls Are: Growing Up Female with the Mass Media* (New York: Times Books, 1994), p. 98.

4. The literature on African Americans in Los Angeles is rich and fast-growing. See, for example, Quintard Taylor, *In Search of the Racial Frontier: African Americans in the American West, 1528–1990* (New York: W. W. Norton, 1998); Dolores Hayden, "Biddy Mason's Los Angeles," *California History* 68, no. 3 (fall 1989): 86–99; Douglas Flamming, "African American Politics in Progressive-Era Los Angeles," in *California Progressivism Revisited,* ed. William Deverell and Tom Sitton (Berkeley: University of California Press, 1994), pp. 203–228; Douglas Flamming, "A Westerner in Search of 'Negro-ness': Region and Race in the Writing of Arna Bontemps," in *Over the Edge: Remapping the American West,* ed. Valerie J. Matsumoto and Blake Allmendinger (Berkeley: University of California Press, 1999), pp. 85–104; and William Deverell and Douglas Flamming, "Race, Region, and Regional Identity: Boosting Los Angeles, 1880–1930," in *Power and Place in the North American West,* ed. Richard White and John M. Findlay (Seattle: University of Washington Press, 1999), pp. 117–143.

5. Des Barres, *I'm with the Band,* p. 2.

6. Beth Bailey deftly traces the significance of these changes for one western community in *Sex in the Heartland.* More general histories of women's lives in the period include Rosalind Rosenberg, *Divided Lives: American Women in the Twentieth Century* (New York: Hill and Wang, 1992); and Ruth Rosen, *The World Split Open: How the Modern Women's Movement Changed America* (New York: Viking, 2000).

7. Anthony Giddens, *A Contemporary Critique of Historical Materialism* (New York: Macmillan, 1981).

8. The definitive Joplin biography is Alice Echols, *Scars of Sweet Paradise: The Life and Times of Janis Joplin* (New York: Metropolitan Books, 1999). Previous works include Peggy Caserta, *Going Down with Janis* (New York: Dell, 1974); Ellis Amburn, *Pearl: The Obsessions and Passions of Janis Joplin* (New York: Warner Books, 1992); and Laura Joplin, *Love, Janis: A Revealing New Biography of Janis Joplin with Never-Before-Published Letters* (New York: Villard Books, 1992).

9. Grace Slick with Andrea Cagan, *Somebody to Love: A Rock-and-Roll Memoir* (New York: Warner Books, 1998).

10. Arthur Salm, "As a Groupie, *Band* Author Topped the Charts," *San Diego Union-Tribune,* October 20, 1988.

11. Tom Hayden, "Port Huron Statement," excerpted in *A History of Our Time,* ed. William Chafe and Harvard Sitkoff (New York: Oxford University Press, 1983), p. 229. The best general history of the period is David Farber, *The Age of Great Dreams: America in the 1960s* (New York: Hill and Wang, 1994).

12. Des Barres, *I'm with the Band,* p. 2.

13. Ibid., p. 4.

14. Barbara Ehrenreich, Elizabeth Hess, and Gloria Jacobs, *Remaking Love: The Feminization of Sex* (Garden City, N.Y.: Anchor Books, 1987), p. 11.

15. Douglas, *Where the Girls Are,* p. 119.

16. On sexual containment, see Elaine Tyler May, *Homeward Bound: American Families in the Cold War Era* (New York: Basic Books, 1999), passim.

17. Des Barres, *I'm with the Band*, pp. 12–13.

18. Ibid., pp. 15–16.

19. Christine Stansell, *City of Women: Sex and Class in New York, 1789–1860* (Urbana: University of Illinois Press, 1987); Kathy Peiss, *Cheap Amusements: Working Women and Leisure in Turn-of-the-Century New York* (Philadelphia: Temple University Press, 1986); Shirley Ann Wilson Moore, *To Place Our Deeds: The African American Community in Richmond, California, 1910–1963* (Urbana: University of Illinois Press, 2000); Elisabeth Lapovsky Kennedy and Madeline D. Davis, *Boots of Leather, Slippers of Gold: The History of a Lesbian Community* (New York: Penguin, 1994).

20. Des Barres, *I'm with the Band*, p. 31.

21. On the history of American courtship, see Beth Bailey, *From Front Porch to Back Seat* (Baltimore: Johns Hopkins University Press, 1988).

22. Des Barres, *I'm with the Band*, pp. 38–44.

23. Nicholas von Hoffman, *We Are the People Our Parents Warned Us Against* (Chicago: Elephant Paperbacks, 1989), p. 1.

24. Des Barres, *I'm with the Band*, pp. 45–48. Many commentators have seen the Be-In as the beginning of the end for the counterculture. "Up until then," said Linda Gravenites, longtime Haight resident and close friend of Janis Joplin, "people came because they were full to overflowing and were sharing their fullness. After that, it was the empties who came, wanting to be filled" (quoted in Alice Echols, *Scars of Sweet Paradise: The Life and Times of Janis Joplin* [New York: Metropolitan Books, 1999], p. 157).

25. Des Barres, *I'm with the Band*, p. 53.

26. Ibid., pp. 54–64.

27. John Burks and Jerry Hopkins, *Groupies and Other Girls* (New York: Bantam Books, 1970), pp. 67–68.

28. Early in the history of the American republic, the practice of "treating" developed among urban working-class youth. Young men would pay for food, drink, and entertainment for young women, who were expected to reciprocate with sexual favors of one kind or another. See Christine Stansell, *City of Women*.

29. Des Barres, *I'm with the Band*, pp. 96–97, 102.

30. Ibid., pp. 71–72.

31. John Burks, Jerry Hopkins, and Paul Nelson, "The Groupies and Other Girls," *Rolling Stone*, February 15, 1969, p. 15; expanded as Burks and Hopkins, *Groupies and Other Girls*.

32. Des Barres, *I'm with the Band*, pp. 90, 74.

33. Burks and Hopkins, *Groupies and Other Girls*, p. 55.

34. Ibid., p. 16.

35. Des Barres, *I'm with the Band*, p. 81.

36. Ibid., p. 80.

37. Burks and Hopkins, *Groupies and Other Girls*, pp. 84–85.

38. Des Barres, *I'm with the Band*, p. 131.

39. Ibid., p. 213.

40. Willis, *No More Nice Girls*.

41. Des Barres, *I'm with the Band*, p. 187.

42. Ibid., pp. 180, 187.

43. On California's long-standing history of utopian and spiritual seeking, see Robert V. Hine, *California's Utopian Colonies* (San Marino, Calif.: Huntington Library, 1953); and Kevin Starr, *Americans and the California Dream, 1850–1915* (New York: Oxford University Press, 1973).

44. Des Barres, *I'm with the Band,* pp. 214, 219.

45. Ibid., pp. 224–225.

46. Ibid., pp. 224–225, 236, 240.

47. Ibid., pp. 236–237.

48. Ibid., pp. 256–257.

49. Pamela worked through this emotionally draining mess in a second volume of memoirs, titled *Take Another Little Piece of My Heart* (New York: Berkley Books, 1993).

50. Ibid., pp. 3, 8–9.

51. Ibid., pp. 132–133.

52. Des Barres, *I'm with the Band,* p. 225.

53. Des Barres, *Take Another Little Piece of My Heart,* p. 294.

CHAPTER 8. THEY PAVED PARADISE

1. Between April 1, 1990, and April 1, 2000, Douglas County grew from a population of 60,391 to 175,766, an increase of 191 percent (U.S. Census Bureau, 2000 Redistricting Data [P.L. 94-171], Summary File and 1990 Census).

2. Susan K. Appleby, "Douglas County: History and Guide to Cultural Resources" (M.A. thesis, University of Colorado at Denver, 1995).

3. See www.highlandsranch.com; Cathleen Ferraro, "Growth Spree on County Line Road," *Rocky Mountain News,* September 22, 1994, p. 66a; Michael E. Long, "Colorado's Front Range," *National Geographic* 190, no. 5 (November 1996): 80–103. The 2001 population figure is courtesy of the Highlands Ranch Community Association.

4. The figure of woman as American haven-keeper is explored in Dolores Hayden, *Redesigning the American Dream: The Future of Housing, Work, and Family Life* (New York: W. W. Norton, 1984); Marjorie DeVault, *Feeding the Family: The Social Organization of Caring as Gendered Work* (Chicago: University of Chicago Press, 1991); and Christopher Lasch, *Haven in a Heartless World: The Family Besieged* (New York: Basic Books, 1977).

5. "Highlands Ranch Facts at a Glance," Highlands Ranch Community Association Records, Highlands Ranch, Colorado; *Highlands Ranch Community Guide,* published by Mission Viejo Company, 1997.

6. Appleby, "Douglas County."

7. "Highlands Ranch Sold," *Rocky Mountain News,* August 2, 1997, p. 1.

8. *Highlands Ranch Community Guide,* 1997.

9. "Reserve Defends Line between Town, Country," *Rocky Mountain News,* August 23, 1993, pp. 18a, 19a; Steve Ormiston to author, May 20, 2002.

10. Wilderness, of course, presents problems of its own. See William Cronon, "The Trouble with Wilderness; or, Getting Back to the Wrong Nature," in *Uncommon Ground: Toward Reinventing Nature,* ed. William Cronon (New York: W. W. Norton, 1995), pp. 69–90.

11. "Creeping into the Open Space," *Highlands Ranch Herald,* August 1, 1997; "Douglas' Wide, Open Spaces May Cramp a Bit," *Rocky Mountain News,* August 4, 1997.

12. "Rattlesnakes, Hawks, Coyotes Are Also Residents of the Ranch," *Highlands Ranch Herald,* August 15, 1997.

13. "Incorporation Talk Shifts from 'Not Yet' to 'Maybe,'" *Highlands Ranch Herald,* July 28, 1997, p. 3.

14. "Women with Clout: Residents of Highlands Ranch Become Movers and Shakers in Various Civic, Cultural Projects," *Rocky Mountain News,* July 2, 1995, p. 35a.

15. The most comprehensive examination of women's travel issues to date took place at a 1996 conference in Baltimore, funded by the Federal Highway Administration and organized by the Drachman Institute at the University of Arizona in cooperation with Morgan State University. See "Women's Travel Issues: Proceedings from the Second National Conference, October, 1996," U.S. Department of Transportation, Federal Highway Administration, Office of Highway Information Management, HPM-40, publication no. FHWA-PL-97-024. Conference organizer Sandra Rosenbloom, director of the Drachman Institute, has been a pioneer in the field of gender and transportation.

16. "Growth Spree on County Line Road," *Rocky Mountain News,* September 22, 1994, p. 66a.

17. See www.parkmeadows.com; *Denver Post,* August 18, 1996, pp. 1a, 10a.

18. "Big Traffic Hike If Mall Is Built," *Denver Post,* April 3, 1995, p. 2b; "It's a Mall World after All," *Denver Post,* August 18, 1996, pp. 1a, 10a.

19. "Arapahoe Fearing Impact of Huge, New Douglas Mall," *Denver Post,* August 27, 1996, p. 3b.

20. I am indebted to Judy Morley for information on current Highlands Ranch covenants.

21. "Town Center Would Provide a Downtown," *Rocky Mountain News,* June 7, 1998, p. 4g.

ILLUSTRATIONS

Territory of Shaumpishuh, from "Land Agreement between Henry Whitfield and the Sachem Squaw" (September 29, 1639). Courtesy of the Massachusetts Historical Society. / *1*

"A Section of the Lewis and Clark Expedition, the Sources of the Missouri River, and the Meeting Place of the White Men with the Shoshone Indians," by Laura Tolman Scott. Reprinted by permission from Grace Raymond Hebard, *Sacajawea: Guide of the Lewis and Clark Expedition* (published by The Arthur H. Clark Company). / *11*

Route of Magoffin and Doniphan Expeditions. Reprinted by permission from Stella M. Drumm, editor, *Down the Santa Fe Trail and into Mexico: The Diary of Susan Shelby Magoffin, 1846–1847* (New Haven: Yale University Press, 1926). / *35*

"Map of the History and Romance of Wyoming," by Grace Raymond Hebard. Courtesy Grace Raymond Hebard Collection, American Heritage Center, University of Wyoming. / *67*

"Grace Raymond Hebard, Her Map," by Clara Frances McIntyre. Courtesy Grace Raymond Hebard Collection, American Heritage Center, University of Wyoming. / *93*

"Martinez Map of New Mexico, after 1602." From Fabiola Cabeza de Baca Papers. Courtesy of Center for Southwest Research, General Library, University of New Mexico. / *115*

Travels of Jo Ann Robinson, by George Pearl. Courtesy of the artist. / *139*

"Meanders," by the author. / *157*

Impressions of Highlands Ranch, Colorado, by Florian Brożek. Courtesy of the artist. / *181*

INDEX

Text:	10/13 Sabon
Display:	CgEgiziano Black and Sabon
Designer:	Nola Burger
Compositor:	Integrated Composition Systems
Printer + binder:	Maple-Vail Book Manufacturing Group
Indexer:	Carol Roberts